I Can Begin
Again

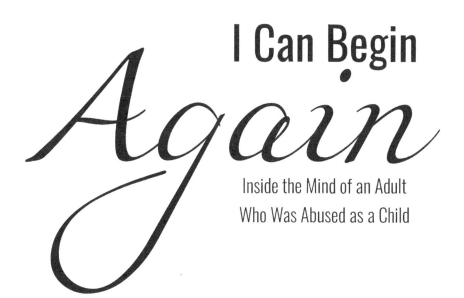

I Can Begin Again

Inside the Mind of an Adult Who Was Abused as a Child

Nola Katherine Trewin

Copyright © 2011 by Nola Katherine Trewin.
Copyright © 2021 Revised by Nola Katherine Trewin.

All rights reserved. No part of this book may be reproduced or transmitted in any form or by any means, electronic or mechanical, including photocopying, recording, or by any information storage and retrieval system, without permission in writing from the copyright owner.

This book was printed in the United States of America.

ISBN: 979-8-9852471-0-7 Paperback
ISBN: 979-8-9852471-1-4 E Book

To contact the author:
nolakatherine.blogspot.com
icanbeginagainbook@gmail.com

Book Notes

I Can Begin Again will take you into the complex and perplexing mind of an adult who bears the scars of child abuse. The silent voices of adults abused as children beckoned the author to tell her childhood sexual abuse story. For 30 years, she struggled until she finally listened and obeyed God's call to reach out and help others who are stuck in the grips of this devastating affliction.

Her intensely personal story will help adults abused as children understand who they are and why they behave the way they do. It will prove they do not have to remain stuck in their pain, and it will show each of them how to reclaim the power stolen from them as a precious, innocent child.

For those who have endured abuse of any kind, this revealing account will encourage them to believe they can do more than survive. They can begin life again.

Throughout her story, the author gives insights to those who live with one shattered by child abuse. She hopes that understanding will heal relationships often torn apart because of the wounded child's confusing behavior. She also desires to open the eyes of abusers who have no clue what they are doing to their precious, innocent victims. It is her prayer that her story will save other innocent children from becoming victims.

There are many subjects covered in her book, and everyone who reads it will take from it something of value. So, please, won't you join Nola Katherine in her search for her precious, wounded child as God, the Master Artist, guides her brush while painting the canvas of her life for you? Cry with her, laugh with her, and be touched, perhaps even changed, by the power of her story. And then share it with others—everyone knows someone who has suffered abuse.

About The Author

Nola Katherine has led Bible studies, prayer groups, and retreats on forgiveness. She has spoken to small groups and churches, has been the guest of Dr. Gene Getz on his weekly program, Renewal Radio, and interviewed on Today's Issues with American Family Radio. However, her most purposeful moments have been unexpected one-on-one encounters with those who suffer from the devastating effects of child abuse.

For this reason, she has chosen to overcome her fears and allow herself to become a vulnerable, open book. She desires others to experience the freedom she now has from the horrific power her abusers had over her for over 40 years. She believes that no one should ever have to carry their abuser's anger, guilt, and shame.

Nola Katherine lives in the Dallas area with Jake, her soulmate of 52 years. Her three children, spouses, and five grandchildren bring her immeasurable joy and keep her young. She is thankful to God for His presence in her life and for watching over her precious wounded child on the bumpy road to wholeness.

In Memory of Sharon Wilkinson

I dedicate this book to Sharon, who finally had her breakthrough. Now in Heaven with Jesus, her precious inner child has been set free from the evil imposed upon her. Thank you, Sharon, for showing me the way. Someday we will laugh together again. I will always love you.

Sharon and I met while in hospital. We were both there to find answers to things we did not understand. She had no family, so my family took her under their wings. One day she gave me the book *The Giving Tree*. Below is the notation she made in the book.

"To Nola Katherine, who has given so much to so many and deserves so much more herself. I envy you for all the progress you've made. I hope to make that breakthrough someday. Thanks to you and your family for your loving support. Thanks to God for putting you in my life." Sharon Wilkinson, 1990.

Dedication

I dedicate my book to all adults who, as children, were abused.
We are called survivors.

I dedicate my story
to the unimaginable number of children now being cruelly abused.
They are called victims.

I dedicate my life to Jesus,
the One who carried me when I could not walk.
I am blessed.

Foreword

I have chosen to use two letters and a personal experience as a foreword to my book. They each touch the very heart of my story. An abuser of children wrote the first letter, and a woman abused as a child wrote the second letter. The short story is a moment shared with my young son.

I am filled with mixed emotions as I invite you to enter through the doors of my life as an adult within whom lives a precious, wounded, abused child. Because I know there are untold stories like the ones behind the following letters, I welcome you with open arms.

June 26, 1996
Dear Nola Katherine,

I want you to know how grateful I am for your openness in sharing your pain and forgiveness with me in the terrible childhood abuse you suffered. I have needed to meet someone like you for many years. I believe nothing happens by chance, and God plans and arranges the healing we need in our lives in His own time.

I need to tell you about the enormous pain I've carried for thirty years. And though I know in my heart that God, through Jesus, forgives me, I am still often haunted by the shame, guilt, and self-hatred. This pain was the most challenging thing for me to share in my first recovery group because at the time, my youngest daughter was eight years old, the same age as one of the little girls I victimized when I was fifteen years old.

I told the men that if anyone ever did to my daughter what I had done to those two innocent little girls, I would kill them. I am still often tortured by what I did in coercing them into my sickness as a young man. Even though the Lord has forgiven me, and he has led me to a wonderful new life and pathway of healing, I carry this shame and anguish because I can never go back to them or find them. They were neighbors in a place 1,200 miles away, and of course, I have no idea where they are or how their lives are today.

I pray God has shown His grace and mercy on them and healed them. I guess that's one reason I needed to meet you and hear your story. I needed to meet a little girl victim and to see God's grace and healing love in your life. Maybe you needed to meet the fifteen-year-old perpetrator inside me.

I want you to know how sorry and angry I am for what you went through, and for what happened to you in your childhood. You were robbed of your childish joy and innocence. Your soul was murdered. I'm so terribly sorry for the pain and death you suffered.

I am thankful for seeing how the Lord Jesus has reached into your life to resurrect your soul and give you new life, hope, joy, and forgiveness. I pray you will continue to heal and grow spiritually, mentally, and emotionally day by day. I have carried such self-loathing, pain, and self-hatred for so much of my life. I have been unable to forgive myself. But when my brother died, the years of lonely secrets, hidden pain, and dark shame finally surfaced. It was then that God led me into new paths of recovery. I thank Him now, and I thank you that our paths crossed. I needed this next step on my journey. I didn't even know what I had needed, but He knew. Thankfully, I never sexually victimized a little girl again. However, for many years I victimized many, many girls and women with my lust. I turned them into objects of my lustful desires. I have hated myself in my deepest pain, not realizing that I, too, was a childhood victim in so many ways. Pornography was one more tool that fed my addiction. Now I am on a pathway to freedom by God's grace, and you have helped me along that pathway.

Thank you so very much.
In Christ, Jerry.

June 2008
Dearest Nola Katherine,

It has been sixteen remarkable years since I met you and gave my life to Jesus. He sent you into my life at a time when He knew that I needed Him, and He sent just the right person. Jesus used the power of your testimony and ministry to impact and transform my life radically.

You were giving a retreat on forgiveness at a friend's home over a Mother's Day weekend, and I attended because I thought I would support the friend who was giving the retreat. What I did not realize was that the Holy Spirit had already started to work on me. I had had anger and rejection issues for years. There were times that I had contemplated suicide and had been in trouble at schools where I had taught. At least three different principals had reprimanded me for my behavior in the way I treated students with verbal abuse. I even had a letter to that fact put in my permanent record file after numerous complaints by parents. Many wanted their student removed from my classroom.

On the first evening of the retreat, you discussed why God wants us to forgive. The group took turns reading different Scripture passages on forgiveness, which annoyed me. I still have the paper that you gave us with my definition of forgiveness blank. The next day you shared your testimony with the group. I had never known that other people were victims of sexual abuse. Then you shared about Jesus. I had never heard about salvation, let alone a personal relationship with Him.

I went home that afternoon and felt like something was gnawing inside of me. At the urging of a friend, I went back to speak with you to feel better. What an afternoon! At first, I refused to talk with you until you told me that Jesus loved me and gave His life for me. That afternoon I shared about the sexual and emotional abuse of my childhood and was delivered of the anger and hatred that I held so deep within me. You had me forgive those who had abused me and led me in the sinner's prayer. I gave my life to Jesus, and I remember the overwhelming peace that came over me. You even commented that lines disappeared from my face. Supernaturally I was healed! A few months later, you introduced two books to me, which led to experiencing the mighty work of the Holy Spirit.

The Lord showed me what He could do in a life devoted to him—peace, joy, and love not only for my students at school but also for my family. I was even worse with my family and asked them to forgive me. They said that I changed so much. At school, parents called to compliment me.

The next year I joined my husband in the Middle East, where he had been working for almost four years without me. (I was never going to go over there.) There I was to carry on with the Lord's work with many unforgettable experiences for ten years. And all because of God putting you in my life at His right time!

I pray that the Lord will continue to use you in showing what He can do in a person's life.

I love you very much, Lorrie.

Memories

  I had seen her roaming the neighborhood since she was a tiny kitten. Her beautiful calico coat of many colors was hard to miss. My eight-and nine-year-old children and I had discussed the young feline, and so far, I had managed to avoid getting involved with her. However, one day in desperation, she cleverly staged a dramatic catfight in front of my children. They promptly rescued her and then ran into the house with arms filled with the now-grown cat. She looked lost and hopelessly destitute. With great passion, they pleaded their case, "Oh, Mom, pleeeease, can we keep her? She neeeeeds us!"

  Within the hour, my children had acquired cat food and a pet named Patches. Within a few weeks, she repaid their kindness by blessing them with five irresistible, adorable kittens. Katherine and Jay were spellbound as they watched new life birthed and marveled at the new mother's intuitive ability to care for her family. They observed the new babies nurse and sleep and creep around with blind eyes that slowly opened to the world around them. They witnessed the kittens' first wobbly steps and their first attempts to play with their siblings. They were tiny miracles unfolding before my children's eyes every day; it was so much fun for them to watch this furry mass of growing delight.

However, each passing day sadly drew the kittens to the end of their stay with us. One day, as we stood watching this little family sleep peacefully with their mother, I asked my young son to go into the house and get the camera so that we could take some pictures. I knew this might be the last time we would ever see this little family cuddled together. When my son did not respond quickly, I looked down at the little boy whose rigid back and tight muscles kept him frozen, unable to respond. His wide, blue eyes held back a well of tears. Characteralisticly, his bottom lip remained tightly tucked over his top lip, a trait he developed as a toddler when unhappy. Finally, in a voice as sad as the look on his face, he whispered, "Oh, Mom, please don't take any more pictures."

Surprised by his request, I asked him why. "Because, Mom, memories are so painful." He quietly sobbed as I pulled him close to me. His blonde head nestled under my arm as tears spilled down fair, rosy cheeks. Mother and son were transfixed in a capsule of time as emotions mingled together, each understanding the other's quiet, unspoken thoughts and grief.

Memories are like that, I thought. They are indelibly printed in the recesses of our minds like acid burning, burning, burning—they never, ever go away. They are like a movie camera clicking off frame after frame and never allowing us to forget—the happy, the sad, the good, the bad. I did not want to remember either because if I remembered, then I would have to feel, and I did not want to feel.

"Yes, my son, sometimes memories are very painful."

Contents

Part one: 1
The Turning Point

Chapter 1   3
Could Death Be More Confronting than This?

Chapter 2   13
Understanding the Various Aspects of Child Abuse

Part two: 25
Discovering the Wounded Child

Chapter 3   27
Facing the Roaring Lion

Chapter 4   35
Unit 3E—There Is Nothing Shameful about Finding Answers

Chapter 5   43
Family History—You Have to Take What You Get

Chapter 6   53
I Always Hate Personality Tests—I Never Know the Answers

Chapter 7   61
Teddy Bears—in Search of My Lost Little Girl—a dog and a Rooster

Chapter 8   69
Who Took Care of You?

Chapter 9   85
Facing a Fear, Comic Relief, a Special Friend, and an Angel

Chapter 10   95
What Does a Little Bird Have to Do with Faith?

Chapter 11   105
The Battle Between Good and Evil

Chapter 12   115
The Unlikely Love of My Life

Chapter 13   127
Facing the Predator, Touched by a Song, Set Free with a Bed, and a Bat

Chapter 14   145
A Three-Hour Pass, a Long and Honest Talk, the Final Crossroad

Part three: 153
The AAC and the Survivor

Chapter 15   155
The Imperfect Church, God's Training Ground

Chapter 16   163
Yes, Life Can Get Worse—and It Did

Chapter 17   179
A Retreat and a Divine Appointment

Part four: 187
Finding God

Chapter 18   189
Such Faith Is Sure to Be Tested

Chapter 19   205
It Is Not That You Have Been Waiting on Me—It Is that I Have Been Waiting on You

Chapter 20   213
God Sees a Bigger Picture I Cannot See

Part five: 223
The AAC'S Journey

Chapter 21   225
Connecting All the Dots—the Church, the Abuse, the Enemy of My Soul, and Jesus

Part six: 265
Reconnecting With My Precious Child

Chapter 22   267
The Canvas of My Life Completed—Well, Not Just Yet

Part seven: 277
Guidelines to Help You Begin Again

Postscript	303
Acknowledgments	319
Praises for *I Can Begin Again*	*323*

I can begin again

With the passion of a child

My heart has caught a vision

Of a life that's still worthwhile

I can reach out again

Far beyond what I have done

Part one:

The Turning Point

Chapter 1

Could Death Be More Confronting than This?

The foreboding sound of heavy metal doors clanging shut behind me blatantly defined my life in that cruel moment of shame. One of the night nurses on Unit 3E of the adult psychiatric ward selected a key from the silver chain around her wrist and locked the now-silent door behind us. Jake and I exchanged glances—no need for words. After a few moments of instructions, the nurse kindly told my husband he must leave. Soft lights cast eerie shadows in the deadly silence of this unfamiliar place as strangers quietly began to rummage through my hastily packed bag.

"I'll be okay," I whispered as I tiptoed to kiss his tightly drawn lips. Without warning, I felt the warm security of strong arms around me, hugging me, not wanting to let me go. I could see the reflection of pain in Jake's clear, glassy blue eyes—eyes that possessed so much love and concern for the woman he held in high esteem. Though I sensed his helplessness, I couldn't reach inside and find the strength to comfort him. I had nothing left to give. Except for my shallow breath, there seemed to be no life within me.

Once again, the imposing sound of the strong metal door disturbed the quiet of the evening, this time putting a wall of separation between us that we both chose not to remove. Like a small, abandoned child, I stood with my face pressed against the narrow window and watched as my mate of 22 years disappeared into the elevator. I wanted to cry, but there were no tears. I wanted to scream, but there was no voice. I wanted to run, but there was no place to go. The reality of our decision began to sink in as my heart said goodbye. Methodically, I turned from the door and watched my few possessions being taken away and locked up.

"This is for your protection and the protection of others."

I was too numb to care.

I privately wondered if the survivor, who lived within me, would be able to rescue me this time. There had been so many times before when I'd thought I would go to that place of no return, over the edge, but I had always managed to come back, to hold on, and to survive just one more time. But no more; this was it. There was no turning back. I would either find the answers I needed to do more than just survive—to get well—or I would die.

Silently I cried out, "Oh, God, will I survive? Will my family survive? How will we ever get through this? Please help us! Please, God, help me!"

But in that woeful moment, the One who had been there so many times before seemed so far away.

I barely noticed the barrage of instructions tossed at me, until stern words caught my attention. "As of now, you are on a seventy-two-hour suicide watch, which means that you cannot leave the unit for any-

Chapter 1

thing. You will have all your meals in the unit. You may not have any visitors or phone calls, and a nurse will check your room every fifteen minutes."

I started to protest that I was not suicidal.

"This is standard procedure for everyone who checks into this hospital. You have no choice."

Suppressed anger rose to my temples and throbbed in sync with my beating heart. It grasped at my taut muscles. Veiled anger turned inward, deepening the numbness I felt. It anesthetized my mind and emotions while sending shock waves of pain throughout my body. If only I could stop the pain.

These were the rules, and I had to follow them. I wanted to yell and tell them to stop, to lock me up, and leave me alone. I sighed and reluctantly turned to find my assigned room.

Could death be more confronting than this?

Dear Reader, I believe every minute detail of our existence fits onto a large canvas that we call life. This colossal picture often remains obscure until one day we stand back and begin to see the genuine character of our emerging painting. Just as an artist who can create a beautiful masterpiece knows that mistakes will sometimes add character and depth to his painting, we who have struggled to survive also know our life's canvas would not be complete without its shadows of pain. The scene I painted above is the first stroke on this canvas of my life.

Over 30 years ago, I began feeling the urge to write my story. Although the seeds were planted long ago, I could never have imagined just where those seeds would take root and sprout. Finally, I could no longer deny the still small voice speaking within me. I spent an entire day searching through two large boxes full of notes and untold pages about my life. The task of organizing all this information was overwhelming until I stopped digging, went to my computer, and began to tell my story.

Before I continue, you need to know a few important things about me. First, I am an adult abused child *(AAC).*[1] In other words, my dignity, my power, and my God-given rights as a human being were stolen from me as a small, innocent child. As an adult, I bear the scars of those atrocious violations. While I have experienced incredible healing by God's grace, my inner abused child will always be with me, living in my skin, and she will always carry the memory of the wounds of abuse.

Almost everything about an AAC is confusing, and as you read this book, you may sometimes find my story confusing as well. If this happens, well, I have succeeded in giving you insights into the life of an abused child who must eventually learn to survive in an adult world.

And even though I refer to this book as my story, you are actually reading my experience: the accumulation of knowledge that results from direct participation in events. My knowledge is neither black nor white but has many variables. An AAC's life is often inconsistent, uncertain, and unexplainable.

Some of my thoughts may seem repetitive, but with reason. Usually, we must hear an idea over and over before we finally understand it. Some words, often repeated, connect my story, my experiences. I hope you will read with understanding patience.

As you read, keep in mind the venue where many of the events transpired: a psychiatric hospital.

Now, please stop and reread the last four paragraphs and remember them so that when, later, you stop and scratch your head and say,

---

1 Adult Abused Child (AAC): adult (within whom lives an) abused child.

"What?" you will recall my warning. The life of an AAC, in most instances, is challenging to comprehend.

To be clear, I am not writing this to dwell on the past for my sake. My past is behind me, and I have no desire to go backward. Therapeutic writing years ago helped me find healing and put my story together. But now, I have three reasons for writing this. Firstly, I feel called to open the doors of my life for those of you who are stuck in the pain of child abuse. My heart desires that you will find the courage to open the locked doors of your life and find hope that leads to wholeness.

My second motivation is my unrelenting desire to honor God and give glory to Him for all that He has done in my life through Jesus Christ and His Holy Spirit. To bear the title of Christian is a great privilege, but to be a Christ-follower, one must go beyond merely carrying His identity. As Christ-followers, we are called to bring hope to hurting humanity. Therefore, I am to open my heart and pave the way for others to know His immeasurable love—strong and powerful, yet so gentle that human words fall short in defining it.

To know that *I know* the God who *knows me* is a gift to be guarded and protected. It is sacred. It is a gift that every Christ-follower should earnestly pray for every human on earth to possess. And although human boundaries limit me from understanding it or explaining it fully, I have experienced the presence of God's love. My gift back to God is to tell His story in me—to share my experience with His wounded children. Jesus proclaimed that He came for the sick, the brokenhearted, the sinners. He came to set the captives free. He did this for me; He can do it for you.

Thirdly, Jake, my husband, encouraged me, and my three children, Katherine (Kat), James (Jay), and Kimberly (Kim), consistently begged me to write my story. Even my daughter-in-law, Zoe, pleaded that I owed it to our family to tell my story. "Yours is a great story of faith, and who knows what future generations will face? They need to know about you."

I agreed with her because I believe the America I know is slowly passing away. (It is noteworthy that those words appeared in the first edition of my book in 2011. Ten years later, they seem prophetic.) I shudder to think about what my grandchildren and the generations after them may endure. Perhaps someday, an aged, worn book discovered on a dusty shelf or in a long-forgotten trunk stored away in an attic will find its way into the hands of one who has lost all hope. Perhaps it will bring renewed faith in the God of a faithful, ancient forebearer. I sincerely pray that God's story in me will live on for many generations to come.

The never-ceasing cries of abused children past, present, and yet to come keep calling my name. Ten years ago, I wrote that the website Enough.org published the following statistics: one in four girls and one in six boys are sexually victimized before reaching adulthood, and in one study, one in four women and one in six men reported experiencing sexual abuse as a child. They also noted that the magnitude of child sexual abuse is overwhelming and primarily unrecognized and under-reported. When I went back to Enough.org to update the statistics for this revision, I was so overwhelmed and upset by what I read that I decided to challenge you to visit the website for yourself. You will be shocked to learn how bad the sexual abuse of children has become.

It was the unbelievable, ever-increasing, sick exploitations of babies, toddlers, and young children on the internet and the trafficking of innocent boys and girls that forced me to face my overpowering fears and find the courage to tell my story. But before that was possible, I had to travel down many paths and learn many lessons so I could remove the sackcloth of mourning and exchange it for pure, God-breathed redemption. I fervently pray many will read my book, hear God's voice, and find their pathway to wholeness.

Finally, think about this. For every sexually abused child, and every AAC, one or more predators exist. I hope that many who crossed over that sacred line and became abusers of children will read my book and may yet understand the devastating consequences of their actions. I pray that my account will persuade abusers to be repentant and seek help before it is too late—before they decide to abuse another child.

The casual reader was not in my mind when I wrote my book because it is not easy to be open and honest about my innermost, secret realm of self. Vulnerability scares the heebie-jeebies right into the very core of my being, but I know I must take whatever risk confronts me. If just one tormented, hopeless, defeated child of God (and we are *all* God's children) finds freedom, finds peace, finds joy, finds healing, then my suffering has value. Most importantly, if one discovers God through my journey of pain, shame, sorrow, mistakes, and invaluable lessons learned, it gives meaning to my life. I must dare to be vulnerable.

I write to family members, friends, therapists, ministers—to Christians and non-Christians—who are touched in some way by one like me. Figuratively speaking, I want you to crawl into my skin to understand better the heart and soul of an AAC—the abused child who will someday live in the skin of an adult.

I hope you gain insights about adults who were abused as children; they are often misunderstood. Their sometimes erratic behavior is the result of wounded, fragmented, and even split personalities. They are desperately screaming out to those closest to them for understanding and unconditional love. However, they cannot always receive nor reciprocate the love and acceptance they crave.

I invite you to look inside my world, where suppressed anger, suicidal depression, alcoholism, divorce, pornography, and confused sexuality tormented this AAC. You will begin to understand why she trusted no one and struggled with relationships. You will see what caused her to have severe panic attacks, forcing her to find dark places in her mind to hide when she felt unsafe.

I will unmask what it means for a child to be exposed to pornography and the evils that lurk in porn's deadly pathway. I pray you will grasp the devastating, lingering effects that pornography has on anyone lured into its deception.

You will feel this mother's painful journey with two terminally ill children. And you will rejoice with her in her many victories. By the end, my expectant hope is that you will look at the world around you through the clearer eyes of understanding, acceptance, compassion, forgiveness, love, faith, and hope.

I am compelled to address the church, the Body of Christ, and how it failed my wounded soul. People say, "If you don't like something, change it—but if you can't change it, change the way you look at it." I had to change my preconceived view of the religion I embraced because Christianity, more times than we want to admit, fails Christ's cause. Unfortunately, God is the one who gets blamed for our shortcomings.

Within my church experience, you will find my wounded child trying desperately to survive in an adult world that should have brought healing but instead caused the wounds of my childhood to fester. Please understand that I wrestled long and hard during the writing of my church experience. I often paced the floor, wrung my hands, cried out to God for direction, and felt I could not move forward. I struggled with the information I was putting forth, fearing its negative impact. But then I would feel God's Holy Spirit pulling me back into my story, encouraging me to continue. Ultimately, I hope my story will cause all who read it to look anew at their walk of faith, their rela-

Chapter 1

tionship with God, and their relationship with others.

This book is about my life, but it is not about me; it is about something far beyond the one who writes it. Once again, please understand the words I share with you are simply my stories and a part of my life experiences that impacted me greatly. I believe many of them will impact you as well. It will not be an easy book to read, but I promise you it will give any soap opera a run for its money. But above all else, it is my sincere desire to bring good; in no way do I write intentionally to offend or bring harm.

As you read my story, I ask you not to judge me, but I warn you at times, you will be tempted to do so, even to stop reading. However, I beg you to persevere to the end. I promise it will be worth it.

In some instances, I have used fictional names for doctors, ministers, therapists, and so on. For the most part, I have avoided using specific names of organizations and groups of people. I have used the first names of family and close friends. I desire to be as sensitive as possible without losing the authenticity of my story.

It is important to note that the italicized text after a paragraph represents the inner voices inside the adult's mind who was abused as a child.

Also, the occasional appearance of a symbol following text indicates that I am changing horses in the middle of the stream, so to speak. Just be aware that I am interjecting a thought or a story or taking you in a different direction which in most cases will end with another symbol.

It's time to move on! Grab a cup of hot tea with three lumps of sugar, rich cream, and a scone. (I had recently been to England when I wrote this!)—or whatever special treat you desire.

I, meanwhile, will need pencils for sketching, plump tubes filled with an assortment of alluring colors, and several good paintbrushes.

Please, come along with me as I begin to paint the picture of my life for you. Better still, let's do it together. Embrace me, cry with me, rejoice with me, ponder with me, grow with me, and experience the events of my life with me as we wash across the pages of time. I will sketch in the outline, and then together, we will paint in the dark shadows and glimmers of light. At times, we will stand back and examine our unfinished painting. Then we will begin again until all the brilliant colors of my life unfold the power of my story.

Chapter 2

Understanding the Various Aspects of Child Abuse

In this secular hospital environment, I accepted some new, specific terms: dysfunctional family, codependency, lack of boundaries, disassociation, fragmented and split personality, denial, anger, latent development, abandonment, wounded child, history of origin. These words' therapeutic meanings would prove invaluable to me as they slowly unveiled my understanding of the wounded child living within me.

When I was growing up, the term *abused* was not used as it is today. I heard it used once when I overheard my mother talking about a classmate who was attacked by a man as she walked home after school. This was in the mid-1950s. Even though I was young, I remember making a personal connection with the word in my mind.

I was 17 years old when I first spoke the words "I was abused." In retrospect, I do not know how I even knew what happened to me was abuse. Perhaps children just know things without always understanding them or requiring a definition. Now, I needed not only to accept the definition but also to understand what *abuse* truly means.

Terms of abuse

So that we can see the elements of our canvas more clearly, let's pause for a moment to look at some of these definitions.[1] The following traits, relevant to the AAC, begin to manifest in very young children.

Sexual abuse happens when a child is expected to fulfill or participate in the sexual needs of another person. It is *never* a child's responsibility to sexually satisfy anyone, ever. When any person—whether an adult or a child—coerces, forces, tricks, or threatens a child into having any kind of sexual contact with them, that person is guilty of sexual abuse. Touching the private parts of a child or having intercourse with a child is abuse. Exposing a child to pornographic pictures or films, telling sexual jokes or explicit sexual stories, or taking sexually explicit photos of a child is abuse.

Sexually abused children may suppress and shut down their sexual development, or, because pleasure is associated with the abuse, they may become promiscuous. It is important to note that God created us as sexual beings for procreation. He gave us a bonus by making sex pleasurable. Pleasure is the normal response to sex, and no one should feel guilty or shameful for feeling sexual pleasure. However, when guilt and shame are associated with the pleasure of sex, that is God's red flag trying to reveal that something is very wrong.

---

[1] The information that follows is my compilation and interpretation of notes taken while in the hospital, in various counseling situations, and workshops. I have no direct reference for this material. There appears to be variations to the definition of abuse available on the internet.

An addiction to sex, masturbation, and promiscuity will often result from childhood sexual abuse, leading to feelings of guilt and shame. Exposure to pornography alters brain chemistry and has lasting, devastating effects. No stone is left unturned for sexually abused children. They are forever changed, and *every* aspect of their lives *will be* affected.

Sexual confusion: To my knowledge, no studies support that sexual confusion is sometimes the result of sexual abuse; however, I and other victims of childhood sexual abuse who have shared their experiences with me have experienced sexual confusion as a result of the abuse.

Neglect is when a parent fails to feed, protect, nurture the child, or provide essential necessities. For example, leaving a child unattended when they are not ready to care for themselves puts the child in a potentially dangerous situation; this is child abuse. Substance-abusing parents are often neglectful of their children's needs.

Physical abuse is when a child is slapped, pushed, burned, punched, or beaten by a person of authority. Visible evidence may include scratches, burns, bruises, welts, or broken bones. Intangible scars of physical abuse remain long after the injuries fade and the bones mend. Children are powerless to protect themselves from those entrusted to love and protect them.

Emotional abuse is ridicule, screaming, or any verbally abusive attention directed at a child by an adult. When a child witnesses verbal abuse directed at others in the family unit—for example, spousal fighting or harsh discipline of a sibling—this vicariously damages the child's emotional well-being and is abuse. When parents ignore or do not take an interest in a child, do not hug them, or are generally emotionally disconnected from their child, severe emotional scars result in devastating consequences.

Spiritual abuse is the ultimate result of any abuse inflicted on an innocent child. Our Creator's greatest gift to humanity is that of a baby, a child. His intent in creating marriage and sexuality between one man and one woman was the continuation of life. Adults have this precious gift to nurture and to pour love into one who will, in turn, someday nurture and pour love into their child. But when children become devalued to the point of feeling worthless, it increases the chance that eventually they may degrade their offspring. Out of that kind of behavior will be born a mistrust of even their Creator, God. All children born on this earth deserve the right to know their Creator, to know His love, and to understand their worth in Him.

Dysfunctional families create unfavorable conditions that interfere with the healthy functioning of a family unit. At times, in all families, function becomes impaired by stressful circumstances, but a healthy family will return to normal within a reasonable amount of time after a traumatic event. But for a dysfunctional family, unresolved issues become monsters that refuse to go away. These monsters have long-term effects upon the children who come from dysfunctional families where abuse has occurred:

- When children are disrespected or shamed, instead of feeling valuable, they feel worthless and insecure, so they end up controlling others as adults.
- When children are unprotected, they learn they have no boundaries; anyone can do anything to them, and they will remain silent. But as adults, they often become filled with rage, anger, and resentment.
- When goodness is stolen, children believe they are bad; as adults, they often become rebellious and live in a world of denial. Reality becomes skewed.

- When needs and wants are denied, an abused child may become either anti-dependent or overly dependent. They often develop addiction issues or physical and mental illnesses. They will continuously be searching for love and acceptance.
- When innocence is thwarted, maturity is often latent; emotional development progresses very slowly. These individuals will exert no control over their lives—or will try to control every facet of their life. They may even exhibit both traits simultaneously. Real intimacy will elude them, no matter what.

Fragmented and split personalities create vicious cycles that overshadow the victims of child abuse. The affected individuals are very complex people, and their thought processes do not flow down the same channel as those of non-abused people. Circumstances dictate what part of their mind will react to any given situation. What was that again? Circumstances dictate *what part of their mind* will react to any given situation. Can a mind become fragmented, disunited, or even split? Suppose it is suddenly forced to disconnect from reality because it cannot resolve conflicting and confusing circumstances. In that case, is it possible for the unity of the mind to be altered and possibly even destroyed?

Those with real multiple or split personalities are unaware of their erratic behavior. However, those who are fragmented usually know they are unpredictable; they are just clueless about why they behave the way they do and clueless about changing.

Those with fragmented personalities are extremely *ambivalent*, which means they have "simultaneous and contradictory attitudes or feelings toward an object, person or action" and are in "continual fluctuation (as between one thing and its opposite such as love/hate)."[2] Victims of abuse can get angry at someone they love, but they can also hate that person at the same time.

Appropriate and inappropriate anger begin to war with each other. This war can throw victims of abuse into anxiety, depression, and unacceptable, ambivalent behavior. They want to die, but they want to live. They want to be good, but they do bad things. They love, they hate. They want sex; they hate sex. These conflicts lead to unbelievable confusion for victims and those who live with them. Victims survive by stuffing their confusing contradictions deep inside where they cannot feel them, never dealing with what they deny.

You can find a lot of information about personality disorders on the internet. In researching this topic, be sure to use discernment. If truth be told, I think most of us would find that we suffer from some form of personality dysfunction. However, I do not think everyone should be given the same label or put into the same category, because we are all unique.

Codependency is one of the various vicious cycles. Every victim of abuse enters a secret underworld inhabited by survivors of every type of abuse that leads to various vicious cycles. One of those cycles is what many call *codependency*.

The core of codependency is when an individual's emotional stability is predicated on the dependence of another. For example, I might say, "I feel personally validated because you depend on me to take care of you. When you become self-sufficient and no longer need me to support you, I will need to find someone else who needs me so that I will feel good about myself. I need to keep you under my thumb."

---

2 https://www.merriam-webster.com/dictionary/ambivalence

Codependent people tend to behave in inappropriate ways that adversely affect relationships. If a codependent person stunts the growth patterns of another, it is detrimental to the relationship and both parties. It becomes another form of abuse.

The aspects of an abuse victim

The adult abused child (AAC) is the main character in this scenario, where the wounded child, the victim, and the survivor emerge as the precious child withdraws.

Adults abused as children are self-centered and self-absorbed. They can only give complete attention to their own thoughts—even though they may, at times, be prone to think of others before themselves. They remain fragmented and stay in the shadows and sidelines with their wounded child. Although each person handles things differently, almost all adult abused children follow certain character traits and patterns. Although they are not "normal," they are normal in the world of child abuse, and they all share some common traits:

- adapt to the stresses and changes in life, as they are very fine-tuned.
- empathetic toward others and successful in most anything they set out to do.
- struggle to understand the thought processes of an ordinary person, not realizing that everyone does not process thoughts in the same way they do. These misunderstandings usually lead to conflicts in relationships.
- have unrealistic expectations of others to meet their needs.
- lack self-esteem from within, so they look for ways to fill the pillaged spaces in their minds through their relations with oth-

- ers. That is why they typically become controllers and caretakers.
- deny their dysfunctional past, their pain-filled feelings, and their inability to be intimate.
- have extreme issues with distrust and are hypervigilant, which means they are always on the lookout for possible danger, even though they will deny the perils they see.
- often are physically ill, depressed, sensitive, and easily offended.
- have difficulty celebrating the God-given uniqueness and beauty of their existence. They can only see ugliness, where self-loathing gives birth to the denial of anything good within. Unworthiness reinforced over and over does not allow healthy self-worth to develop. Sadly, they may never recover.

The precious child, the innocent one, is born with the expectation of being loved, nurtured, and protected and is God-breathed into each of us. We come packaged in magical contentment, but we are also vulnerable. When the precious child's trust is broken by neglect or sexual, physical, emotional, or spiritual abuse, the little child will find many ways to compensate for the shame that has stolen their innocence. The resulting powerlessness will lead the AAC into a life of varied, often destructive, unmanageable behaviors, while the precious child becomes lost, quiet, holding God close to her heart.

The wounded child is the ambivalent, angry troublemaker who openly carries the scars of abuse for all to see and causes much grief for the AAC. Busy guarding secrets, appearing and disappearing, the wounded child causes much confusion—while looking for love.

The survivor is the protector who is always quietly present, always watching, and who steps in when things get tough and has a strong faith in God.

The victim always feels the wounds of abuse and is continually trying to find a way to heal the wounded child's secrets. Victims stay stuck like glue in the deception of depression, suppressed anger, bitterness, and unforgivingness, until one day the reality of abuse is confronted, and they grieve over the loss of their precious, wounded child and acknowledge that not only does God love them but they too love their precious child and the survivor they have become.

Discovering the various aspects of me

For me, the following questions therapists asked me to determine the effects my childhood had upon my personality produced surprising results:

- Does everything around you need to be perfect?
- Do you seek approval from others to feel good about yourself?
- Do you overdo for others while denying your own needs?
- Do you go to extremes, either taking on too much responsibility or avoiding and ignoring responsibilities? Do you do both?
- Is it hard to trust others?
- Are you other-focused, or are you self-absorbed? Or are you both?
- Is it difficult for you to have intimate relationships?
- Can you express your feelings, either negative or positive?
- Do you feel lonely in a room full of people?
- Is it impossible for you to tell others what you need from them?
- Do you tend to migrate toward unhealthy relationships/people?
- Are you aware of others' needs more than your own?

- Is it challenging to deal with anger or criticism?
- Is it hard for you to respect authority?
- Do you feel that you must give false impressions of who you are, socially or professionally?
- Is it difficult to play and have fun?

When my test was evaluated, I was told that almost everyone can answer yes to a few of these questions. However, I answered yes to all of them, indicating I probably had a personality disorder and needed help. The results were not easy for me to hear, but they were eye-opening.

As surely as I knew the term *abuse* connected us—the AAC, the precious child, the wounded child, the victim, and the survivor—I also knew it was God who connected our threads of hope. For weeks I was given tools to work with and knowledge to process; now, I had to figure out what to do with all this information. I was overwhelmed.

Eventually, I began to accept that I had a fragmented personality. What you are about to read is my perception of what happened to me and does not come from clinical studies or any other source. I believe our Creator gave us a way to escape mentally from traumatic situations we cannot cope with. He has given us the capacity to store unwanted experiences away in our minds so that we can survive, and for me, it looks something like this:

The core of who I am—my soul—is the precious child within me, and she is the one who quietly held me together. Early on, the strong one, the survivor, took the wounded precious child and put her into a safe, well-guarded place of protection. The wounded child split and left the precious child in her safe place and joined the survivor who took care of her. Eventually, the mixed-up, confused adult within whom lived the mixed-up abused child emerged as the victim. The problem came when the adult did not know what to do with these seemingly other entities that kept popping in and out of her mind, her life, causing much confusion.

I know you must be thinking this explanation is strange, but you will begin to see this scenario unfold as you continue to read my story. You may notice hints of a split personality, which I was not even aware of until I wrote this book. Again, this is just my way of understanding what happened to me, why I do the things I do, and who I am.

I think we can agree that the mind is a marvelous creation, and it has astonishing abilities we humans hardly tap into or understand. For the abused child, it is truly a gift.

Understanding child sexual abuse is a challenge for those who never experienced it. It is hard to understand the AAC's often disturbing patterns—because laced within those patterns are unique individuals who can bring many marvelous gifts into their relationships and into the lives they lead. They are called survivors—those who have lived through affliction—because they have developed valuable skills to help get them through life. Yet, the roots of abuse established lifelong patterns that affect every area of their lives, and they impinge on the core of every relationship they encounter.

The wounded child I was trying so hard to figure out held the missing link to understanding. Perhaps if I could understand her, I would then be able to find my precious child. I spent hours in pursuit of her. I listened. I took notes. I answered questions, filled in blanks, charted my history, wrote endlessly, and I cried out to my God. Slowly, powerfully, reason took my hand and gently led me toward awareness of my precious child's wounds. I started paying attention to what I was learning.

I can begin again

With the passion of a child

My heart has caught a vision

Of a life that's still worthwhile

I can reach out again

Far beyond what I have done

Part two:

Discovering the Wounded Child

Chapter 3

Facing the Roaring Lion

My "painting" must begin with sketches—the first step in a plan to lead us through this maze of trials, errors, and successes. Let me first draw a few characters into the background where my story began: the adult psychiatric hospital.

I entered in July 1990, at the age of 46, to work on issues surrounding child sexual abuse. However, the final downward spiral into the seemingly bottomless pit I found myself in, at that point, began in September 1989.

My husband's father, who was in his 70s, had undergone major heart surgery; he faced a long rehabilitation. In the meantime, Jake's youngest sister returned to Michigan to attend to some personal matters, leaving her teenaged son with us in Texas. While Jake's sister was there, a severe pancreatic attack almost took her life. Because of her parents' situation, I helped her after being well enough to return to Texas.

Our two older children were away at college, but our 12-year-old was, of course, still at home. By the time Christmas morning rolled around, everyone was out of the hospital, and despite all the stress, we managed to celebrate the traditional all-day event that we cherished. My father-in-law continued rehab as an outpatient, and Jake's sister prepared for additional surgery after the first of the year.

As the chills of January 1990 crossed over into February's dreariness, life seemed to be getting back to normal when Clark, a therapist in our church, recommended that I attend a weekend workshop for abuse survivors. He and I had briefly discussed my childhood issues, and he thought it might be beneficial for me to attend the rather expensive three-day event. The workshop unexpectedly opened Pandora's box. I was just beginning to absorb its impact when storm clouds began to roll my way once again.

The frantic voice on the phone belonged to my sister. "You have got to come and get Mother. I can't take care of them both!"

Our 80-year-old mother had suffered a severe asthma attack several days earlier; instead of getting her to a doctor, typically, my sister was just going to let her ride it out. Instinctively, I knew Mom was critical. I tried giving Sis some slack because her husband was dying of cancer. She had already lost one husband to cancer, and I knew this was a difficult time for her.

As I drove into the driveway of my sister's house, unwelcome images flashed across my mind—I deliberately pushed them away, denying them access to my already grumbling spirit. Heaviness filled my legs as I stepped onto the concrete porch, opened the heavy wooden door, and walked inside where dark memories lived.

Icy terror struck the pit of my stomach when I saw my petite, white-haired mother gasping for air. She was inhaling small amounts of oxygen and barely able to exhale. Carbon dioxide had caused her body to swell to almost twice her size, and she was incoherent to the point that she hardly recognized me, the youngest of her five children. I turned to my sister and asked her why she had not called me sooner. My tone of voice did not betray the anger I felt.

Giving neither of them a choice, I told my mother I was taking her to an emergency room. The 45-minute trip across town was agonizing; I pleaded with God to help Mom breathe. Selfishly, I wanted her away from my sister's influence, and I wanted her closer to my home so that I could take care of her and my family.

Emergency room attendants wasted no time tending to my mother and quickly assessed her need for life support. A lung specialist informed me he was not sure he could pull her through this attack.

Family members came in and out of the ICU throughout the evening, perhaps silently feeling they had come to say goodbye. Visiting hours came to an end, and I was left alone watching my mother struggle for each breath—trying somehow to breathe for her—unaware that I was there for a divine appointment. During the quiet, dark hours of the night, I tried to comfort my frail but strong-willed mother as she fought the arm restraints that dug into her tender skin.

"Mom, please try not to fight. You need to stay calm so that you can breathe."

Her white hair, tinged with yellow nicotine, was drenched in sweat. The few lines in her face appeared uncharacteristically deep.

"Let me go! I want to go!"

I reached out and gently touched the clammy hand of this woman who stirred so many mixed emotions within me. I tiptoed, stretching to get over the cold bed rail so that I could whisper into her ear.

"Mom, where do you want to go?"

Her voice became strong and determined. "I want to cross over the river."

"What do you mean? What river?"

Feeble, shaking hands attempted to point toward the ceiling. "That river, the one right there! I can see Grandma and Grandpa, and there's Mama, too. Please let me go. I want to go over to the other side of the river."

I did not understand the significance of my words back to her that night. I wanted to tell her it was okay to go, but instead, I pleaded.

"Mother, you can't go yet. I need you to stay with me just a little while longer. Please, stay with me just a little while longer."

A week later, to everyone's surprise, except perhaps mine, I took Mother home with me to recuperate. I knew it would not be easy, but I didn't care. I wanted to take care of her. Consequently, our time together became the best memory I have had with my mother.

While with me, she looked better than I had seen her in years, and the sweet, good-natured side of her I had occasionally glimpsed while growing up began to emerge. We experienced tender and fun times, and I felt close to my mother for the first time in my life. But it did not last. I had to let her go. She returned home to her life, and our relationship returned to life as we had known it before she tried to cross the river.

February waved goodbye, and just like the old English proverb, March came in like a lion. Chewy, our golden retriever, produced 12 large, golden puppies within just a few hours—but when puppy number ten was only halfway born, she stopped pushing. The take-charge caretaker that I am quickly delivered a limp puppy. When stimulation failed to produce life-giving breath, I put my mouth over hers and breathed life into her lungs. She squealed; I praised God, and Chewy reluctantly lay back and gave birth to two more babies.

As exhaustingly joyous as the whole event had been, somehow I knew that a litter of 12 might not be such a good thing. At the advice of a local golden retriever club, I rotated these fluffy darlings every two hours. Chewy only had ten places at the dinner table, so to speak, and I needed to make sure they all got their fair share.

As spring went on, trying to meet the family's needs was challenging. Weeks of rotating puppies night and day; trips across town to clean house, shop, and bathe Mom; my sister's husband's death; and Jake losing his job about did me in. The kids came home from college for the summer, and I began to have flashbacks. The workshop I'd attended in February had dimly exposed my 46-year secret life, and now I could no longer ignore the warning signs given to me. I was exhausted.

Early summer, a dark, menacing cloud began to overtake my body. The Texas heat encouraged sleeplessness. I found myself getting up in the night and staring into a place of void for long hours at a time—unable to think, unable to focus, unable to deny the previously dormant, unwanted images that had begun to flash across my mind. Depression resurrected a new wave of despair over me as its shrewd black hole began to crack open and suck me into its grip, depleting my mind, body, and spirit of hope.

I had danced with this fickle intruder of spirit since I was 16 years old, but now the trespasser was different somehow. I felt strangely numb; for the first time in my life, I could not function. I mentioned to Jake that I was struggling, and we agreed that I probably needed some help.

I sought out a therapist that our COBRA insurance would pay for and made an appointment. With hair and makeup in place and a smile on my face, I walked into this man's office and simply related the past few months' events. He agreed I had been under a lot of stress and probably needed to be on medication. He gave me the name of a psychiatrist.

I Can Begin Again

A week later, dressed and groomed as though I had stepped out of a magazine, I met Dr. Kamen in the hallway. He directed me to his office and invited me to be seated. To this day, I cannot tell you all that happened during my time with him. Did I see trust in him, or was I just desperate to trust? Did he see the void in my eyes? Did he hear the emptiness in my voice? Did he sense my shameful secrets or desperate unspoken cries? Had I even offered him more than my usual response—the same answer I used at the workshop?

"I was abused; I am depressed."

Did I open a tiny window that allowed this perceptive stranger to see into my child-soul—or had this simply been a divine appointment?

"Nola, you're scaring me! I met you an hour ago in the hallway, and you looked as though you didn't have a care in the world. I would never have guessed what you are carrying inside of you." His words were unrelenting. "How much longer do you think you can do this?"

I drew my lips tighter, unable to raise my head, daring tears to roll down my cheeks onto neatly folded hands. My voice barely audible, I whispered, "I don't know."

"I don't normally recommend hospitalization the first time I see someone, but I suggest you go to the phone, call your husband, and have him meet you at the psychiatric facility near the hospital."

I sat in numb silence, not wanting to breathe. Breathing meant living, and it was just too hard to live. How could I tell anyone—especially my husband and my children—that I felt this way when I had so many reasons to live? I was not suicidal; I did not want to die. I just wanted the pain to stop. I just wanted the constant, never-ending, all-consuming, secret pain to go away.

If I had been capable of feeling, I would have felt terror at the thought of going into a psychiatric hospital. If I had been capable of reason, I would have made excuses that I could not leave my family

for the proposed three-week hospital stay. If I had been able to feel shame, I would have turned away and run for my life. I was an expert at minimizing and denying. But this course, this divine appointment, had been set in motion in February when I attended the survivors' workshop where, for the first time in my life, I had learned that a precious child lived inside me, and she was worthy of love and protection.

The workshop—led by Mia, a well-known counselor associated with a rehabilitation center in another state—quickly assessed my fragile state of mind. A simple test revealed I had no boundaries: anyone could walk into my space, and I would not retreat or object.

Repeatedly, Mia asked me a question I could not answer. "Who took care of you?"

I would just shake my head and say nothing while the distant voice of my aunt whispered in my head. "You weren't raised. You just grew up."

My outward appearance suggested I was anything but fragile. The facade I wore was both a curse and a blessing—a blessing because it helped me survive by giving me a way to hide from the secrets that picked away at the core of my being, and a curse because I was as sick as the secrets it hid. By keeping my secrets hidden, I subconsciously denied them. The disguise I wore kept people out, the abused child locked in.

Mia told Clark, the church therapist who also attended the weekend event, that she would do little work with me during the sessions. She also cautioned him to be careful of my delicate mental state. At the end of the workshop, Mia met with both of us privately and strongly recommended that I check myself into a hospital to deal with my complex childhood issues.

I could not comprehend the magnitude of what Mia was saying about me. I had ambivalent feelings—resolve because someone had looked beyond the many masks I wore and dared to give me honest feedback, and restraint because I was deathly afraid of removing them. I came away from the workshop feeling drained, confused, and helpless as I went back to life as usual.

Little did I know the cold winds of February would usher in a roaring lion that would turn my life inside out. And now, in July, the time had come for me to face it.

I took a deep breath and raised my head. My eyes met Dr. Kamen's unyieldingly perceptive gaze, and with resignation in my voice, I agreed to call my husband.

The doctor led me to his private phone. Taking control of my emotions, I methodically told Jake what the doctor had advised. However, I was much too responsible to drop out of my family's lives on such short notice. It was late Friday afternoon; we decided to wait until Sunday to proceed. I needed time to prepare my children, get the house in order, and meet with a cousin I had not met before. Otherwise, the timing was perfect for me to get away—and it would only be for three weeks.

The older children would be busy with their summer jobs. My youngest was visiting a friend in Denver, and Jake would be home to stay with our daughter upon her return in two weeks. I cannot begin to imagine what I must have put my family through initially. The children had never heard me talk about depression or abuse. But, like their father, they loved me and supported my decision to go into the hospital.

Chapter 4

Unit 3e—There Is Nothing Shameful about Finding Answers

I can't recall much about my first 72 hours in the hospital. I couldn't sleep, and my body became increasingly tense; the physical pain was almost unbearable. Dr. Kamen prescribed an antidepressant, and eventually, I began to level out . . . somewhere between a high-wire performer and a zombie.

Rules on 3E were strict, and the routine became demanding once the suicide watch was over. Up for meds, off to breakfast and the morning meeting, down to the gym for physical activity, then to lunch, and then the fun began. Meetings! Meetings! And more meetings! Cognitive therapy, occupational therapy, group meetings, therapy sessions, doctor's meetings, psychological testing, art therapy, music therapy, optional spiritual therapy—but worst of all was Barb, the psychologist who probed and prodded for information about my past. Visiting hours followed dinner, and then we had an all-unit evening meeting before bedtime.

Jake visited every evening; initially, he was the only one I wanted to see. After the evening meeting, I was off to my dreaded bed for a night of tossing, turning, and thinking, thinking, thinking. I could not shut off my brain, and the black hole of depression continued its never-ceasing attempt to swallow me. I wanted out—out of my skin, out of my brain. But no matter how hard I tried, I could not find my way out. My mind was caught in a prison of despair that twisted my ability to be in touch with reality. I knew where I was, but I couldn't understand how or why life had managed to lock me up—whoever *me* was.

For the first time in my life, I questioned my identity. I was a wife, a mother. I was a daughter, a sister, a friend—but really, who was I? Resistant surrender began to settle on my raw emotions like a giant black hawk covering its prey. I felt my will to fight slowly slipping away, my resolve to survive waning. But my determination to live had not yet succumbed to the dark powers that wanted to defeat me. My silent pleas to God were continual.

"Please, God, help me!"

Would morning ever come? If only I could cry . . .

My first all-unit encounter in the meeting room felt ominous. However, I was oblivious to the fact that I was meeting my new temporary family. Michael, who managed the third-floor unit, was an attractive, exuberant young man with a thin mustache, magnetic smile, and caring eyes. He also led the twice-daily all-unit gatherings of patients on 3E. With protective authority, he began the morning ritual.

"State your name, tell us how long you have been here, why you are here, and what your goal is for the day."

My thoughts flip-flopped all around the inside of my head.

"What? I must speak? Goals for the day? Are you kidding me?"

I wanted to bolt from my chair and run to . . . what? A locked door? With my legs crossed, foot swinging, muscles taut, I sat poised like a stone statue, my hands gripping the seat of my chair. And I listened. I listened to snippets of tangled lives much like my own. My nurturing, sensitive side emerged for just long enough to help me set aside my fears.

In this setting, I decided to use my full name. Symbolically, Nola had been the part of me that had always been strong but was now very tired and needed a break. If there was indeed a precious child within me, her name was Nola Katherine, and I had come there to find her.

"My name is Nola Katherine, and I am depressed. Last evening, I checked into this hospital. My goal is just to get through this day."

I have had countless unexpected encounters with people who briefly brought varied and diverse attributes to my life, but the memories of some on Unit 3E remain with me. They brought new colors to my life's canvas as I watched their stories slowly unfold before me. They were all good people from many different walks of life—intelligent men and women who were mostly highly educated. Hearing their stories, I began to realize I was not alone. Perhaps some could understand the depths of my pain and not judge me if I dared to reveal my secrets. More importantly, I realized none of us were mentally ill or insane. We all lived in crazy, mixed-up worlds and were just trying to figure out the why of it all. We wanted to learn how to do more than just survive. We wanted to live.

Let me introduce you to some of them. Depression was an epidemic. Just know that we were all depressed, so I don't need to repeat the obvious.

Bill was in his twenties, tall and slender. Thick black eyelashes made you look twice at his beautiful dark eyes. He was kind and polite, but he was already well into the disease of alcoholism. He had lost his job and his girlfriend.

Jimmy was overweight, shy, sweet; his father's abuse heightened his low self-esteem.

Becky, mid-forties, was an attractive blonde executive whose husband had divorced her five years earlier. She could not move on.

Cheryl was a lawyer whose marriage was crumbling. She sought help to deal with her circumstances and with the potential loss.

Sue was quiet, sweet, and brain-damaged from an incorrect prescription medication. She cried all the time.

Jean, about my age, was also a victim of childhood sexual abuse.

John, mid-twenties, was gay and had been sexually abused by his mother. He could not cope with the confusion he felt.

Gary had AIDS and was trying to process the devastating diagnosis.

Jane's successful 50-something husband had left her and her young children for a younger woman.

Jody, suffering from postpartum depression, had attempted suicide after the birth of her fifth child.

The one we secretly called Barbie had a nine-month-old baby she could not bond with; she was having difficulty being a mother.

Jack, who once had an exceptionally high IQ, worked for a large corporation doing detailed analysis. He was struck by a car while riding his bicycle. His head injury left him with intellectual impairments, and he was having a tough time accepting his disability.

Suzanne, a single mother and businesswoman, had been drugged and assaulted by her associates while on a business trip.

I heard countless disturbing stories of abuse—alcohol, drugs, domestic, child, sexual, physical, emotional, verbal. Many troubled souls came through the doors of 3E for short stays, but there were three who impacted me deeply.

On my first night in the hospital, a slender, personable strawberry blonde walked up to me.

"Hi! I'm Sharon. I've already been here for six weeks."

She then put her index finger to her temple and twisted her hand back and forth to signify that she was *crazy*, tilted her head, crossed her eyes, and offered me a contagious laugh.

"And I'm gay! Now we have that out of the way; I'll show you around."

In one of the darkest hours of my life, Sharon made me laugh. My entire family came to love and embrace her. In time, she trusted me with her secrets—horrific things that she was incapable of telling the staff or her small group, not even her doctor. Sharon's inability to talk eventually enabled me to talk about what happened to me. I saw the confusion, terror, shame, and fear trapped beneath a quick smile, a warm heart, and a witty sense of humor.

She was released from the hospital when her insurance would no longer pay for her stay and was then admitted into a county hospital but could not stay for an extended time. When Sharon got home, she called her mother and told her she was going to shoot herself. Her mother called the local police, who promptly arrived at Sharon's house and spent hours trying to coax Sharon to safety. Because of Sharon's persistent refusal, tear gas was tossed through a window, hoping to force her out. However, she put a gun to her head and pulled the trigger.

My sweet friend was alone and felt desperately lonely. She needed more from life than this world could possibly give to her. I was heartbroken for this precious child of God. Wicked, sexual child predators destroyed her life, yet through it all, Sharon wrote beautiful poetry and believed in Jesus. Based on what she told me, she was not gay; instead, she feared men, and being gay was her way of avoiding intimacy with them. Sharon, who was wounded, was now healed, set free, and with Jesus.

Julie came onto our unit like a bull in a china closet, immediately getting everyone's attention. If we met her coming down the hall, we would hug the wall opposite her. No one wanted to make eye contact with her, and we would rather have died than talk to her. She appeared very tough, and everything about her screamed out a warning: "Don't mess with me!"

Honestly, I was scared to death of her. However, I will never forget this stout, robust young woman with big deep-set eyes and a wide, square jaw.

Once, while sitting near Julie during art therapy, I noticed her working on an incredible drawing of a vast city skyline. I decided to compliment her artwork. Much to my surprise, she looked at me with soft eyes, smiled, and graciously thanked me. From that moment on, I had a new friend.

Julie had bipolar disorder. In all my life, I have never seen anyone so misunderstood, so judged. When I looked behind her mask, I found a dear, loving, talented person who just wanted to be loved unconditionally. I don't know what happened to Julie, and I still get tears in my eyes when I think of her.

And then there was Joe, who came in and out of our lives in a flash. I talked with him when he first arrived on 3E and saw the all-too-familiar depths of depression with which he struggled, so I was shocked when, in just a matter of days, he appeared happy and upbeat. He convinced his doctor to release him. The day after his release, we were called into the meeting room and told that Joe had taken his life.

Chapter 4

During my next session with Dr. Kamen, I told him I had seen myself in Joe and begged him not to release me until he knew for sure that I had made significant strides toward recovery. I knew I was capable of convincing everyone that I was just fine.

That was the day when I looked denial in the face and began to accept the truth about my fragile state. God had put me there for a reason, and there was nothing shameful about wanting to find answers. I needed to pay close attention. I had a lot of work to do, and I needed to get busy.

Chapter 5

Family History—You Have to Take What You Get

Sometimes, before beginning a painting, an artist will cover the canvas with a "wash": a mixture of paint and water. When you do this, you never really know how it will turn out because water mixed with paint can take on a mind of its own—much like our family history. Sometimes it's good, sometimes it's not so good, but you just have to take what you get. I have only retrospectively realized the importance of finding out as much as possible about our origins. My family history will become the wash for my life painting. I invite you to pick up your brushes and work with me—but our task will not be easy.

My work began when Barb, a psychologist, appeared in my room with a pen and notepad in hand. She had come to help me start the challenging process of washing through distant spaces of time with the hope of revealing untapped memories, unspoken truths, and stowed-away secrets. I had many years of crucial information to explore and sift through.

Needing a quiet, out-of-the-way place to work, we settled into comfy burgundy chairs positioned at the end of a long hallway in front of a window. The hot summer sun peeking through the glass gave welcome relief from the cold, air-conditioned building. I was always cold. As usual, I crossed my legs, and my foot began its anxious swing. I was not sure what she meant by *history* and was a bit uneasy about our meeting. Barb, professionally poised, came ready to listen. She asked me to tell her about my father. Despite my shutdown emotions, my knack for organizing detail allowed me to state the facts. Methodically, I began.

> Dad was born in 1899. He was almost 45 when I was born, and he always seemed like an old man to me. He had a tough life growing up—one of nine children, the third youngest. His mother died shortly after giving birth to the last baby. The baby died too. Dad was only three years old at the time, and he had a younger brother, Ben. They lived on a farm in Oklahoma. My mother told me that my grandmother walked to town to buy food one day and hemorrhaged to death. My grandfather was a heavy drinker and an alleged womanizer, so who knows where he was when my grandmother needed him. All Dad's brothers were heavy drinkers too, but thankfully, my father was not.
>
> I am amazed Dad even survived childhood. He was born with a severe cleft palate and lip. According to my mother, my grandfather refused to have his son's deformity corrected because he boasted that no woman would ever have my dad looking like that; he wanted to be sure to have someone to take care of him when he got old. But by the time Dad turned 18, he had worked and saved enough money to have

corrective surgery. The surgeon did an excellent job—I was not aware of Dad's condition until my mother told me about it when I was a senior in high school.

There was only one girl born in this family of boys, Eva; she was a victim of incest. Her father—my grandfather—fathered her two girls, making them both my aunt and my cousin. One of her girls, Ruby Ellen, was lost to the family.[1] No one knew what happened to her. Family members told my mother her other daughter—Beulah, whom we call Billye—was sold, aged 13, for $400 and some land to a man in his 40s. She gave birth to a boy and a girl by this man, and when she was 19, she took her children and ran away. The man found Billye and kidnaped her children; she never saw them again. They were only three and four years of age at the time.

Billye made her way to California, where she became a companion to an elderly lady who had no heirs. When she inherited the woman's estate, she remade herself, started a business, became active in her community, and married a prominent businessman, who tried unsuccessfully to find her children. I grieve to think about what those poor children suffered, and I cannot even imagine the pain of never knowing what happened to them. Billye was named Woman of the Year by the governor of California in the 1950s, but I think she always feared her past would surface and destroy the image she worked so hard to achieve. Considering every-

---

1 Several years after the first printing of this book, Ruby Ellen's granddaughter, Rita, found me. When we met, she brought documents, and we were able to put many missing pieces into place. Ruby Ellen died from cirrhosis of the liver and is buried in a pauper's grave in Washington state. Clearly, she had a terrible, sad life.

thing she went through, I can understand why. I identify with Billye in many ways.

The day I entered the hospital, I met with Ruth, a cousin looking for her birth family. She looked very much like Billye and was the illegitimate daughter of Ben, my dad's younger brother. I took her to meet my mother, who claimed no knowledge of Ruth's existence. I suspected otherwise because she was unusually quiet that day and has never spoken of Ruth since. The timing of Ruth's coming into my life just now seems ironic—when I, too, am searching for answers to secrets.

Dad's mother, a schoolteacher, was of Cherokee Indian descent. After her death, my grandfather sold the Oklahoma farm, put his family in a covered wagon, and moved to New Mexico Territory. Mom says that he arrived with a wad of money in his pocket but handed most of it over to booze and gambling. He bought some farmland, where they lived in a dugout—a large hole dug into the ground and covered with hay, and who knows what else, for a roof. I think you could say they were dirt-poor. I cannot imagine what life must have been like for Dad and his family. He never talked about it.

I told my father's story with no emotion; they were just facts. Barb persisted—I had not told her anything about my father and me. Uncertainty lingered. I was not sure where this session was going to take me.

Well, there isn't much I can tell you, Barb. I didn't really know my father. He died in 1980, and I know it sounds odd, but I developed a relationship with him after he died. Daddy was a quiet, distant person who lived his life withdrawn into himself. I can't remember ever having a conversation with him when I was growing up. He just didn't talk. He was a good man, but he just wasn't involved in my life. Considering his childhood, I'm surprised he didn't become an alcoholic like his father, or worse. I do believe he loved my siblings and me. He just didn't know how to show it since he didn't have any role models since his mother died, and his father wasn't much of a father.

After Dad's death, I went into therapy for the first time. Depression had plagued me since I was a kid, and after he died, I got much worse. Through treatment, I grew to understand my dad better. My mother was always telling me that Dad never wanted children. In my young mind, I translated that as *Dad did not want me*—but in retrospect, I think he was afraid of having a deformed child, or maybe he just didn't want to bring children into this troubled world. I no longer believe he did not want me.

I was always concerned about my dad's spiritual beliefs. He became a Mason as a young man, and the Masons became his religion. He once told me he believed in Jesus, but he seldom went to church, and he didn't rear his kids in the Christian faith. It's all very confusing to me.

Toward the end of his life, Dad was in and out of the hospital a lot. I would go and sit with him, read from the Bible, and pray for him. One day, lying in his hospital bed, he began to speak words from the Old Testament; Masons appear to know many Old Testament texts.

"I will give you a plumb line in the wilderness. From dust, you were made, and to dust, you will return."

I had only seen my father cry once, and that was when

his last brother died. But that day in the hospital, he sobbed, and the fear in his eyes broke my heart. I asked him if he was afraid.

He said, "Yes, I'm afraid."

Drawing close to his side, I picked up my father's soft, aged hand.

I said, "Oh, Daddy, don't you see that Jesus is the plumb line in the wilderness that God gave us to get through this life, the one who directs our path to God and life eternal? Can't you see you have nothing to fear if you believe in Him?"

A peaceful silence followed, and the unmistakable presence of love filled the small hospital room. My father slowly nodded his head in affirmation.

He whispered, "Yes, I guess that I do."

I watched peace settled upon my dad—a peace that never left him from that day on. His fear of death vanished.

When death became imminent, Mother called me to the hospital. Alone with my dad, I stood beside his bed as he slept. His skin had a youthful glow—his face free of wrinkles. Picking up his frail hand, I closed my eyes and began to pray softly.

I felt a tug at my hand; when I opened my eyes, they met his clear, blue gaze.

"Daddy, what do you need?"

There was no reply, just the gentle tug at my hand. It must have taken every ounce of my father's strength as he struggled to pull both our hands to his moist mouth. Finally, he firmly pressed his lips against the back of my hand—a kiss—seeking to touch the heart and soul of his distant, youngest child. My hand fell from his grip, and he quietly slipped back into himself.

This was a man who did not know how to say, "I love you" and seldom showed affection, even toward his wife. He was a man who, not by choice but because of his childhood, had been a detached parent. Yet in that one brief, final kiss, my father said to me what he could not speak with words. It is only in retrospect that I fully appreciate and understand that precious God-given moment with my father.

A surge of emotion. Tears suddenly rushed into my eyes and just as quickly disappeared. I would not welcome tears here at this moment. I continued.

> It has been ten years since we buried my dad. It seems like yesterday. I will never forget the day because it was bitter cold and snowing; he always hated the snow. I have wondered if it was because there was never enough heat or clothing to keep him warm as a child, but not on that day. I knew where he was.
>
> My lack of grief over my father's death remains a mystery to me. How do you grieve over someone you don't know? When I saw my children crying, I cried; I felt their sorrow. Yet there was an emptiness, a repressed sense of loss that seemed buried deep inside me, which I carried for several years before finally seeking the help of a counselor.
>
> The opportunity to role-play happened during my first session with David, the therapist. He explained that he would take on my father's role, which would allow me the chance to say things to my father that I could not tell him when he was alive. Hesitant, I agreed to his suggestion.

He asked, "What would you say to your father if he were here right now?"

It was many long minutes before I mustered the courage to speak.

"Why didn't you protect me when I was abused? Why didn't you love me?"

Through the voice of this wise counselor, I heard all the things I had needed to hear from Dad but never did.

"I am sorry you were abused and hurt as a little girl. I am sorry I was not there for you. If I had known, I would have protected you. Please forgive me. I love you. I appreciate the person you have become."

Those responses enabled me to take three baby steps I didn't know I needed to take: I accepted that my father probably did not know what was happening to me, I forgave him for not being there to protect me, and I acknowledged that he truly did love me. He did the best he could do, considering his childhood circumstances.

I paused to process what I had reported to Barb. Perhaps I had not fully understood its value at the time—but was my time with David a priceless gift for me to embrace now?

I stayed in therapy with David for a short time, only touching the tip of the iceberg and not disclosing much information beyond admitting to being a victim of child abuse. Looking back, I believe this discerning man knew there was much more I was not saying.

During my last session, he told me a story about a large

basket of shamrocks, in full bloom, given to him and his wife. One morning they got up only to discover their two-year-old son had taken his toy bat and beaten all the blossoms off their lovely plant, except for one. They were disappointed, but in time the shamrocks came back to life and thrived wonderfully.

"Nola," he said, "you remind me of that basket of shamrocks. You have been beaten down and beaten down. And now you only have one blossom left standing. I believe that someday you will come back in full bloom, more beautiful than ever."

Again, I paused as I began to realize that the story of the shamrocks lingered in the soil of my soul. Had David planted seeds of hope in my heart for a time such as this?

After the role-playing session, I began having dreams about being with Dad in old familiar places. Instead of just watching him from afar, together we fished, worked in the garden, played dominoes—we talked and laughed and hugged. My father became so real to me that I began to have a sense of knowing him, having a relationship with him. The slightest memory would trigger tears. Eventually, I began to grieve the loss of my father.

It was Kim who helped me move through that period of grief. She and her granddaddy had a special bond, even though she was only three when he passed. It was her enduring memory of him that kept him alive—remembering special moments. I learned to love my father through the eyes of my child.

One night Daddy came to me in another dream. He told

me he had come to say goodbye and that I needed to talk to my mother—warning me that she would not be with me much longer. I never dreamed of him again. I miss my dad.

For the first time since I had entered the hospital, I felt something more than physical pain. A single teardrop slowly slid down my cheek. Barb was not going to let me slip away from the moment so easily.

She asked, "Why was your father warning you to talk to your mother?"

I quickly took control of my emotions, stuffing them, denying them, doing anything to keep them hidden. The momentary expression of grief was lost in my now-rigid body, and I began to ache all over again. Dr. Kamen had expressed great concern over my ability to feel physical pain but not emotional pain. I did not understand it either.

We would talk about my mother another day.

Chapter 6

I Always Hate Personality Tests—I Never Know the Answers

Despite the demanding hospital schedule, I had much-needed time to process and reflect. The busyness of life had enabled me to avoid confronting my past, but now I had the rare opportunity to walk away from daily responsibilities. I had permission to pause and seriously look at the canvas of my life. Now was the time to give careful thought to the changes I needed to make.

I had walked through the first weeks on 3E very much in a daze. In the beginning, I resented the camaraderie of the patients who had been there for a while. Their laughter and joking irritated me. I judged them, thinking they could never understand or relate to me in any way. All I wanted was to be left alone, and I made my feelings quite clear to everyone right off the bat.

But time has a way of changing things. My peers had also figured out how to hide behind locked doors where shame and pain crouched in distant corners, begging to be found, hoping to stay lost. Eventually, I embraced their struggles and let my guard down. Friendships formed, and reluctantly I began to feel I was in a safe place.

Although the staff was persistent in getting patients back into life as quickly as possible, focusing seemed hopeless in those first few weeks. I resisted progress, but I could not wrap my thoughts around why. I sat through countless training classes, wondering what these trained professionals were trying to show me. Some days were torturous for me.

When I tried to forget, I remembered, but remembering only made me try to forget all over again. I kept hiding and surfacing, surfacing and hiding, never knowing just who was disappearing or emerging. Denial was my game. Confusion was its name.

I began to understand that the threads of knowledge given to me daily in this place represented my life, and they desperately needed to be rearranged. But how would I ever sort *me* out of those tangled strands? And what had forbidden me access to them for over 40 years? There were times when I thought I really might go mad, but I had to keep trying. Every day that I hung in there, each day that I worked hard and stretched beyond my limits, I found my hopelessness grabbing onto the golden threads of hope that dangled before me. As I began to see that my life circumstances were anything but normal, reality slowly fell into place. Emotional chaos had become my "normal," but living in confusion is not normal, not what God created for His children.

The very thought that I might be able to begin again gave me hope. Ever so slowly, methodically, I began to untangle the strands of my life that would ultimately enable me to open locked doors where hopelessness and hope held hands.

Chapter 6

The first of many doors I opened centered on the confusing signals and messages I sometimes radiated to those around me. Those who crossed my path pretended not to notice, or cared insufficiently to notice, or didn't know what to do with me and just walked away. More importantly, I did not know what to do about the confusion that tormented me. If I was going to change, I had to look inside and dig as deep as possible to understand who lived inside of *me*. In the solitude of my hospital room, I allowed my thoughts to revisit worrisome memories to try and figure out the cause of my sometimes troubling patterns of behavior.

As I continue with my story, recall that the italicized text represents the inner voices living within the AAC (me). At times you will hear my inner voice as I awaken to many things I had not previously understood.

I was usually in the kitchen when Jake came home from work, but I recall one day being in the family room when he stepped into the entryway. I don't remember what I was doing, but Jake immediately stopped dead in his tracks and looked at me.

"What happened to you today?"

I looked up at him and simply replied, "Nothing!"

"Well, you're not the same person you were when I left here this morning!" I can still hear the puzzled, matter-of-fact tone in his voice.

I shrugged; he walked away. I paused, wondering what this meant. *How many times has he been greeted by this unsuspecting stranger that mysteriously appears and disappears? Who else has seen her?*

Another incident. My oldest daughter was only five years old when one day she suddenly turned to me with tears in her eyes, tiny hands perched on slender hips.

"Mommy, what happened? You were so happy a minute ago." *How many times has my mood turned on a dime, leaving my children feeling dismayed, confused, and hurt?*

Even my handwriting gave way to confusion. As a teenager, I left a written message for my mother one morning, telling her I had gone out with a friend. Later, she asked me who had written the note. When I told her I had, she looked surprised.

"That is not possible. This is not your handwriting."

But I knew I had written the note.

After that incident, I became aware that my penmanship seemed to change drastically from time to time. Some days it was hardly legible, while at other times, the very style of my writing took on different characteristics. *Why did this strange phenomenon suddenly begin in my teens? What were these drastic changes in my handwriting trying to tell me? And why do these frustrating changes continue to haunt me?*

As a cheerleader in high school, I recall feeling that I was sitting in the stands watching rather than being on the football field performing. The same thing happened if I stood in front of my class giving a book report or playing my clarinet in a band competition. Anytime I was the center of attention, I just seemed to go somewhere else where a kind of darkness engulfed the space around me. *Why am I afraid of drawing attention to myself?*

It seemed that whenever I felt unsafe or threatened, or scared, I just faded into the background. *Where is this dark place that I go to hide? And what is this overshadowing darkness that I feel? Why do I feel so unsafe? Why do I want to hide? Why do I sometimes dance with the darkness?*

Sometimes when someone is standing over me, watching me do something, I get fearful, and my mind shuts down. I can't think clearly. Sometimes I feel so alone and lonely—deserted. *Feelings of panic assault me when people are too close to me. Why?*

While setting the dinner table for my mother-in-law, she once commented that I set the table properly for a change. When I replied that I always set it correctly, she quickly informed me that I seldom did. I was baffled and angry because I just knew I always set her table the exact same way. *Why do I sometimes do things and then deny that I did them? Why am I constantly changing horses in midstream? What compulsion fuels this strange behavior? Have my confusing mannerisms created the many issues I've had with my husband's family and others?*

Occasionally, someone will comment about something I supposedly said that was totally out of character for me, and I will think, "But I would not, and did not, say that!" Or people would comment on the way I felt about something when I knew the opposite to be true. I would get angry at people for making up things about me and wonder what in the heck their problem was. *Anger seems to come unexpectedly from nowhere, unbridled, unexplainable. Why? And why the confusing messages? I am beginning to see something is very wrong with me.*

Some people seem to love and respect me, while others reject me. Some have walked away from me. I have walked away from many. Perhaps I built walls of protection around myself so no one could get inside? But then I am told I have no boundaries at all; I don't protect myself! *I am so confused. I don't understand. Why?*

I have often felt deserted, unloved, and suspicious of others, unable to trust. *Why does the bad so often overshadow the good? And why do I not trust?*

Sometimes I have made inappropriate, unwise choices that simply made no sense to me. Sometimes evil danced all around me, and sometimes I danced with evil. I had no control. *Why am I so powerless?*

Jake once asked me if I knew that I occasionally asked him if he wanted a divorce (at least ten times). I was bewildered because not only did I not recall his answer, I did not understand why I would even ask such a question. *Did I fear he would leave me or stop loving me? Or did I feel so unworthy that I needed reassurance? Perhaps I just wanted to run away.*

If Jake and I argued, I would either go into a rage to defend myself, or else I would bow my head like a scolded child and turn childish emotions inward.

Sometimes, in a group discussion where someone challenged me or said something that made me feel unsafe, unappreciated, or devalued, I would feel myself becoming childlike—powerless. I would often snap out of it and carry on, but at other times I would sink into a depression that would last for days or even weeks. *Does my outward demeanor change as I withdraw into myself? Why do I feel so fragmented and detached from reality? And why am I always depressed? Why do I always see the negative side of everything, and why am I always on the lookout for danger?*

I am often called a perfectionist. It is true, except that I never achieve perfection. I will work endlessly trying to make something exactly right—my house, a painting, a project, the way I look, my kids. I need everything around me to be perfect, yet nothing in my life is ever perfect.

Even unimportant things control me. I will write a letter over and over, trying to get my handwriting to look correct. I get upset when I cannot do things perfectly. If I find something in disarray, I get angry because *someone* has messed up my space. I know I am the guilty one, but I will blame others.

It seems am I at war with myself. Why do I put so much pressure on myself and those around me? Why do I strive for perfection and then fall short? Why do I have such unrealistic expectations of others and then find fault when they disappoint me? Why can't I just be me and let others be who they are? Why am I so angry?

But wait! There is so much evidence to challenge *all* of the above. An entirely different side to me exists. Some know me to be calm, stable, reliable, and wise. I am hardworking with determined values. I am quietly confident, dedicated, kind, loving, thoughtful, and good at heart. I am a person who loves God and desires to serve Him. I love my husband, my children, and people in general. I am optimistic, positive, and secure in my faith.

Doesn't this define who I am? *Or is this troubled one the one I keep hearing about—the wounded child that lives within me? Has she been screaming at me for all these years, hoping to get my attention, hoping I would feel her pain? Is she the one causing all this confusing conflict? I am trying so hard to find her, but is she trying to find me too? And who is holding us together?*

Who am I?

Shades of tenderness, clouds of sadness, lights of joy, shadows of darkness, great moments of peace, rages of anger—what were they trying to tell me? *God, please, help me to understand.*

I always hate personality tests. I never know the answers.

Chapter 7

Teddy Bears—in Search of My Lost Little Girl—a dog and a Rooster

Everyone thought it strange initially, but before long, just about every patient had one: a teddy bear! I had brought two with me when I checked in. One was white and had been a Christmas present from my son. I tucked her in my bed each day because she symbolized the part of me that had struggled so hard to survive; she simply needed to rest. The soft, cuddly brown one begged to be held and became my symbolic wounded child. She went everywhere with me. One day, during my free time, the three of us curled up together on my stiff hospital bed in search of the lost little girl we longed to know . . .

The little girl flipped through the pages of the large old book. "How does it all end?" The smell of ages past lingered on the worn, yellowish-brown pages. The once luxurious brown leather cover was falling apart. The Bible had belonged to her dad's father, whom she did not know because he died before she was born. She never saw anyone read it and wondered how it had gotten in such a state, but she sensed its mystery as she felt an ancient power drawing her deeper into its grasp. Her heart seemed to dance as she once again turned to the last chapter of Revelation. She often went there, searching to understand how it would all end. How strange that one so young would be so concerned about the end of life when her life had just begun. It all sounded so odd, and she was never sure if she had gotten answers or only more questions. "If God is the beginning and the end, then how did it begin, and how does it end? What was before the beginning, and who made God? Where did He come from, and who made whoever made Him? How did it all get started?" Her desire to know about God seemed insatiable.

There had been many West-Texas-hot summer days like this one spent on the screened-in porch of the yellow Santa Fe company house. Lying on her back, she paused to search the baby-blue sky with its cottony clouds to find tigers and bears that turned into dragons and castles, kings and queens. Stories unfolded. Leaving her imaginary friends in the sky, she sat up and balanced the cumbersome book on her lap.

"Why would God want to keep dogs out of the city anyway?" she mused as she read Revelation 22:14–15. "Now, murderers and those immoral guys, that's okay . . . but *dogs*?"

She shook her head quizzically. The child was quite sure that God loved dogs and cats too. He was always sending stray cats for her to feed, and she knew that her dog, Lady Bug, with her white coat and great black patches, was a gift from above. Her pet was her constant

Chapter 7

companion and soulmate, the only living being allowed to enter the closed doors of the little girl's heart.

Summer nights would find the two of them sneaking into the small living room, where the only air that moved came from the noisy window cooler. Away from the sweltering heat and giant buzzing Texas mosquitoes, they would catch a few hours of restful sleep and then slip back to her room before dawn. By then, the bugs would have mysteriously disappeared, and the heat rested for a spell. Cold winter nights would find them snuggled together under thick, heavy blankets. A trip to the small space heater in the living room was just too far away.

A tattered, homemade quilt tossed on the grass found clear, cloudless summer nights calling the little girl to lie back and gaze into the blackest of black skies, where she witnessed billions of brilliant stars; they beckoned her to imagine far beyond their limits until she would become frightened and look away. Lady could have cared less, but the young girl yearned to know all about the mysteries she could not see.

Mischief and adventure became twins to be shared, worthy of any consequence. They made kites out of flour paste, old newspapers, and sticks. Cotton rags, if too heavy, would cause the kite to crash. They crashed a lot.

The girl and her dog walked the railroad tracks for hours on end and cautiously played in the enchanted forest of the nearby creek. The sight of a snake would send the child away screaming, with a bewildered Lady chasing after her. She hated snakes!

A rarely possessed balloon could quickly be turned into a water balloon, but she had to be careful with them in such a small town; her sins would be sure to find her out. Getting caught once was enough for the two of them.

A trip to the gas station down the road for a five-cent Coke was a rare treat; if the girl was lucky, she might even be able to buy a bag of Tom's peanuts to pour into the bottle. Yum!

If the pair came upon a giant anthill in the middle of a dusty path, they would stop and agitate the red, stinging creatures with a long stick. The child found strange delight in standing over the insects and watching them scurry around in a panicked state of confusion. She wondered if they were afraid of the dark, ominous shadows that lurked over them, disturbing their peace—and she wondered why she wondered. At times, she also felt a dark presence standing over her, and sometimes she was afraid.

If they couldn't find ants to bother, they would perhaps find a small horny toad. The child loved the adorable, ugly creatures. They brought out the tender side of her as she turned them onto their backs and gently rubbed their tummies until they trustingly fell asleep in her hand. Sometimes the little girl felt that she, too, was held gently in the palm of a trusting hand. Again, she wondered.

The two companions enjoyed a small circle of friends. They watched through the slats of the pig pen as the bald pink piglets squealed and wallowed in the red mud. Giggles and barking ensued. Together they marveled when fluffy yellow balls of feathers emerged from white shells and became plump, white chickens almost before their eyes. But there was always a price to pay for these stolen moments of happiness.

Slaughter day for the pigs would find Lady and her forever friend walking as far away as possible to avoid hearing their entertainers' final squeals. And then, almost every Sunday morning, they faced the ungodly sight of headless hens hopping all over the yard after bare hands had wrung their necks. She wished to change things, but somehow knew she was powerless. She stuffed her emotions deep inside.

Chapter 7

She learned one day, with no help from her BFF, that roosters have no sense of humor. The chicken coop was home to a bunch of hens, but only one imposing, colorful rooster. Sunrise would find the little girl standing on the front porch, mocking that silly old bird. As he strutted around with his head held high and his chest stuck out, the competition would begin. He would crow, and she would crow back to him, each turn getting louder. The girl could always tell when she was getting his goat and would double over with laughter when she heard him flapping his wings in frustration.

A distant voice warned, "You better stop that! Someday that old boy is going to get you!"

Disobedience prevailed; one day, he did.

She was about six years old when she decided to gather eggs out of the henhouse alone. She had watched her dad do it many times; nothing to it. She called Lady to join her as she skipped across the spacious yard to the aged wooden tin-roofed chicken coop. The old dented bucket for gathering eggs hung high from a rusty nail just outside the henhouse gate. She stretched on tippy toes to reach the bucket, but when her fingertips touched its bottom, it came crashing down on her head, causing a bit of a stir among the chickens and a bump on her head.

Perhaps this should have been a warning to leave well enough alone, but there was a determined, stubborn side to her that never wanted to listen to the voice of reason. Lady sat watching, unusually quiet, her tail twitching in anticipation. The girl unlatched the gate, picked up the bucket, and confidently stepped inside the smelly chicken pen. She fastened the gate securely behind her; she was, after all, wise enough to know that escaping chickens would not be a good thing. She cheerfully turned around . . . only to find the joy of doing a grown-up's job suddenly snatched right out from under her.

Her body suddenly plastered against the locked gate, she found herself eyeball to beady, vengeful eyeball with the rooster! His mass of colored, ruffled feathers hovered over her; his wings spread wide. There was no time to retreat. She was trapped. The very first peck on the top of her already aching head told her she had gotten herself into a heap of trouble this time.

The chase began. Lady, the cheerleader, encouraged the chaos and perhaps alerted her father to the trouble in the henhouse. Before too much damage had been done—though the hens probably didn't lay eggs for a week—her father quietly rescued her from her perilous plight.

But the child wondered where her mother was. She needed a hug.

Although done with grown-up jobs and roosters, her adventurous, strong-willed, and sometimes rebellious spirit stuck to her like flour paste on a stick. Those traits would prove to be both her strength and her weakness.

As the years passed, the girl and her companion no longer sought the adventures of the past. Lady Bug was content to dream of chasing rabbits, while the growing child found a new friend in a little blue parakeet. As sure as Lady had given her the gift of love and companionship, Dickie Bird would lead her to the threshold of faith.

The knock at the door was intrusive. I did not want the little girl who had come to visit us to leave. I wanted more of her, but there were so few memories. I could barely find my parents anywhere in my stories, especially my mother. Who had been there to teach me, to protect and comfort me, or wipe my tears when I cried? I began to think seriously about the question I kept being asked: "Who took care of you?"

Chapter 7

I did not remember being taken care of. I found little joy, no laughter in my memories. I wanted to know why.

Barb had interrupted my childhood adventure, and I knew she had come for more information. We decided to continue my family history in the sunshine.

Chapter 8

Who Took Care of You?

Again, I welcomed the warmth of the sun coming through the window at the end of the deserted hallway. Texas summers get progressively brutal, but for me, the cold air-conditioned interior of the building was just as harsh. I settled into the familiar chair with my arms wrapped around my security blanket: my brown teddy bear. She was always there for me when long days brought conflicting emotions and feelings.

The protective arms of Unit 3F continued to do their magic as I slowly allowed myself to peek over the walls I had built around me—but I still spoke in generalities when it came to my childhood secrets. Details of the abuse remained locked away inside. I knew they were there—I had many memories—but I would not, could not speak of them. Dr. Kamen and Ron, my therapist, wisely understood my inability to talk and gave me time to process. They were patiently waiting for me to trust them, but trust did not come easy.

Sitting in the chair opposite me, Barb pressed on with pad and pen in place, repeating her final question from our last session.

"Why do you think your father was warning you in your dream to talk to your mother?"

I had not been able to answer her then, but now I sat pensively considering the last dream I had of my father. I felt overcome by numbness. I wanted to give Barb the answers she sought, so why was I hesitant? I was starting to stand in front of my locked doors and look at them through different eyes.

Let us pick up our brushes and continue with the wash, the background for my painting.

> Barb, I believe God was speaking to me through my dream because He knew I needed answers, and my mother was the only one who could give them to me. David, the therapist I saw after Dad died, encouraged me to talk to her about the sexual abuse. I have always felt she knew about it but did nothing to stop it. I'm a mother. I would know if that was happening to my child, especially a young child . . . she had to know, and she did nothing. I am very angry with her.

My voice is flat; I speak with no emotion. *Where is my anger?*

> David had warned me that Mother's response might be negative, so I was somewhat prepared. But it still made me angry; it still hurt when she denied knowing anything. However, it was a beginning, and my dad was correct: I needed to get answers that only she could give me—answers that would perhaps explain what I did not know.

Chapter 8

Eventually, Mom admitted that one of her older brothers raped her when she was 15 years old; she later told me the abuse began when she was younger. I strongly suspect I am the only person she ever talked to about it, and she was close to being 80 years old at the time. I still cannot believe Mom held that in for all those years.

My words spoke back to me about my own secrets—the ones I protected and guarded, the ones I had a death grip on, the ones I refused to talk about.

I suppose that's why my mother was constantly sick and always seems angry or bitter about something. I know a sweet and loving person lives underneath her pain because I caught glimpses as I grew up. However, the fact remains I don't really know my mother any better than I knew my father.

I was beginning to see that perhaps I was just as complex and perplexing as my mother, but I wanted to deny the similarities.

My mother's attitude toward God is confusing to me. Although reared in the church, she talks about it with hints of bitterness. I've heard her make snide remarks about her brother who raped her. She calls him a hypocrite because he is a prominent deacon in his church. My uncle never came to my mother to ask for forgiveness, and I have a big problem with that.

Mother's mother was in her mid-fifties when she died; I never knew her. I was told she dragged all six of her kids to church every time the doors were open, but she acted like anything but a Christian at home. It appears she had a mean streak. I found this out from a cousin because Mom never talked about her; it never occurred to me to question why.

Did she also blame her mother for not protecting her? And what had happened to my grandmother that made her so confusing and harsh?

Now, as I think about it, Mom seemed to have a mean streak too. I recall her hitting my brother, almost five years older than me, hard enough to flip him over a chair. And she did seemingly unkind things to me.

Strange yet familiar parallels were beginning to emerge—and I wondered about the three of us. Had my mother somehow twisted her mother's actions and that of her brother's around God and the church until they became a monster in her mind? Was the AAC's judgment of her mother unjust?

Mom's father eventually married Georgia, who became the only grandmother I knew. She was the first person I told when I was baptized because she always talked to me about Jesus the few times I saw her, and I know she prayed for me. Grandad, who lived to be in his 90s, was always a sweet old man in my eyes, but it appears that was not always the case. He was a farmer and extremely strict on all his kids. One of my aunts died at the age of 16 from a heat stroke. She had not been allowed to come in out of the heat while chopping cotton, even though she had complained about not feeling well.

Chapter 8

I'm sure my mother had to work hard as she grew up, but she didn't work to keep our house clean. As a schoolgirl, I would spend every Saturday cleaning; something about me could not handle clutter, uncleanliness. I resent her terribly for that. Now, as an adult, every time I go over and clean her house, it just makes me angry all over again. If only, she would just halfway try to pick up after herself.

Somewhere along the way, my mother started going to fortune-tellers and reading her horoscope. That is where she put her faith, and I suspect it was part of what kept her and her family in spiritual bondage. She was not at all happy about my becoming a Christian. When I begged to be baptized, she flatly forbade it, refusing to give me an answer when I asked her why. I did not understand then, and I don't understand now. I'm still angry at her over that one.

It seemed to me she always said things to hurt or embarrass me in front of people, especially my friends. One Christmas Eve, my brother, who had come home from college, started giving me spiked eggnog. My mother knew I had plans to go to a midnight Mass with a friend and did nothing to intervene. I was only 15, and we had just moved to the town, so this was a new friend. Anyway, my mother thought it was funny that I went to church drunk. She later told the story to the parents of a boy I was dating. I was so embarrassed, and I just could not understand why she would do that to me. I could never understand why my mother didn't like me. I never wanted my friends to come over to my house.

About a year ago, I confronted her again about the sexual abuse. I had been trying to connect my feelings with reality, so I went to her house searching for childhood pictures, hoping they would trigger memories that would help make sense of my life. I noticed that everyone in our family seemed ordinary in the photos, except for me: I never smiled. I don't think I was a happy child.

As I began to pull my story together for Barb, reality came to life within me.

> Determined to get answers, I pushed until my mother finally began to talk. I kept telling her that not only did I have actual memories of abuse, but I also had physical and emotional memories I could not connect to reality. One of the feelings I had was extreme defiance, and I associated it with my birth.
>
> Reluctantly, she told me that Dad's oldest brother lived with them when she was pregnant with me. My father traveled with his job and was gone most of the time. The anger she'd harbored all those years suddenly snapped, her voice defiant.
>
> "He was after me all of the time. The whole time I was pregnant with you, I had to fight him off me. Every night I had to push my dresser up against the door to keep him out of my room."
>
> As soon as the words tumbled out of her mouth, I remembered: this same uncle had molested me.
>
> I told her.
>
> She demanded, "Why didn't you ever tell me all of this was going on?"
>
> Determined, I replied, "And why didn't you ever tell anyone about your brother raping you?"

Without hesitation, she flatly replied, "Well, no one would have believed me!"

The moment of truth arrived. Mother understood; no one would have believed me either. She just looked at me, defeated, resigned, finally permitting me to confront a family member. However, the thought of doing so felt very unsafe.

Could the emotions associated with my mother's defiance of my uncle have been transferred to her unborn child? If so, I wondered what other reactions I might have sensed from her. I allowed myself to dig deeper as I dared to ask myself: Had my mother, almost 35, really wanted a fifth child? Had I felt unwanted from the womb? Is this why I felt so detached from her? And where was my sister when Mom locked my uncle out of her room?

My heart sank when I realized that my poor sister would have been 12 at the time and very vulnerable and defenseless.

Previously, talking to my mother had paved the way, but now talking to Barb about her allowed me to force my way through locked doors where my precious child remained hidden. My words were giving me the courage to begin facing the secrets that had caused her to hide. For the first time, I realized my mother was not unlike me, and I had to face the fact that she was in just as much pain. We had each controlled our lives in unhealthy yet different ways to survive.

I flashed back to a dream—a river, and the pleading words of my father: "You need to talk to your mother."

And my own pleading words to my mother: "I need you to stay with me—for just a little while longer."

Barb listened intently and watched with eager anticipation as my mask of denial slowly began to fade. She had earned my trust, and I continued to tell her my story. I could feel an unseen force leading me, step by step. Without my faith, I knew I would not have been able to continue. The darkness was just too dark, and I was afraid.

> My mother used sickness as a way of escape. Since she had confessed that she was often sick in bed, I asked who took care of me when my sister was away at school. With a strange chuckle, she told me there were times when I went the entire day without getting my diaper changed because she was too sick to take care of me. I froze in disbelief. This was long before disposable diapers and special creams for diaper rash, and since she did not nurse me, I wondered if she gave me a bottle of cold milk. Was I not held but kept in my baby bed with a bottle propped against something? Is that why I had earaches? My oldest brother once told me I cried a lot. I wanted to ask my mother if I was ever comforted when I cried or left alone—but I could no longer ask questions—I could not bear to hear the answers.

I wanted to weep for my precious child. Reluctantly, I gave voice to the lingering memories that haunted me.

> Once, when keeping a friend's toddler while she was at work, I had a sudden overwhelming urge to shake the child. I forced myself to back away and leave the room where she was playing with my toddler. It scared me so badly that I immediately told my friend I could no longer keep her sweet little girl. I had no idea what it was about this child that caused such horrific feelings, but I strongly feel it resulted from something that had happened to me as a child. My sister was only 13 when I was born—what young girl can handle such

Chapter 8

stress? What ill mother can deal with a screaming child with an earache? I cannot remember what dreadful event caused my reaction, but I know it came from a very dark place.

Barb suggested I might want to explore abandonment and physical abuse issues. I had never thought about those being relevant. She questioned me about the safety of my children.

As a parent, I have been a firm disciplinarian. No one disciplined me; I was like a wild weed growing up. I was determined not to let that happen to my children. I did spank them, but I never physically abused them. I was a very protective mother—a good mother. I hardly ever let them cry, and I picked them up the minute they whimpered. And I was quick to feed them and change their diapers. I could never harm or neglect a small child.

My words echoed in my head, and I began to wonder if the inner anger I was finding in myself had unknowingly spilled over to my precious children. Were my spankings much too quick and much too harsh? They were such good children and not deserving of anything but kindness from me. I recalled finding a stash of wooden spoons hidden behind some bookcases. Had I been so out of control that my children feared me? The reality was unbearable for me to grasp. I could never harm a child. Never! Where were these thoughts coming from? Stricken with sorrow, I had to move on.

When I went to Mother's house to look through her pictures, I came across a photo of my brother and me with some young men who worked for my dad. Mom had mentioned I learned to speak Spanish because I was around these guys a lot, and she also revealed they sometimes took us into town and bought us candy and stuff.

I tossed the photo in front of her. "How do you know one of these guys didn't abuse me?"

With no emotion, my mother told me that one day she heard me screaming, and when she went outside to investigate, she found one of the men sexually abusing me.

When I asked her what she did, she said, "I told him to leave the house and not come back."

I asked, "What did Dad do when you told him what happened?"

"Well, your dad would have killed the man if I had told him!"

In a flash, the monotone of my voice changed as I shouted my disbelief to Barb. The stark reality of what I was saying was like a sharp slap across my face. I continued, with angry energy in my voice.

> If it had been my child, I would have done serious harm to that man. I was a toddler, still in diapers, running around outside where young men were working. And my mother was in bed, too sick to watch after me. And then she protected the jerk!

Giving voice to my mother's confessions pushed denial away; reality intervened. I had to face facts. I was not making this stuff up. These things happened to me, and they were not acceptable.

> I'm beginning to wonder just how many times something like this happened to me. I have vivid memories of my bot-

tom hurting and burning and itching, but I don't remember why.

My first memories are of being five or six years of age; I can pinpoint the time only because I can remember the surroundings and the house where I lived. I remember having repetitive dreams about being in these long tunnels, looking for a place to hide. I have this *knowing* about something, but I don't know what it is that I know.

I recall one incident when I was about six. My mother took my temperature with a rectal thermometer, commonly used back then. I can still remember her troubled look when she commented that my private area was red and swollen.

Sharing the memory of my mother's words confirmed that my emotional memories were just as real as the actual physical ones I remembered but had repeatedly denied.

Typically, I would bypass anger and settle into denial, but not on this day during this session. The magnitude of what I had just told Barb was enormous; the rage that lurked just below the surface threatened to burst through the strong armor that kept me from exploding. Even though I had been imploding all my life, I was still not capable of outwardly facing anger, not yet. I didn't want to say anything else about my mother. Wisely, Barb did not press me further but shifted the interview to my siblings.

Soon after I was born, Jack, my oldest brother, ran away from home at 15. He never wanted to talk about his childhood, but eventually, he confessed that he'd never felt wanted or loved. My brother told me he was often beaten with a razor strap because our sister, just two years younger than him, always blamed him for things he didn't do. I always knew he held resentments toward her, but I never understood why, and I'm sure I don't know the entire story. Jack told me the last time Daddy beat him, he grabbed the belt out of Dad's hand, threw it in the fireplace, and ran out of the house. He came back home after everyone went to bed. Dad never touched him again. I suspect our father was punished in the same way and disciplined Jack the only way he knew how. I see a lot of hurt on my brother's face when he talks about our parents.

I was beginning to understand that adults often repeat their parents' behavior and that children are vulnerable and easily molded into both good and bad behavior.

Shortly afterward, Jack left home and joined the Merchant Marines. Eventually, he ended up in the army and fought in the Korean War, where he was injured and received a medical discharge. That was the same year Mother suffered a stroke that temporarily paralyzed her on one side of her body. She was only 41 years old, and I was six. When I asked Jack what he remembered most about her, he said she was always sick in bed. Now Jack is an alcoholic and is twice divorced from the mother of his three children. I have always been close to Jack and his family.

I was only two when my sister ran away at 15 to marry a 19-year-old man. I think they lied to get their marriage certificate because she was just a child. Since she had to take care of everything and everybody growing up, I guess I really can't blame her for wanting to get away.

Chapter 8

I've had a difficult time feeling close to my sister. She and I are different, just as my mother and I are different. She is a sweet, loving person, but I think I subconsciously put a thick wall between us because I believe she knew about the abuse.

Sis lives in the same town as my mom and won't let anyone else help take care of her, but then complains because she must do everything. Her first husband died of cancer, and her second husband recently passed with the same disease. I know her life has not been easy, and I feel sad for her. Her son is only six years younger than me, and her daughter is ten years younger. They are more like a brother and a sister to me, and I love them very much.

Confusion flashed through my mind; ambivalent feelings for my sister paralleled those I have for my mother. I love her, but I resent her. She had been my caretaker but abandoned me when I needed her. She did not protect me. Feelings jumbled up in my mind, realizing that my uncle had probably abused my sister as well.

Alice Ann was the third child born to my parents. She was only 20 months old when she died. I was told my dad was devastated by her death. I have always wondered if they both resisted getting close to me because of losing Alice Ann. I wish she had lived . . . then maybe I would not have been born.

Perry is almost five years older than me. We have mostly had a close relationship. He, too, is an alcoholic but stopped drinking for a while after a dreadful accident took his middle child's life. Perry is divorced from the mother of his three

81

boys. His youngest son became a father at the age of 16, and he and his young son have had a tough time. I love those boys and have prayed often for them. My brother does not believe in God and has traveled down some very dark roads; I grieve for him for many reasons.

Perry is my mother's favorite. A close family friend who took me under her wing once told me, when I was about 12, that she'd scolded my mother because all she ever talked about was Perry.

"No one even knows you exist," she told me.

I don't think she meant to be unkind, but her words stung; I knew what she said was true. I don't fault Perry for being the favorite. It was not his choice to make.

After Jake and I were married, he wrote to the hospital where I was born and requested a copy of my birth certificate. When we received it, we were surprised to see that I was a twin. Jake asked my mother about it, but she denied it. He wrote to the hospital, and they sent the certificate back with the word *twin* removed. I think my mother would have told me if a twin had died, but she would never have confessed to giving up one of her children. I have never wanted to open that door, but sometimes I wonder.

While I only have tidbits of information about my family history, I know enough to question what was really going on. I wonder how many secrets my siblings have but refuse to mention. A reliable family source confided that I was not the only victim in my family. She also admitted to being victimized once, and I have no doubts about her story.

And what about the secrets my parents kept to themselves . . . and their parents before them? Where does it stop? I can account for two generations of incest, and I am beginning to believe it has been a long, generational sin that has plagued this family.

I will probably never know all the reasons why my siblings ran away from home at such early ages. My mother once said that when I was born, she had told my father she had made a mess of the first two, so he could raise the other two. I suppose that is when she washed her hands of raising me.

My mother's sister often came to visit us. She would tell me, "You weren't raised; you just grew up."

I do not think any of us were raised. We all just grew up, like our parents before us and, I suspect, their parents before them.

I don't recall ever being told, "I love you."

I sat quietly, choosing not to speak any more about my family. For the first time, I felt their pain. And I wondered sadly—who took care of any of us?

I felt emotionally drained; my body seemed to never stop aching. It had been a long and challenging day.

Since I had been on 3E, I kept hearing about shame, but I could not wrap my mind around what such an emotion meant. But Barb's next daring, invasive question rolled the cold stone of shame right over me, allowing its sting of conviction to speak to me.

"Nola Katherine, who else abused you? What did you tell your mother that you are not telling me?"

With my chin resting on my chest and my eyes cast downward, I could not say anything more, and the session ended. I was not ready to deal with the underlying shame I was beginning to feel.

Chapter 9

Facing a Fear, Comic Relief, a Special Friend, and an Angel

Visitation time, gym time, mealtime, and free time became treasured moments for all of us on 3E. We each had grueling sessions that drained our resources, and we desperately needed respites. The medications I was taking began to punch pinholes of light through the black veil of depression. Consequently, I could now embrace shared laughter and fun.

"Come on, Sharon, it's time for someone to hold the door open for you."

We giggled as I grabbed the slender, freckled arm of my new friend and pulled her into the long cafeteria line. Sharon was always holding the door open for the rest of us, tossing morsels of dry humor our way to make us laugh and help us momentarily forget why we were there. I suspect her humor was more for her benefit than ours. We all loved her and cherished her ability to bring light into our dark and cloudy spaces.

I was blessed to have visitors in the evening. Sharon never had any guests and would manage to drop by my room, staying just long enough to make us smile and perhaps feel like she too was part of a family. Jake brought her a bouquet of flowers. To Sharon, it was a pot of gold.

Sharon had with her several thick volumes of her poetry. I felt honored when she told me she wanted to show them to me. One day we went into her room and innocently closed the door. She had started to trust me and tell me as much as her wounded child would allow about her childhood. I was horrified at the stories she shared and overwhelmed by the look of stark terror that hung relentlessly in the windows of her soul. Anyway, I got so flippin' mad when one of the staff nurses threw open the door, suspicion all over her face; given that Sharon was gay, I suppose she expected us to be engaged in some despicable act. What she found was Sharon stretched out face down across her bed and me sitting cross-legged on a floor covered with books. I let the nurse know in no uncertain terms that she was way off base. We were never bothered again, but this became a defining moment for me.

When I returned to my room that day, I questioned why I had been so defensive when I had no reason. Or did I? Sharon was wounded, and in her pain, she reached out to women for intimacy. I could not blame her, considering her precious child's cruel treatment by the men who attacked her. Being gay, in Sharon's mind, protected her from ever being with a man again.

I could no longer deny that my own story was much like Sharon's. Had I stuffed my confusing sexuality so deep inside I could not see that the sexual abuse imposed upon me as an innocent child had become a predator too?

Abusers leave, but the effects of their actions stay with the victim forever. Sexual abuse confuses sexuality, compounds it, and stuffs its shame and guilt into a dark, forbidden place. This was a door I did not want to open, but I knew I didn't have a choice if I was going to find all the answers I needed.

Once again, my two companions and I curled up on my never-soft bed and relived one of the most cherished times of my life: a time when a small corner of my child-soul found healing, and a place I needed to revisit and process questions I had previously dared not ask.

After graduating from business school, I moved to the Dallas area to look for a job. I moved in with my sister and her family and eventually worked in the accounting department of the company where my brother-in-law worked.

JoAnn came to work there about the time my first marriage ended (I will talk about that later), and we quickly became friends. She owned a small cabin that rested on five acres of land outside of Dallas, and occasionally we would go out on weekends and ride horses around a nearby lake. Sometimes we would detour through the grounds of a monastery not far from her property. I always got a rather mysterious feeling as we rode our horses through the unfinished chapel. The wall-less shelter with its concrete floor, massive square pillars, and finished roof offered shade from the intense summer sun. There was always a sweet, cool breeze sweeping through.

What I cherished most was the gift of laughter JoAnn gave me. Laughter was one of the missing links in my childhood, and to discover its healing power was truly divine. For the first time in my life, I allowed the wounded child within me to play.

Each summer, JoAnn's father led the famous Old Chisholm Trail Ride from Grapevine, near Dallas, to the small town of Saint Jo, Texas, near the Oklahoma border. In June 1967, having convinced her father I was an experienced rider, she asked me if I wanted to go along. I wasn't exactly a skilled rider, but . . . oh well. I was up for the adventure.

Like her father, JoAnn loved to have fun, usually at others' expense, and she knew she was in for the time of her life watching me try to stay on a horse for three days. I did not disappoint her. JoAnn arranged for me to ride her mother's horse, Pam, and before I could even think about changing my mind, I found myself packed and ready to go.

Reddish-brown, big, tall, and proud describes Pam well. And one more thing: she was much too smart for a greenhorn like me. The first morning out on the trail ride, she bloated out her belly when we put the saddle on her so it wouldn't be tight. I forgot I was supposed to check the saddle before I got on her.

Just before we crossed a long, steep, narrow dam, the entire herd of horses took off at breakneck speed at the exact same time. I tried to hold Pam back because I wouldn't say I liked swift gallops; I liked slow gallops, at most. But there was no stopping her. Instinctively she wanted to keep up with the others, and so off she went—and off I went, literally! If only Lady Bug could have seen me. I would have taken a mad rooster in a henhouse over this anytime. And this was only the first day.

The saddle slipped sideways, and I slid sideways with it, shooting off Pam's back faster than a bullet from a gun. When the dust settled and the air returned to my lungs, I slowly lifted my head and opened my eyes. Pam, nonchalantly, returned my gaze while casually chewing on a blade of grass. I'm sure I saw a smug grin on her face.

Fortitude possessed me, or maybe I was in denial; I had no choice but to dust off, buck up, get on that horse, and let her catch up with the others. With wide eyes and a dry mouth, I stuck myself to that animal like a fly to honey. The survivor in me was never short on stubborn determination when she really needed it!

Aside from my life almost coming to a sudden end, the first day wasn't so bad, and I had learned a valuable lesson. As I moseyed along with the other 30 or so participants, the cloudless skies stretched for endless miles ahead of us. The scorching June sun parched my lips, even under my straw cowboy hat, and the backs of my hands slowly turned bright red. I had forgotten to wear gloves. But it didn't matter. Something within me roused, and I felt a peace and happiness I had never felt before.

My new adventure captured my imagination and carried me back in time. I tried to relive the certain hardships my ancestors must have endured as they migrated by covered wagon from Georgia, Mississippi, and Oklahoma to settle in Texas and New Mexico. Whole clans traveled together, which I suppose accounted for the fact that both my grandfathers had married their cousins.

Long hours spent ambling past vast prairies reminded me of roaming buffalo and my Cherokee ancestors. I wished I could hear their stories, now forever lost.

As the sun began to close in on the western horizon, the trail riders came to a stop just ahead of me. I was suddenly famished. At least we didn't need to find our own food and water; I was thankful for the chuck wagon that followed behind us. It was full of delectable country vittles and cold water.

We rode 41 miles the first day and camped near an old cotton gin. That night I had no trouble falling asleep under a star-studded sky that reminded me of long-ago summer nights spent lying on an old, tattered quilt, wondering about the mysteries of God. I was so tired I didn't think about what might be crawling around on the ground beside me. I hate snakes.

However, the dawning of a new day told me this carefree venture might not have been such a good idea. I could hardly move—and this was only the second day. My bowed legs didn't want to walk, and every muscle in my body protested when I moved. To make matters worse, my right knee, which had hit the ground just after my chin the day before, was swollen. A kindhearted retired cowboy came to my rescue. He bathed and massaged my swollen knee with liniment and told me, "You're doing great. You ride like you were born in a saddle."

Well, that was all the encouragement I needed! After riding with the chuck wagon gang for a spell, I wanted to get back in the saddle and relish every moment I had on top of Pam. I noticed JoAnn hadn't laughed much since my ploy for attention the day before.

We traveled only 38 miles the second day and spent a much-appreciated night in a high school gym . . . with showers!

After 92 miles, we made it to Saint Jo. The local cowboys promptly dunked us in the horse troughs located around the old town square. If you kicked and squealed, you got dunked again. They didn't know how good that cold water felt, so we kept on kick'en and squeal'en. The event ended with a Texas-style BBQ.

My first and last trail ride was an unforgettable, fun experience mostly because wherever you found JoAnn, the joy of life was sure to be lurking close by. These were stories I would, indeed, someday tell my grandchildren—but surely our trip to Washington, DC in the fall would not be nearly so adventurous. Or so I thought.

We borrowed JoAnn's mother's camper pickup truck and set out with a number two washtub, a Coleman cookstove, lots of food, sleep gear, and just enough clothing for the ten-day trip. In September 1967, it seemed a reasonable and safe thing for two young gals in their early 20s to do.

I was mesmerized by the beauty of the southern states and the incredible history they held. It was all so different from the flat plains of

Chapter 9

Texas, where there was nothing but miles and miles of nothing but miles and miles, where strong winds frequently tossed red dirt into the spacious sky, changing daylight into darkness, breathing into wheezing, and people into the salt of the earth.

Our visit to the nation's capital was remarkable. I wished for more time to spend there. Moved to tears, I stood frozen in disbelief and bewilderment at the perfectly aligned white crosses in Arlington Cemetery, trying to understand the thousands of lives that war had claimed for my freedom. I found no peace there.

I mourned that fateful day in Dallas as I stood near the Eternal Flame of our fallen president, John F. Kennedy. My grief still fresh, I recalled being close enough to their passing car to touch it—the President and Mrs. Kennedy looking directly at me. Life had given me a precious gift. Minutes later, the shots were fired. The city stopped breathing; for a moment, I stopped breathing as the same eerie silence lingered near his tomb that day

Our time in the capital city passed much too quickly.

On our way back home, we managed to get lost on Mount Mitchell in North Carolina, the highest point east of the Mississipi. At first, we didn't know we were lost, but eventually, we realized we were climbing higher and higher as it kept getting darker and colder. We didn't have a clue where we were or where we were going.

We were growing anxious when suddenly, in the black of night, a small log cabin appeared in the bend of the road. JoAnn brought the truck to a stop, and we sat there for a long while, just staring at the wooden structure. There was not a soul in sight. For once, we didn't find anything funny about our predicament.

Cautiously, we got out of the truck and slowly opened the cabin door, where we were welcomed by the warm glow of a small space heater, spotless showers, and hot running water. We didn't hesitate. We just grinned at each other, ran back to the truck for soap and towels, thanking God all the way!

Refreshed and warm, we climbed back into the unheated camper and piled everything we could find on top of us, and slept like babies. I think we skipped supper.

The following morning, we found our way off the magnificent mountain and continued our trek homeward, making as many stops as possible. Consequently, we failed to reach the campground where we had planned to stay before it got dark. Back then, campsites were very primitive and had no lighting at all.

As we drove into the pitch-black campground, once again, there was no one to be seen. JoAnn parked the truck parallel to a picnic table, where we quickly set up for supper.

We lit a candle and put it on the table beside the stove, which was low on fuel. JoAnn looked for a paper cup while I retrieved a plastic milk jug half full of fuel from the camp box. We quietly soaked up the peace of the evening as I poured the white liquid into the paper cup.

Without warning, the fuel splashed out of the cup and hit the lighted candle. In a flash, my hand, along with the fuel-filled milk jug, was covered with fire. Our eyes followed the flame as it flew to the cup, the stove, the table. We glanced at each other in total shock and disbelief, realizing it was heading toward JoAnn's mother's truck, parked alongside.

JoAnn took command. "Quick! Get away from here, set the jug down, run away from it!"

For once in my life, obedience was not a problem. But then the most incredible thing happened: a man with a fire extinguisher strolled out of the woods and casually put out the fire.

When he had accomplished his mission, he gazed at us and said, "Good night, ladies. Have a good evening."

We stood speechless as he disappeared back into the lightless woods.

Shaken but humbly thankful, we ate cold beans that night—in complete silence.

When daylight peered through the clouds the next morning, we quickly prepared for the day and then searched for the man who rescued us from the fire. But there was no man around for us to thank; we were the only ones at the campsite.

I will always believe the man who visited us that night was an angel sent by God to watch over us. And occasionally, I wonder—if we went back to Mount Mitchell, would we find a heated cabin sitting in the bend of a road?

And there's one other thing: the fire did not even leave a red mark on my hand.

JoAnn made my small world so much bigger and happier. She gave me so much, but in retrospect, I feel I gave her so little in return. I was such a needy person. She was probably the first person in my life I really loved. But there were limits to my ability to love and be loved, and our relationship scared me.

Even though there was never even a hint of anything physical between us, I did not understand the unspeakable, conflicting sexual issues surrounding my relationship with JoAnn. We pulled away from each other, and both began to date again. God had a perfect plan for each of us, which has included our lasting friendship.

A soft tap on my hospital door beckoned me to return from my wistful thoughts. I opened my eyes and saw that Sharon had come to remind me of the time. I had never noticed until now that her smile, her personality, and her sense of humor reminded me a bit of JoAnn.

I smiled back at her, hugged my teddy bears, and then looked at my clock. I had two appointments scheduled back to back.

I was unsure what, if anything, I would reveal about my visit with my forever friend. There were extenuating circumstances in my life that I was not ready to face just yet. Still, I was beginning to rearrange the threads of understanding and hope that I was finding along the way, in this place, where God was calling me to trust Him as I had never trusted Him before. Memories of my special friend had brought joy to my uncertain world, and for just a moment, I felt a twinge of happiness.

Chapter 10

What Does a Little Bird Have to Do with Faith?

My psychiatrist, Dr. Kamen, and my therapist, Ron, were beginning to push me. It had been almost three weeks since I had allowed total strangers into my private space, and I was not telling these professionals what they wanted to hear. I could get into everybody else's issues, but not my own. In my small group, I was the attentive listener, the comforter, the friend. I could encourage others to talk, but I would only share in generalities about my stuff, never allowing honesty to make me vulnerable. I sincerely wanted to move forward. I had begun to progress as I talked with Barb, but I still couldn't bear to look her in the face and tell her, or anyone else, about the wounded child the survivor in me protected.

My next appointment was with Ron, my therapist. I always dreaded my sessions with him because his silence felt like fingernails scratching on a blackboard. He would just sit there, usually looking at the floor or the ceiling, waiting for me to say something. If I sidetracked, he would put me on the spot, asking why I needed to talk about something else instead of myself. I resented his behavior and his mannerisms. For some reason, I could not open up to him, and I was always relieved when our sessions ended. This day was no different than before. Eventually, his silence became his gift to me because he was forcing me to talk.

I met with Barb back at the sunlit window. Having admitted in a previous session that this was my second marriage, I began to feel dread. Before bringing Jake into the picture, we needed to visit those years leading up to my first marriage, and I did not want to go there. However, I knew I must allow Barb to travel with me down pain-filled roads where God's tender mercy and grace miraculously found their way into the deep ruts of my soul. For this part of our canvas, dark shadows must fill the empty spaces where the purest of white strokes will expose the bright light of hope. Today, perseverance will guide our brushes.

> Because my dad worked for the railroad, we moved around to different parts of West Texas. When I was in the second grade, we moved to a small town near Abilene—and this was where most of the abuse I can remember happened.
>
> Ironically, it's also where I found God.
>
> Mrs. Gray, whose husband worked for my dad, lived in the concrete Santa Fe Railroad bunkhouse next door to my house. Her son, Wayne, and I became friends, and I frequently went over to visit. I loved being with Mrs. Gray because of her kindness. She told me stories about a man named Jesus and started taking me to church. I have often wondered if she sensed a deeply troubled child who needed God.

Chapter 10

Images flashed across my mind as sweet memories flooded my soul—recalling that I felt so happy whenever I was in the small white church. I can still see the beautiful, large picture that hung over the baptistry behind the choir: Jesus holding a lamb beside a stream of flowing water.

I loved Sunday school and the hymns we sang. I loved the peace I found there and the people who knew my name and freely gave me hugs.

I clung to the preacher's words as he spoke about God's love and about being born again if I would believe in Jesus to forgive my sins. He didn't know he was tossing lifelines for me to grab. Nor did I.

Although pinpointing exact dates is tricky for me, I was around nine or ten years old when God's Spirit spoke to me through the words of a song that drew me to the altar of prayer. "Softly and tenderly, Jesus is calling, calling for you and for me."

I slipped off the long wooden pew and walked toward the front of the church. Before my knees touched the first step leading to the wooden altar rail, it seemed the entire congregation was on their knees around me, soaking me in prayer. The pastor's wife wrapped her arms around me, held me close, and wept as she prayed over me. Tears wrenched from somewhere deep within as I professed my belief in Jesus and invited Him into my life.

The pastor's prayer of sanctification called for the Holy Spirit's anointing to set me apart as holy for God.[1] At prayer's end, I knew I was somehow different. In retrospect, I believe on that day God commis-

---

1   In John 17:17, Jesus prayed for his disciples. "Sanctify (set apart, declared holy) them by the truth; your word is truth." (NIV)

sioned special angels to watch over me because he knew there would be many spiritual battles fought over me, His wounded, abused child.

As soon as I got home from church, I told my parents I had been saved and sanctified. I got no response. I don't know why my parents were always silent.

I will always be thankful to Mrs. Gray and the small body of believers who prayed me into the mystery of a transformed life through Jesus.

I still seek understanding. As a child, I had been reborn—not in the flesh, but in my soul—but I wonder why the wounded child living in me was not transformed too?

My intimate relationship with God began when He used a small blue parakeet, given to me by my sister, to seal my faith. Dickie Bird soon became my new best friend, and whenever I was at home, he was almost always on my shoulder. He would stop at nothing to get my attention.

If I was attempting to study, he would be chewing on the corners of my schoolbook. If I was writing, he was on my hand, trying to take away my pencil. If my record player was on, he would jump on the record and try to go for a spin. It was a hoot to watch him go sailing from the vinyl disc, flapping his wings wildly.

We kissed and whistled and talked to each other like any friends would. And like Lady, he filled an empty place in my little girl world.

My greatest fear was that someday I would forget about my little buddy and walk outside with him on my shoulder.

Chapter 10

And sure enough, one day, it happened. When I went out the back door to hang laundry on the clothesline to dry, I heard Dickie's wings flutter in my ear, and then he was gone.

Screaming, I ran back into the house to seek my mother's help. She casually looked up from her newspaper and suggested he might have headed for the trees down at the creek, about a hundred yards from our house.

Confusing emotions. Why didn't she go with me? I'm a mother; I would have gone with my child to help find her bird.

In West Texas, trees are sparse, leaving many wide-open spaces where a little bird can get lost. I raced out of the house, sobbing so hard I could barely see. Panic pounded against my chest as I ran down the long dirt path. The blistering summer sun mingled sweat with my tears. For the first time in my life, I cried out to God.

"Please, God, please help me find my bird!"

When I reached the edge of the creek, I stopped and looked into the forest of mesquite trees, wondering how I would ever find him.

I called his name and waited.

I called again . . . and this time I heard him. It was as though he was waiting for me.

"Hello, my name's Dickie Bird" — wolf whistle — "Whatcha do'en?"

I looked up, and there he was, sitting calmly on a limb, looking down at me and chatting away. He flew down onto my shoulder, and as I wrapped my small hands around his hot, panting body, I thanked my God over and over again for helping me find him.

Strong faith was born in my heart on that day because I knew that God hears and answers prayers. However, I did not realize such faith would be tested. I did not know it then, but that day would also change my life's direction.

My life experiences from birth until I met Jesus assuredly revealed something about those earlier years. When I look back, I can see the confusing roles I played. I was a good kid and sweet, a shy kind of girl that most everyone liked. I always had friends, but I was continually changing them, never really staying close to anyone for any length of time. I think I was crying out for help all my young life, but no one was listening, not paying attention. I rebelled against authority and sometimes found myself in trouble at school.

I recall being told not to go over and play on the playground with the big kids. What did I do? I went over and played with the big kids. I was late getting back to my class, but I didn't care.

Once, when the teacher left the room, all the boys started throwing chalk erasers. I was the only girl in the room to get into trouble right along with them.

I was always getting in trouble for talking and passing notes in class, but my worst mistake was underestimating a football coach overseeing the study hall. He had repeatedly told me, a girlfriend, and several boys to stop talking and had warned that we would get paddled if we did not stop. My friend and I thought he would never spank a girl, so we ignored the coach. Well, guess who got lined up with the boys and spanked with a wooden paddle with holes in it? That cured me from talking in study hall.

Chapter 10

During recess, I would play baseball with the boys, which is how I learned to hit a hard, straight ball. One day, I got hit right smack in the middle of my tummy with one of those hard fastballs. I thought I was going to die and decided it was time to find something else to do.

Chewing gum in class, stealing some small thing out of the Five & Dime, cheating on a test, skipping my homework—if there was a rule, I wanted to break it. I never wanted to be told what to do. Once, when Lady was in heat, Mother told me not to let her outside. Of course, I opened the door, and off she went. Puppies followed.

None of these were severe infractions by today's standards, but they were shameful acts back in the 1950s. For me, they were symptoms. I had no shame; I was left to my own devices. There was no one there to pull me aside and help me be any different.

Was I predestined for more significant offenses, more painful failures because of the things I would not talk about?

No one gave me an incentive to learn, so I did what I had to do to get by. No one had read to me or taught me that learning was a good thing. I recall when I learned to spell *envelope*; I went around the house all day saying, "e-n-v-e-l-o-p-e." It was such a big word, and I was so proud of myself. But no one stopped to listen; no one patted me on the head; no one said, "Good job." To this day, I remember feeling disappointed, sad, unimportant.

Another defining moment happened when my fourth-grade math teacher towered over me and chastised me for not getting 100% on a test. I think I only missed a couple of problems. She announced to the entire class that she had taught my brother math, and he was a whiz.

"I know you can do better than this. You are just freezing up on tests!"

All eyes focused on me, the space around me turned dark, and for the first time that I can remember, I disappeared into the darkness. From that moment on, I hated math.[2]

This teacher's action ultimately caused me to just sail along with the wind when it came to my education. I had a very "I don't care" attitude.

Why did this teacher's action impact me so strongly? What about this situation caused me to disappear into the darkness around me? Surely, I was angry, but did I suppress it, turn it inward? Was this all because I had learned that adults have power, and I had none?

I had a talent for music and art—but even those gifts, just like me, were not regarded as special or important. I begged for a piano for years, but my mother told me Dad, who played the fiddle by ear, would not allow a piano in the house. I now wonder if that was true. Anyway, when I didn't get one for my 13th birthday, I was so disappointed that I refused to ever look forward to birthdays again. I still dread them.

---

[2] While I was in a depressed state of mind, the hospital tested me; the results indicated my intelligence was on the high side. Until then, I'd believed I was not very smart. A machine monitored my heart rate during the testing; my intense anxiety about math caused it to triple, and I could not verbally solve even simple equations. This is an example of how children are influenced by the power adults have over them.

Chapter 10

After I graduated from high school, a teacher told me I was a big disappointment because I had done nothing with my artistic talent. He said I was one of the best artists he had ever seen. I was so surprised because no one had ever told me I was talented, and I was not capable of seeing it in myself.

As surly as these incidences defined my early childhood—no encouragement, no sense of value, just surviving-the years after I met Jesus until I was fourteen eventually defined who I became.

Small towns can be difficult places to grow up, especially if you think you are different. But they can also be places where lifelong friendships and memories are born. After I invited Jesus into my life, my behavior and attitude started to change. My Christian family and friends meant everything to me. I was in church every time I could get a ride there. But good memories are often overshadowed by bad ones.

When I was 14, my father was transferred to another location, and I was taken away from the security of my church family at the end of my freshman year in high school. I was heartbroken at the very thought of moving away from my Christian friends. A sense of foreboding began to settle upon me, even before I said my final goodbyes.

It had been a long session with Barb, and I needed a break. Tomorrow would be another long day.

Chapter 11

The Battle Between Good and Evil

Barb gently pulled me along as I struggled to unwind the threads of my life. I slowly began to accept what the staff had been trying to tell me for weeks. Sometimes my personality fragmented, and I often disassociated from reality. Simultaneous but conflicting attitudes and emotions called after me, and I followed them as though I was running with a wild wind. I survived by hiding in my dark sanctuary because I was afraid of the unsafe world around me.

When the wounded child came out to fight with another's wounded child, life got messy. While attempting to crawl out of the box of past behavior, she would sometimes fall back in, pulling others with her. She acted out inappropriately to bring attention to the devastating pain she secretly carried. The AAC longed to find and touch the core of the precious child stolen from her. The wounded child's brokenness begged for the AAC to please love her, but the adult could not hear her wounded child, and she did not know why.

Recognizing these conflicting attitudes helped me understand my lack of boundaries, my inability to take care of myself, and the wounded child that lived within me. The victim whose shoes I had walked in all my life started to take form in my mind. I began to see that I was indeed a complicated person.

My session with Barb continued.

> The town we moved to was small, like the one we'd left behind, but different in ways that would change me. Summer Saturday nights would find the back two rows of the drive-in theater full of drunken teenagers. After my first night out with a group of kids, I went home and cried. My first day in the new school was no better, as there seemed to be a tug-of-war within me. One side warned me, pleaded with me to hold on to my faith, while the other pulled at me, encouraging me to let go. A spirit of dread began to surround me and would not let me go. I no longer had my church family or Christian friends to support me, and I had no protection or guidance from my family.

Had the abuses that stole the innocent soul of my precious child begun to create a monster that was taking control of me? Deep inside my spirit, I knew my life would change, and I also knew I was powerless to stop the changes from happening. Were there tormenting demons hovering nearby?[1] Did they have their prey in sight? Had

---

[1] Ephesians 6:12 "For we wrestle not against flesh and blood, but against principalities, against powers, against the rulers of the darkness of this world, against spiritual wickedness in high places" (KJV).

they been lurking in the background, knowing that the abused child was like a stray sheep without a shepherd to guide or protect her and that she was rendered incapable of making wise choices? Is this when the precious child disappeared and the wounded, abused child took over—the survivor born?

Subtle changes began during my sophomore year. The following summer, I went to Dallas and lived with my sister and her family to work and make money for the coming school year. I returned home to begin my junior year and quickly became part of the in-crowd, doing everything the popular kids did. Temptations dangled in front of me—the principles of my faith began to slip away.

Almost overnight, I became uncharacteristically concerned with learning, and my grades improved drastically. Elected to the student council, I became the recording secretary. Cheerleader and Football Sweetheart highlighted my senior year. I joined the school band, landed the solo clarinet position, and was selected to participate in an All-Star Band concert. I was one of the art editors for the school paper and the yearbook, and my science teacher even presented my science project in a state competition.

Everything about my life pointed to a well-balanced, happy teenager, but nothing could have been further from the truth.

I lived in guarded fear that people would discover I was not what I appeared to be. I told no one, not even my closest friends, about my past, the depression, or the struggles. No one had a clue about my secrets, and only the wise would have noticed my sometimes-strange behavior. Teachers indeed must have turned their heads.

Was this when I began to dig deep holes to bury my guilt and shame? Was this when my facade, concealing something unpleasant, was created, and when I put on my first mask—the mask of deception? Was I reaching the age of accountability? Was this when the AAC was born?

> I began dating a popular football player who was also in my junior class. Everyone liked him, and I wanted to be associated with him. Dee's laughing eyes and quick smile earned him the title of Best All-Around Boy in our senior year; at the same time, I was runner-up to the same title for girls. We had become one of the school's sweetheart couples, and my girlfriends always wanted to know when we were going to get married.
>
> From the very beginning of our relationship, I denied that Dee was already well into the disease of alcoholism. Since I was well into the disease of victimization, I also denied that we were a deadly combination.
>
> As a child, I had learned that I could not say no; I had no boundaries. While under the influence of alcohol, I gave in to Dee's sexual advances. When he asked me why I wasn't a virgin, I had no choice but to tell him I had been abused. It was the first time I said the words aloud—the first time I openly admitted it to anyone, even myself. I hated sex, but I was numb to the power it had over me. I could not say no to it, but it brought no pleasure—just guilt.
>
> The first signs of suicidal depression emerged when I was 16. I began to have constant thoughts of death. I wanted to end the pain of living.

Chapter 11

Did the black abyss of depression invite the demons of suicide to begin their evil dance in my mind, where their poisoned darts hit their target and almost claimed an innocent life? Did the raging private war within turn into self-hatred, behavior becoming even more erratic, bouncing like a ball between good to bad?

One day, when I was home alone, I decided to turn on the gas heater in the living room and put an end to my insane life. Just as I reached for the jet connection, Dee appeared at the front door and saw me through the window. The moment passed. He never knew what he had thwarted.

Did God's angels bring him there to stop me?

After he graduated from high school, Dee went away to college, and I enrolled in a business college about 70 miles from home. When I graduated from there, I moved to the Dallas area and got a job at the company where my sister's husband worked; I rode to work with him each day. A year later, Dee and I were married. I knew I was making a mistake, but I had made my bed and thought I had to lie in it.

Dee was raised on a large ranch owned by a state senator. His parents were hardworking, kind people, devoted to Dee's mentally challenged younger brother. They showered me with love, and I loved them very much. However, the good things in our marriage were overshadowed by so much that was wrong.

After enrolling in a local college, Dee joined a fraternity, which only became an open door that fueled his addiction to alcohol. His excessive drinking brought turbulence into our strained relationship, and with each passing year, his drinking increased. Dee began to come home late at night, feeling no obligation to explain his tardiness. We began to have awful fights, which only once almost became violent. He threw his fist into a wall rather than into my face.

One Saturday night, I went to a party with him and slowly realized it was a party for gay people. Dee worked part time for a popular shoe store, and I became suspicious of his male coworker (this was long before people openly professed to be gay). That night, I went into that dark place where I hid—except I took something with me this time. Denial defeated me; I gave in to the demon that chased me and drowned my fears in a bottle of Southern Comfort. I sorely regretted it the next day. I had never allowed myself to drink to that extent before.

After that, I stopped drinking. Not only did I see the adverse effects of alcohol on Dee and our marriage, but I was also beginning to see its impact on both my brothers' lives. I no longer wanted anything to do with it. I had personally slept with the demon of alcoholism, and I was afraid to stay in bed with it because I wanted so badly just to go to sleep and never wake up. Taking care of myself was so uncharacteristic, but I had the good sense to stop drinking for once.

Did God protect me from giving in to this addiction that ran through my family's veins? Would I have destroyed my precious child had I chosen to continue to drown my pain in alcohol's unforgiving comfort?

Although I functioned in a deep state of depression and unhappiness, no one knew the personal hell I lived in—not

Chapter 11

my family, not my coworkers, no one. But my suppressed boiling rage would sometimes fuel unexpected, unpredictable behavior that I am sure was not missed by those around me. I wore my facade with its many faces while my masks became an intricate part of my identity.

Dee began to invite his coworker to our apartment. Then he began to disappear for days at a time, again feeling no need to account for his whereabouts. I begged and pleaded with him to stop drinking, but my words fell on indifferent ears. I could no longer live with his lies, his drinking, and the unknown.

I didn't know what Dee had gotten himself into—but whatever it was, it terrified me. I moved into an apartment without giving him my address or my phone number. However, Dee was the type of person who could look you in the eyes and tell you a lie, and even knowing full well that he was lying, you'd believe him anyway. He convinced someone in my family to give him my unlisted phone number. I never told my family the real reasons for the separation. They began to pressure me to reconcile with my husband, so out of frustration and to shut everyone up, I invited him to move into my apartment. The reunion was short-lived; we got into a fight on our first day back together.

I locked myself in the bathroom, intending to slit my wrists. I had never wanted out of life as much as I did at that moment. Suicidal depression has no mercy. Its evil voice told me life was hopeless, and there was no other way out of my marriage or the underlying effects of the secrets I carried. I was determined to end my life, and Dee knew it. He knocked down the door and stopped me. So, the one who kept pushing me over the edge was strangely the one who kept pulling me back again.

Or was it God's angels again?

Later that evening, my unlisted phone rang, and Dee answered it. I heard him say he would "be right there." He told me a friend had car trouble and needed some help; he promised to return shortly. The meal I had just prepared was waiting on the table.

I offered to go with him, but he walked out, closing the door in my face. He never returned to my apartment. There are no words to describe the rejection, the defeat, the abandonment, the hopelessness I felt. The unseen forces I felt around me were powerful and frightening. I had to flee from them, or else I knew they would pull me into their unrelenting grip, and I would not survive. It was three days before I heard from him at work. I told him I was filing for a divorce. I was thankful there were no children.

We had been two immature kids with no responsibility and no understanding of what love meant. We were in need of love but not in love, each perishing in our own twisted search for significance, hoping to find it in each other but destroying each other in the process. I felt great pain for Dee's family. They deserved much better from both of us.

Months later, I stood alone in a courtroom full of people. I felt as though every ounce of blood drained from my body and spilled on the floor around me as the harsh whack of the judge's gavel ended almost four years of marriage. Divorce is never right. It leaves its bitter mark upon the soul. I felt exposed as the failure I was; divorced labeled me flawed.

But as I left the cold stone courthouse and walked back

to my office, I felt a strong determination and hardness of soul walking with me. I held my head high, and for the first time in many years, I could breathe. Nothing was going to break me. I would let no one ever hurt me again.

Denying that I was dying within from the never-ending pain of child abuse, I vowed to remain strong, not knowing I would be broken before I finally understood that real strength comes from God and not oneself.

The following three years were good. I was successful in my accounting job. I discovered that not only was I good with numbers, but I also loved the challenge of working with them. I even landed a promotion to a job that required an accounting degree, which I did not have. I bought lots of new clothes and a car, made new friends (including JoAnn), dated, traveled, and just lived life. The deep longing for God in my life slowly began to return. I began to seek the principles of my faith that I had walked away from as a teenager. They were well-deserved peaceful years.

I met Ann, Janie, and Phylis, young Christian women who needed a roommate. I wasn't sure they would want a divorced woman living with them and was nervous about meeting them and confessing my sin. My facade had probably never been thicker.

I will always be thankful to these three godly women for taking a chance with me because their lives influenced me; I saw in them what I had abandoned. I began going to church and was finally baptized. They were an important part of God's plan for my life, and we have enjoyed over 50 lasting years of friendship, though we traveled down different paths.

And then Jake came into my life.

From the time I left my church family at 14 until my baptism at 23, it seems I was a lost soul. I do not understand the person I became during those years; I know I was changed when I found the essence of who I am in Christ, but I succumbed to invisible dark forces that seemed to control me ever so quickly. I walked away from godliness into the arms of this world—where godlessness prevailed. I did things I did not want to do and lived in the denial that my actions, though often the results of sexual abuse, were sinful. However, the one thing I know for sure is that the part of me that was strong and good and held me together came from God.

Please keep in mind I could not share everything about my life in this book. I needed to preserve some of my dignity. Sadly, in today's world, promiscuous sex, getting drunk, smoking, doing drugs, and for sure divorce are common place. There seems to be no shame. Even sadder, in today's culture, they no longer seem to be viewed as sinful acts. However, if you lived in a small town in the '50s and '60s, these acts labeled you unfavorably. I truly do not recognize the person I write about during that time in my life.

Chapter 12

The Unlikely Love of My Life

The canvas of my life is beginning to take on a form of its own. It may seem out of control, but don't worry; there is a plan. Isn't that just the way life is? Everything seems awry, but before we know it, we realize a plan was in place all along. Thank you for hanging in there with me; soon, you will see where all this work is taking us.

My session with Barb continued. She knew she had to be diligent, or I might stop talking. "Tell me about your marriage to Jake. Surely this has not been an easy relationship."

By the world's standards, my marriage should have failed years ago. Jake and I met in 1967 at a party the day before Halloween. Even now, I cringe thinking about the costume I wore because of the recent changes in my life. A friend loaned me her long black "fall," a hairpiece that fit at the top of my forehead, leaving my own dark bangs exposed. It looked very natural. I also borrowed a white majorette uniform, which looked like a one-piece bathing suit covered with fringe that jiggled when I walked. It fit my 5'1", 102-pound frame like the long white gloves that covered my arms. Black high heels complemented my sheer stockings, black seams running down the back of my slender legs. I carried an empty champagne glass even though I had become a teetotaler. I did not drink, nor did I do any of the other things I was putting out there. The long black fake eyelashes were the icing on the cake that caught every guy's attention at the party. But it was Jake who took command of the night.

How could I exhibit such shameless behavior? Where was my shame?

After the party was over, he walked me back to my apartment. I couldn't help but notice his handsome features. I never expected to see him again. I perceived a quality about him that caused me secretly to think I was not good enough for him. He told me he liked my hair.

Much to my surprise, he called me the following week and asked if I would have dinner with him.

Again, I had to borrow the hairpiece—a frantic process that continued until I finally got caught in my deceit as we looked at pictures of my trip to DC. I'd had short hair just one month before we met. But by this time, Jake had fallen in love with me and politely overlooked my indiscretion.

I was beginning to see that unintentional deception followed me like a lost puppy.

Jake's phone calls continued as magical chemistry began to form between us. He was a never-ending fountain of information when talking about his family and was an entertaining storyteller: country clubs in Iowa and Dallas, trips in his father's airplane, family-owned farms, priests, lawyers, a state senator, and a large land company in Louisiana. If Jake had aimed to impress me, I obliged him. This West Texas gal was captivated.

Being the oldest child in his family, he had two sisters away at college, and his younger brother was still at home. I was quick to note that his family attended church regularly. I was mesmerized by it all but scared to death at the same time. I felt way out of my league.

On the other hand, I mostly listened. I had learned that if you ask intelligent questions and keep people's attention on themselves, they won't focus on you. So, I offered Jake as little as possible about me or my family.

I had small-town roots, and I came from a low-income family. We always lived near the railroad tracks in a company house, and folks from different cultures were our neighbors. I was lucky to get a pair of shoes once a year, and I learned to sew when I was young and made most of my clothes. My parents were uneducated; only one of my siblings finished high school and graduated from college, and I graduated from a small business college.

We didn't have an indoor bathroom until I was in the first grade; before then, we got a bath once a week in a number two washtub in the kitchen. To get a nickel for a Coke or a dime for the Saturday afternoon movies was a rare treat, and we seldom had the money for a coveted bag of popcorn. There were few extras, but thankfully, we had basic life needs.

We celebrated Christmas Eve with no thought of what Christmas meant. My family did not go to church, and gifts were few. Mother made candy from scratch. There was always a lot of family around, but I always secretly dreaded Christmas. I kept my family stories primarily to myself.

Our family dynamics were as different as the dialects we spoke. My thick Texas accent prompted Jake's mother to send his grandmother in Chicago a book on how Texans talk so that she could understand me when we met. Culturally, spiritually, emotionally, and educationally, we might as well have been born on different planets.

Jake was reared in the northern part of the country, having lived in Iowa most of his life. His family roots hinted at wealth and status, and he grew up in an educated, upper-middle-class family. When he was in his teens, the family moved to Texas. They built a large, spacious house, eventually adding a large swimming pool, which seemed lost in their sizable backyard.

Eating in their formal dining room, on fine china, with real silverware and cloth napkins held by personalized napkin rings, was a bit challenging. His father sat at the head

Chapter 12

of the table, his mother at the opposite end. As a guest, I was given a place of honor to his dad's right, a place that remained my own after we married.

Jake had to educate me on certain etiquette, informing me that I should never pick up my fork to eat before his mother picked up hers, and I should never help in the kitchen. My southern roots reeled; not helping was frowned upon.

I had wanted to belong to this perfect family, not understanding that there is no such thing as the perfect family.

Jake had lived a sheltered life. At the age of 25, he had a lot of growing up to do and was needy in his own way. Just as I had seen what I wanted to see in him, Jake saw in me what he wanted to see. Truthfully, he only saw what I wanted him to see. Even when I tried subtly to warn him that I might not be what he expected, he chose to see what I could not see in myself. Jake saw only the good.

Looking back, I wonder how I could have expected him to know who I was when I didn't even know myself. I lived by an image I'd created for myself that was far from my roots. I had learned to hold my head high and to walk with dignity, taking on an air of sophistication. I discovered I had good taste in clothes and wore my choices well. My makeup and hair were always in place. Even Jake's father once commented that I was a classy lady. I guarded every word that came out of my mouth.

When Jake discovered that going to church was important to me, we started attending the church where his family had belonged for many years and where roots went deep. It was a sacramental, ritually oriented church that was lightyears away from my childhood church experience; in the beginning, I had been awestruck. In time, those differences would shockingly come to haunt us and almost destroy our marriage.

Eventually, I told Jake I was divorced and briefly mentioned I was a victim of child abuse. It was hard for me to believe or even accept his response.

"I don't care about your past. I just care about you."

Early in our relationship, I was suspicious when this young man told me he loved me. My walls went up so fast it would make your head swim because I knew his intentions. After all, I knew about men.

However, he had a good quality about him that pulled at me like a magnet, and I wanted to be a part of him. I wanted the hope for a better life that he offered me. So, I began to let my guard down, and after weeks of dating, I dared to trust a man for the first time in my life—as far as I was capable, I began to allow myself to fall in love with Jake. He respected me as a person, and sex before marriage was not an option.

Yet, not long into our relationship, troubling family issues began to surface. When we were invited to his parents' house for happy hour before dinner, red flags popped up all over my brain. I mistakenly thought that *real* Christians did not consume alcoholic beverages. I soon learned that drinking was acceptable in Jake's denomination, but I didn't understand.

I had a genuine problem with even the casual acceptance of alcohol because of my family, my first marriage, and my own struggle to defeat the demon. It chased me during my teen years and early 20s. It terrified me, and I refused to allow it to get a grip on me because of what I had seen alcohol do to the people I loved. Above all, I did not want to bring children into a family where drinking was the norm. I came close to breaking up with Jake over that one issue.

I knew I would need to be strong to overcome the insecurities about my family; little did I know how strong I needed to be to face the issues surrounding Jake and his family. I found that I had little in common with them and didn't think they would understand the world I came from or my internal turmoil. Communication would become our Achilles' heel.

Because I did not have solid roots in any church denomination, I didn't feel I could ask Jake to let go of his. I ignored my concerns over the church and the inner warnings about our background and social drinking differences. We were married just eight months after we met. Jake won my heart, and I stuffed my concerns in my dark place.

I was beginning to see that denial always won, and I always lost. But why?

The first six months of our marriage were heaven on earth. We were so much in love. I kept my intimacy issues to myself and relished the joy of being loved and respected. Despite my intimacy issues, it was easy for me to return Jake's love.

After our small June wedding in his church, Jake whisked me away to the Virgin Islands. This small-town Texas girl's breath was taken away by the beautiful blue-green waters of St. Croix. I felt like a princess living in a fairy tale, hoping never to wake up to find it was all a dream.

Shortly after returning home, we bought three-quarters of an acre of land in the country. It came with a spacious three-bedroom, red-brick house, fully furnished, except for a television.

We were fortunate that a coworker of Jake's was building a new home and just needed to get rid of all his furnishings.

I fell in love with our new home; I'd never dreamed I would live in such a beautiful place. We quickly added two cats to our family to help keep the field mice out. Each day when Jake came home for lunch, Spot and Mittens would escort us down to the end of the road to get our mail. I had more than I ever dreamed possible, more than I thought I deserved. I was safe and happy and loved.

Eight months after we were married, I became pregnant, and nine and a half months later, a beautiful, blue-eyed baby girl with a head full of honey-blonde hair came into our lives. It was a long, difficult delivery, and I was secretly terrified. I had never been around babies and knew less about taking care of one than I did about riding a horse.

But motherly instinct intervened. I never knew love could be so compelling, so consuming, and so strong. I vowed to protect her and never to allow harm to befall her in any way—ever.

It was a promise I would not be able to keep.

My fairy-tale world shattered when our 11-month-old baby was diagnosed with an incurable disease. I was four months pregnant with our second child when our baby began chemotherapy for acute lymphoblastic leukemia, a blood cancer. In 1970, this type of cancer treatment was experimental, and the success rate was practically nil with only the promise of living up to five years. We began a journey with our daughter that would stretch our faith and our marriage to the limits.

However, that was not all we would face. Born in March of 1971, our son became terribly ill just ten days before turning two years old. He was diagnosed with bacterial spinal meningitis, and the prognosis was that our son would probably not survive. If he did live, he faced mental and physical impairment. Indeed, my faith would be tested.

In February of 1977, I found out we were expecting another child—and just two months later, a tragic motorcycle accident took the life of Jake's 24-year-old brother, Tom. Kimberly's arrival the following November was just what this family needed. God's grace was sufficient. Blessings happened when needed the most.

It has been 22 years since my marriage to Jake began, and it has not been easy. We have learned much as we have grown up together, pulling each other through the muck and mire of marriage and all that it entails, the good and the bad.

We brought different strengths and weaknesses into our family, and where one has been weak, the other has been strong. We have laughed, we have cried, and sometimes we have failed. Human love and respect sometimes tottered, but true love never failed us. We have loved our children and made our share of mistakes with them, but true love has not failed them either. I believe this love is not of worldly understanding or from human nature; it came straight from the heart of Jesus.

If I have learned anything in my troubled life, it is that love does not walk out when passion wanes and differences arise or when trials come, and tragedies strike. True love steps in. Our love for each other, our love for God, and His immeasurable grace sustain me. God did not fail me.

Time had run out, and our session had to end. Barb closed her notebook and tucked her hands under her legs. Leaning forward and staring into my eyes, she did not waver or mince her words.

She reminded me that she had spent a great deal of time pulling necessary information from me because I needed to get a clear perspective about my life. She expressed gladness, knowing I understood that my life at that point was like an airplane flying out of control: I was all over the place and didn't know where I was going, much less how to get there. I had been given the tools; now I must figure out what to do with them. It was my choice: remain stuck where I was, or choose to move on. I needed to find a way to unlock the doors I was guarding because if I did not, I would crash.

Barb got up from her chair, gave me a tender hug, and told me I no longer needed her. Then she walked away.

I wanted to run after her, but all I could do was sit in silence with my small brown bear pressed tightly against my anxious heart. I wanted to stop. I wanted to go home. But I knew I could not. I hadn't told Barb the whole story. I had avoided essential details, and she knew it.

For weeks I had been dispassionately telling my story. But that would need to change. I could not recite the secret parts of my life without emotion. These details impacted me and changed me; I could not relate them with the same dignity.

The weight of the burdens I carried fell hard upon me. Once again, the ache began—that deep ache that sometimes recedes but will never go away, that nothing will satisfy: the weight of deception. How many times had I unknowingly tried to deceive not just those around me, but myself? Hiding behind every disguise I could imagine, I tried to cover up the truth and protect, or deny, the wounded child within me. But why?

In this place of refuge where I had lived for such a short time, the many faces I wore stared back at me. They screamed from behind the facade. "Here I am! Please, look at me!"

So many faces: the face of denial, the face of insecurity, the face of fear, the face of panic, the face of abandonment, the face of deceit, the face of depression, the face of suicide, the face of disassociation, the face of sadness, the face of oppression, the face with no boundaries I kept hidden behind my masks so others would not see the real face of abuse.

The face of confusion that pulled all the others into a melting pot reminded me that I also wore the faces of tenderness, goodness, caring, mercy, wisdom, peace, joy, and love—the face of Jesus.

And, last of all, the face of the survivor, which I was so very tired of wearing. Had I not declared when I came into this place that I did not want merely to survive? I wanted to do more; I wanted to live!

But why was I so afraid to open this final door and search for the face of the one I did not understand—the angry one who mocked me and controlled me along with her companion twins, shame and guilt? Did the survivor hold the key that would unlock the door and set us all free?

The AAC begged, "Please, God, give me courage."

Chapter 13

Facing the Predator, Touched by a Song, Set Free with a Bed, and a Bat

Today marks a turning point on our canvas. We will need to let our paint flow freely and swiftly, or we will not be able to capture the very heart and soul of the picture. Perhaps this will be both our most difficult and our most glorious session, where in the solitude of my hospital room, I faced the worst of my perpetrators. He is the one who twisted in and out of my days and nights like an unrelenting, ferocious hurricane, with its reckless, raging winds seeking to devour my precious child. He is the one I protected. He is the one I pretended was safe and trustworthy at every family gathering, and in his home where I sometimes lived, and at the office where we worked.

Through the eyes of my abused child, I—the survivor—picked up my pen and began to write a letter to my sister's husband. (Please note that the following letter is a graphic description of child abuse.)

I Can Begin Again

August 6, 1990

You ruined my life. You took my innocence, my youth, my pride, my dignity, my virginity, my joy, my laughter, my ability to give or receive love, to be intimate—the very essence of who I am. Your selfish acts made me hate sex and caused me to turn my anger inward to the point of wanting to destroy my own life. You threw me into the black hole of depression and covered my mind with your unforgiving darkness. I cannot see out of it. You have affected every area of my life—my relationships and mental, physical, and spiritual health. You gave me your shame and guilt, and I despise you for putting that on me.

Did you have no shame or guilt about what you did? How could you be so shameless? How could you allow a little child to carry your guilt and shame? I am beginning to understand that you were a sick and evil person, and it makes me sick even to think about what you did to me—and maybe to other little girls too. I am so glad you died before you had a chance to hurt my children; I hate to imagine what I would have done to you if you had violated or even came anywhere near them.

I struggle as I remember. I don't want to remember those dark, lost years. They are buried in my mind, but I know they are there. I must think about those first memories of you. I must find you and find that little girl whose spirit you strangled to death.

Because of you, to this very day, I always dread Christmas.

All the family was home the first time I remember you. I do not know how you got me out of the house alone. You drove to the elementary school and parked the car. I could barely see the school building as I tried to look out the car window. I was

Chapter 13

so little. It was very dark. I can still see it all if I close my eyes, but I am afraid of what I will see. My chest is tight. I feel the weight of your body on me; I cannot breathe. How did you get my underwear off? Did I not protest? Had you done this before? You were breathing heavily. I was afraid, and I asked, "Why are you hurting me? What are you doing to me?" You did not answer. You just kept on hurting me, saying nothing. Your breath was hot and heavy above my head. Deep, dark, black darkness consumed me, and I disappeared. I went somewhere else—somewhere far away from you. Was that when I disconnected from reality, or had I done that before too? I remember, when you got off me, I felt this wet stuff run down my legs. I didn't know what it was, and I tried to wipe it off with my dress. It stuck to my hands.

Everything goes blank then.

The next thing I know is that I ran into the living room and jumped into the bed, made up on the couch for my niece and me. I pulled the covers over me, curled up in a ball, and went to sleep. My niece was only two or three years old . . . I must have been between seven and nine. Just a child!

I don't remember the shame, but I know it was there. It had to be there, right along with my hatred of you, but I don't remember that either. Where did you make me put them—the shame and the hate? And why did no one notice my wet dress when I came into the house? Oh yes—now I remember—I was trying to hide. Why? Did you tell me not to say anything—again? And who washed my dress? Why didn't someone notice? Didn't anyone care? Did someone notice and turn away? Where was everyone?

How many Christmases did you steal from me?

I know—I really know—that something had been going on

long before this. I can remember pain and swelling and burning down there long before it happened. But there are so many gaps. How dare you do this to me! How dare you?

You always wanted me to go to the store or go for a ride with you. I never wanted to go, but your wife—my sister—and my mother always insisted I go with you. I was powerless! You could do anything to me. You had power, and I was just a little girl, and I had none.

When did you start showing me those awful pictures and those cartoon drawings of people having sex? How old was I when you first exposed me to pornography? I can never get those images out of my mind—they haunt me, remind me. I hate them, and I hate you. When we sat in your car, and I looked at them, you rubbed me with your finger and put it inside me. I don't remember feeling the shame, but I know it was there. Why couldn't I stop you?

I remember one time—oh, God! You were driving down a country road, and an older couple drove past us. I was sitting next to you, and you had given me more pictures. The couple looked suspiciously at us, and I ducked my head because I did not want them to see me. Where did my shame go? How old was I? Oh, dear God, even then, those pictures had begun to take a strange hold over my mind. What you were doing to me stirred no feelings—all that you had done to me completely shut me down—but what I saw did arouse me, and I became powerless to pornography's evil. I was so vulnerable.

I gave my life to Jesus while you were putting this evil into me. I did not know it was evil, but I was still powerless with you. I trusted you. Did my guilt and shame deepen each time you forced yourself on me? When I became a Christian, could I not face those emotions? Did I just bury them deeper and deeper until I denied they existed and could no longer find them?

When I was 14, we came to Dallas to visit your family. One day, I was left alone with you at your house. Why was I left alone with you? Why did I stay behind? I don't know. I never knew how you managed to take advantage of me. I don't know how you got me there, but my panties were off, and you had me on your bed with my legs spread apart. You were fully exposed and coming toward me, and you told me you were going to put it in. It was not the first time I had seen you. Oh, Lord God! I now recall that you made me touch you and hold you and rub you. I feel sick all over just thinking about it. You would spit in your hand and . . . How young was I? It hurt so bad . . . Is that why you spit in your hand? To make it not hurt? The memory of it . . . I can't even go there. I didn't want to look at you.

Something, thank God, snapped inside my brain, and I kicked you away and ran. All the hate I had for you surfaced; I told you I would kill you if you ever touched me again, and I meant it. But you never stopped. You were so sneaky. You began to harass me verbally. You called me a liar, telling me I said you could put it in, trying to make me feel responsible and that I owed you something. What manipulation! I hate you for all that you did to me.

You left me alone for a while, but then you got into photography—and every time I turned around, you had that damn camera staring me in the face. When I went to Dallas to work so that I could have money for school . . . I can't believe I lived with you and your family. Why did I do that? Was it denial? I felt nothing! I was just so incapable of taking care of myself when it came to you. You bought nighties that you could see through, and you persuaded me to put them on for you. Then you posed me and took pictures of me, all while my sister watched. Why?

Why was I so disconnected from the guilt and shame and anger I must have felt toward both of you? Why did I turn it all inward on myself? Where was my power?

When I went to work for the same company as you, men always came by my desk and talked to me—always coming on to me. It made me uncomfortable, and I did not understand, but now I wonder if you took those pictures to work. Did you show them to your friends? How shameful for me to now think about it! I hate you; I have always hated you. How could you stoop so low?

I feel sick all over. I wish I could throw up.

You even had the nerve to ask me to pose in the nude for money after my divorce. Finally, I was able to tell you no and mean it! But until then, you never stopped hitting on me, and I could never confront you and make you stop. You never gave up. Then you got a boat, and we started going to the lake to water-ski. Oh, dear, God—I had forgotten! You always went out swimming at the same time as me, and I could not get away from you. You pulled me up against you, and you held me, and your hands were all over me under the water. If I moved away, you always followed me, and your family and friends were right there—close enough to see what was happening. Why couldn't anyone ever see what you were doing? What was wrong with everybody?

And what was wrong with me? Why didn't I scream and expose you? Oh, dear God in Heaven, help me! I feel such hate for you!

Every time we got in the boat to ski, you always managed to get me alone—even though the rule was never to pull a skier alone. I could always feel your eyes on me. Those eyes—they still haunt me. There was so much lust in them. Your voice would change when you talked to me, and I could see your body change as you watched me. I disconnected because I could not stand it; I would always go to the dark place to hide from you. You said things to me I did not want to hear. I can still feel my whole body becoming rigid every time I was in that boat with you.

Oh, how I hate you. You are the lowest of scum. You don't deserve justice or mercy, and I hope you got none when you died. I wish you could be here right now so that I could give back to you all the pain you gave me. You are a monster in my mind, and I want the monster to die. I want your haunting presence to leave me. I am going to find a way for this to happen. I am not going to stop, even if it takes another month in this place. I will not stop until you are completely dead in my mind—not until this power you have over me is broken.

God, please help me, give me courage, stand beside me, and help me to let go.

I stopped writing and laid the letter aside. I could no longer force myself through the hell of facing the acid memories rushing through my mind like an unstoppable movie camera.

Every cell in my body had come to life, and it was too much to bear. My tearless body shook uncontrollably as I pulled my comforting companions into my arms and curled up with them on the bed. I reached for the blanket lying at my feet and gently pulled its warmth over us. I had clawed my way to a door I had never wanted to open. I had dared to drag myself into the malignant, heinous, brutal pit of child abuse.

I had looked squarely into the faces of shame and guilt, reliving the unthinkable deeds that fueled them. This detestable pedophile was shameless, totally relentless in his pursuit of me—a defenseless child. His greedy lust and flaming self-satisfying desires were to capture and control my innocence. This stealer of my soul was the personification of evil. They all are.

And yet, it was still difficult to face reality, to believe that these cruel things happened to me. I had to accept that denial was my problem because the memories were not imagined. They were real, and I had always had them; I just didn't know what to do with them. Even worse, I minimized the value of my memories. I told myself "it just happened."

The abuse from this man probably started soon after he married my sister, who was only a child herself. Perhaps I was as young as two or three. What could be worse? And what about all the other abuses I remember—the ones I can't bring myself to mention? Would the pain ever stop? Would I ever stop remembering? I just wanted to stay under the covers and make it all go away.

I had to somehow accept the abuse as my truth; I was a victim and was not responsible for what others had done to me. I was getting so close. Anguish and sorrow for my precious child consumed me.

The following day I read the letter to my psychiatrist. I showed no emotion. He wanted to know where my anger was.

With concern in his voice, he said, "You're reading this as though it's a newspaper article."

"I don't know. This is what happened," I replied.

I read it to my therapist, who had the same reaction. When I shared it with my small group, I found myself comforting them as they shed tears. Several fell sobbing into my arms. They understood.

When Jake came to see me, I read it to him. My husband was furious to the point of being speechless. I had never disclosed any details.

Chapter 13

All he knew was that my brother-in-law had abused me. I also read it to a few of my friends who visited me. They were shocked—except for one, who proved not to be my friend. She judged me and has hardly spoken to me since.

There will always be those who will judge and not understand. Thus, the AAC needs to discern when and where they share their pain.

I forced myself to read the letter over and over, again and again, until its words became a raw reality, and until the relentless, raging fury that sat precariously below the surface of guilt and shame could find its rightful place.

There was yet another divine appointment waiting for the AAC.

I was the last one to enter the large room where so many things took place on 3E. The weekly music therapy class was just beginning, and I slipped quietly onto a chair near the door. The room was packed. I love good music because it brings joy to my soul—but on this day, it brought more than joy. The instructor pushed the button on the cassette player, and an unfamiliar tune fell on my ears. The instrumental introduction began, and then without warning, the lyrics took my ruptured heart, laid it open, cleaned it out, and put it back together again. They reached into the very soul of the AAC—the adult who was abused as a child.

> Alone again in a crowded room
> Cornered by the questions in my mind.
> It's so hard to understand
> How the life that I had planned
> Stole my joy and left me far behind.

I Can Begin Again

Though all I have is lost it seems
In the shadow of a dream that used to be,
I can look beyond the skies
Deep into the Father's eyes
And see that there is hope for one like me.

I can begin again
With the passion of a child.
My heart has caught a vision
Of a life that's still worthwhile.
I can reach out again
Far beyond what I have done
Like a dreamer who's awakened
To a life that's yet to come.
For new beginnings are not just for the young.

I face the dawn of each brand new day
Free from all the doubts that gripped my past.
For I've found in trusting Him
That everyday life starts again
As I look for the things of life that last.

I can begin again
With the passion of a child.
My heart has caught a vision
Of a life that's still worthwhile.
I can reach out again
Far beyond what I have done
Like a dreamer who's awakened
To a life that's yet to come.

> For new beginnings are not just for the young.
> New beginnings are not just for the young.
> New beginnings are not just for the young.
> Starting over again is not just for the young.
> No matter what you've been told
> It's not just for the young,
> It's not just for the young.[1]

My soul had lain dormant in a field of sorrow, stricken and beaten down, but suddenly the long-ago promised hope of the shamrock nurtured its soil. New life tugged at the root of the single, solitary bloom left standing alone within me so many years ago. And it began to grow.

Words echoed from my past: "Someday, I believe you will come back in full bloom, more beautiful than before." The beauty that God had created for this wounded child was indeed coming back, and when in full bloom—as David, her first therapist, had predicted almost ten years earlier—she would be more beautiful than before.

It had taken me three weeks of searching, resisting, denying, and struggling to come to this crossroad, a place of surrender that would ask me to choose a different path for my life. Unrestrained tears began to flow down my cheeks as the words of this powerful song came to life within me. Every face behind every mask and my precious child—the very core of my being that had so stoically held the wounded child, the survivor, and the adult together—began to mesh in agreement that healing could now begin.

God's Holy Spirit whispered, oh so softly, "You *can* begin again!"

I knew that God had just shown me the way toward my freedom

---

1 "I Can Begin Again" used with permission by award-winning artist Larnelle Harris. To hear the song, go to www.larnelle.com.

from every dastardly act inflicted upon me in my life; all I had to do was to walk in His way. Here, again, was a choice, just like the one Barb had offered me in our last session: I could stay stuck, or I could take back my power and move forward. God was *waiting on me* to respond and step into His will and purpose for my life.

The AAC, empowered by the words of a song written by another but intended for her on that day, would never be the same. God had touched her. More divine appointments were awaiting her.

I had a prescheduled appointment with Ron, my therapist, just after music therapy. I walked into the small room with my head held high and a new resolve in my voice. I was surprised to see that Ron was with my psychiatrist, Dr. Kamen. I gave them no time to comment before I recited the words to the song I had just heard. Then, with deliberate determination, I told them I was ready to talk about the others who sexually abused me. Their eyes danced with anticipation, prepared to listen.

I cannot find any words to convey the shame of exposing my wounded child. She was bare, exposed, vulnerable. A part of me died when I was an infant. I wanted my precious child to live again, and if that meant talking, then I would talk. I needed to add seven more names to the list of abusers after disclosing the man who worked for my father, my uncle, and my brother-in-law. It hurt so much, and I cried and cried as I revealed the memories.

"You can be the mommy, and I will be the daddy."
During three different sleepovers with three different girls, I recall hearing those words. I remember disappearing

into my dark place while my body was explored. And now, I can't help but wonder what had been happening to those three young girls that caused them to act out sexually at such a young age. I am a strong advocate against sleepovers.

A teenage boy—a relative—forced me to participate in sexual activity with him. I felt nothing during those encounters and would just walk away, disappearing once again into the darkness.

There was a neighbor who owned a gas station near my house. One day, aged about 12, I went to his station to put air in my bicycle tire. He cornered me inside the station and began to molest me. I was big enough to fight him off before it went too far.

I was in my early 20s when a gynecologist who was examining me began to touch me inappropriately. I froze and could not move. I went into my dark place, where I always hid. Beyond that, I have no memory. I recall leaving the room and stuffing my emotions where I could not feel them. I told no one. *The wounded child buried her shame.*

And finally, there was the memory of one whose abuse I carried with deep sorrow, and I desperately needed to get the anguish out of me. There was a long silent pause before I could open my mouth and talk about my mother's old-maid sister. I grieve to think of the personal hell she had to endure, the struggles. She was a kind soul, a good and giving person who deserved better from this life. I have wept bitter tears of shame for her and my wounded child, but I had to resolve the confusing agony of her actions.

In many ways, my aunt was more like a mother to me than my mom. She helped take care of all of us kids, and I loved her visits. She cleaned the house, fixed my breakfast each morning, played games with me, and talked to me—but she also slept with me. I loved her so very much, but she asked me to touch her inappropriately. I know that she loved me, but I was beginning to understand that it was not my place or my responsibility to fill anyone's needs—ever! I found out long after her death that she had a condition that was not common knowledge in our family. Nature had been unkind to her and gave her both male and female organs. I recall wondering about her deep voice and the fact that she had to shave her face. Yet, she had full breasts and appeared female in other ways.

I needed for the session to end. I felt I had little pride or dignity left. I had said all I needed to say.

The two men sat listening, relieved that I had finally spoken the unspeakable. I thought they were going to do cartwheels as we stepped out into the hallway. They had come to our meeting prepared to confront me, to push me into talking, but I went in prepared to talk. They witnessed God's undeniable grace that enabled me to choose to move forward.

Dr. Kamen reemphasized that I was not the problem; the problem was that predators had violated my sacred space. None of the things that happened to me were my fault. Under the circumstances, my confusion was understandable—abuse from both males and females rebounded in the tormenting sexual confusion I experienced. More importantly, I was not accountable for others' indiscretions, nor did God hold me responsible for others' sins. I was thankful for the wise, affirming feedback I desperately needed to hear.

Chapter 13

Dr. Kamen honored my plea not to let me leave the hospital until he was sure I was in a good place mentally. He had understood that I needed to disclose the details and expose all my abusers. This I had now done. My insurance was about to run out—therefore, time was running out—but he wisely allowed me to stay a while longer. *The adult who was abused as a child felt as though the weight of the world had lifted from her shoulders. She had taken a giant leap of faith toward wholeness.*

Immediately after lunch that same day, the weekly spiritual growth group met. I had come to trust the hospital chaplain, who handed out pens and paper as we entered the room. There were three questions at the top of the page:

1. What losses have you have experienced?
2. How did you feel about the losses at the time?
3. How do you feel about them now?

Under the first column, I wrote, "I lost my precious child."
Under the second, I wrote, "I felt nothing."
And under the third, I wrote, "I am angry!"

I asked permission to read the letter I had written to my predator, and for the first time, I recited my words with the passion they deserved. The letter gave birth to the magnitude of all I had hidden for so long. I was that precious child.

I began to mourn my loss, but more enormous than the grief itself was the untamed, unclaimed anger. An internal explosion began as the words I had written sliced open my broken spirit.

"How *dare* you do this to me!"

I was finally accepting that I was repeatedly abused. I was a victim: a victim of others' sick, sinful lust. They had given in to their selfishness with no regard to the pain they were inflicting on another human being—a child—*me*!

This time, once and for all, I got it! I finally understood that the adults in my life had power over my precious child, and she was utterly helpless to protect herself. That powerlessness spilled over into my adult life, where Christian standards and morals clashed mercilessly with the standards of those who abused me. I wanted, more than anything, to be morally and sexually pure, but in my mind, I thought I never was and never could be. Although I had accepted God's gift of forgiveness and had genuinely believed in and felt the powerful, cleansing blood Jesus shed for me, the voices inside my head constantly nibbled away at the God-truths I learned.

Those voices told me I was a terrible person who could *never* measure up. I could never be accepted. I could never be worthy of all that God had done for me. I could never let anyone find out about me, allow them to know the real me. I could certainly never live up to the pedestal that some had put me on, and I could never afford the luxury of allowing myself to be authentic.

It has been said that you will not know a lie until you know the truth. The voice of my wounded child mistakenly lied to me, as she was lied to by the powers of darkness that sought to destroy this child of God. These lies were not our truth, not God's truth. I carried the guilt of undeserved shame, others' shame, until that day, the day when I allowed God to speak healing into the soul of my wounded child. I would carry it no more! *The AAC and the wounded child continued to heal as the door of understanding stood wide open.*

A part of me sincerely forgave my brother-in-law at the spiritual retreat I had attended years before. However, I was emotionally bound and erroneously continued to carry his guilt and shame and the guilt and shame of all the others who violated me, resulting in suppressed anger and controlled rage. Now I needed to give back everything they had cruelly imposed upon me. More importantly, it was time to take back the most vital thing of all: my power. *The AAC had found the survivor's key she had been looking for. Now she had to unlock the door that had kept her in bondage.*

My next step was anger therapy, which enabled me to confront and deal safely with the suppressed anger that would rear its ugly head and then quickly disappear below the surface of my consciousness, staying hidden until another crippling opportunity arose.

Here I could address those times when I would blindly explode and do and say things that made no sense, even to me. I was like a yo-yo, a Dr. Jekyll and Mr. Hyde, with occasional out-of-control moments that intertwined crazily with kindness, love, joy, and peace.

For the first time, I acknowledged the anger associated with the abuse, realizing I needed to feel the rage and do something about it. Unjustly carved into my personality, this anger was not, nor had it ever been, mine. Like the guilt and shame, I needed to give it back to those who had created it in the first place.

In a small room with only a twin-sized bed, I picked up the bat that had been given to me to help release my anger. A camera in the ceiling monitored my actions. I took the bat and timidly, slowly at first, began to beat the stuffing out of that bed. The more anger I released, the more power I felt rising within me—until finally, God healed the innermost realm of self that only He can heal.

I cried. I screamed. I raged. Yes, I even cursed those who had robbed me of every innocent, kind, and decent thing that was rightfully mine to possess. I do not know how long I was there, but when tears were spent, anger quieted, and rage was no longer present, there came a serene moment when we were set free—my little girl and me. Free to breathe, feel, think, run, play—and, yes, finally free to turn that corner and move on. *God had been waiting on the AAC to give Him the key that would unlock this door so that He could come in and heal her.*

One of the staff who observed my transformation told me I kept yelling, "Get it out! Get it out!" The abused, frightened little girl finally had the voice denied her for so long. It was, at last, her way of being able to shout at her predators, "No, you can't do *this* to me! Not anymore! Never again!"

All my "why" questions were answered. The answer was simple: because I was abused as a child. I got my power back! *The AAC, now empowered, could confidently finish the task God had brought her there to do. There was still important work for her to accomplish. And she had gone too far to stop now.*

Chapter 14

A Three-Hour Pass, a Long and Honest Talk, the Final Crossroad

At the end of my fourth week, I received a pass for a home visit. I felt I had truly earned it.

Dr. Kamen urged me to use this time to tell Jake about what had been happening behind the locked doors of the hospital. Although somewhat anxious, I was happy to be free from the hospital's confining environment and stress, even if it was for a short three hours.

Riding home with Jake in the quietness of our car, I found a new appreciation for many things I had always taken for granted. The greens of the grass seemed greener, late summer flowers' brilliant array of colors teased my eyes, our neighbor's giant maple tree took my breath away with its golden splendor. It was as though I had never seen it before. God's creation came to life before my eyes and touched my soul. I sensed something had awakened in me that had long been asleep. I could not recall a time when Texas was ever beautiful in August.

I walked through the front door of our home with a hint of excitement—but just for a moment. I felt like a stranger there. The silence that greeted me became a sad reminder that I had missed an entire summer with my children. The older kids had returned to college, and our youngest was at school.

But this day was not to be about our kids, and no matter how much I wanted to avoid our issues, I knew we had to face them head-on. Jake and I spent the few hours talking about me, about him, and our relationship. I told him some things that I could not bring myself to talk about to strangers. And though my dignity was teetering on a precarious line, in the privacy of our home, I told him details I had not disclosed to my therapist, my psychiatrist, or anyone else. Even then, some of my secrets would stay between God and me, and I was okay with that.

My husband needed to understand my confusing, conflicting personality. He needed to know why I had difficulty responding intimately from the very beginning of our marriage. I had fallen in love with Jake because he saw me, not as a sex object, but as a person he loved and respected. Because of this, I made myself available to him whenever he needed or wanted me. Regardless of how tired or secretly depressed I might be, I made sure his needs were met. It was my gift of love to him.

For some victims of childhood sexual abuse, the abuse fuels promiscuity because pleasure is associated with the experience; but for others, it causes them to shut down sexually. I fell into the latter category. Growing up, I did not experience a normal sexual metamorphosis, and I believe my emotional response at that time became just one more reason for my suppressed anger. When my girlfriends talked about sex and experimenting during our teenage years, I only pretended to be on the same page; I hated sex and anything related to it.

Early on in our marriage, Jake discovered that bringing *Playboy* into our bedroom enhanced my response. As the years progressed and pornography became more open and explicit, so did our involvement in it. Because I was exposed to these kinds of images at such a young age, they became my sexual trigger. They changed my sexuality, and they became my partner.

That is the evil power of pornography. It grips the mind, the body, and the soul; it will not let them go. Pornography changes who you are. It steals human intimacy. And do not be fooled: porn addiction is not limited to just men. Women fall into its clutches also, and children are especially vulnerable to its evil. Pornography *will* become your partner, even if you do not wish it to be so. It is no respecter of persons.

Simultaneously, my spiritual journey exposed the entrapment of the human spirit for which pornography is designed. Once it becomes your sexual partner, your desire for it is insatiable, and personal intimacy alone is never enough to satisfy the addiction to pornography's power. Spiritually, I knew that sexual response was God-given and holy. It was designed to bring a man and a woman together as one for procreation, a sacred gift that can bring joy and contentment beyond our ability to define when held with respect to God's provision. However, when human beings step out of that provision, we open ourselves to a dark spiritual world that dishonors ourselves and our Creator. When we invite pornography into our lives, we welcome vicious, forceful powers of darkness to work in, through, and against our families and ourselves. As a child, this darkness was imposed upon me, and I was not accountable; but as an adult, I am accountable.

Consider me as I was then: the exposure to pornography, the unresolved sexual abuses by females and males, and the sincere desire to be a godly woman. I did indeed feel like I was on an airplane, flying around out of control—always waiting to crash. And there are thousands upon thousands of women and men just like me. My husband had no clue about the spiritual, emotional, and sexual battles that raged within me during our marriage because, like many other areas in our lives, we did not talk about them, and my thick facade concealed them. But my struggles produced unbearable, consuming guilt. I heaped more and more anger upon the rage I had already suppressed, adding fuel to the depression that had invaded my life as a child.

I had been freed from the addiction to pornography long before the few hours I spent with Jake that day. Learning to be intimate without it was like trying to breathe without air. The battle was enormous. Jake had not yet felt the Holy Spirit's conviction about watching pornography, nor did he understand the demonic influences that came with the package. He had not yet realized his place as the family's spiritual leader, nor the impact of not assuming the responsibility. We needed to deal with pornography and other issues once and for all. I needed him to be all God was calling him to be.

During my recovery process, I encountered sexually confused people or people who thought they were gay who were depressed and unhappy. They found themselves living in dark places from which they desperately wanted to be free. Without exception, they were victims of childhood sexual abuse, and like me, sex caused confusing and conflicting emotions.

Even though I had never actually felt a physical attraction toward women, I secretly struggled with the idea that I might be gay simply because of my lack of sexual response toward men. However, I was very wrong in my assumption, and my time on 3E clarified that I was wounded, not gay. Jesus told the disciples that if they knew the truth, they would be set free. His words enlighten us. When it gets dark enough, you can see the stars, and the darker it gets, the more stars you will be able to see. I finally acknowledged why I was so confused and shared the truth with my husband in my darkest hours. Having seen the truth, I was truly set free from my confusion and fear, just as Jesus promised.[1] God's mercy toward an abused child, especially a sexually abused child, has no limits. Knowledge and truth embrace one another.

In many ways, our real journey together began on that day, perhaps because we started to choose a different path. For the first time in our married life, we talked about feelings and issues that had plagued us. God had been patiently *waiting on us* to find His pathway. He had long been holding the door open for us to walk through, and it was now up to us to take each other's hand and discover what He had there for us. With God's help, we would find our way together. There was much work yet for us to do. Life is all about choices.

My soulmate, my husband, the father of my beautiful children, was the only person in the world I could trust to love me no matter what. He held me close to his gentle heart, where he invited me to live as one with him. Jake now had a better understanding of what he had always believed: I was not a bad person, but bad things had happened to me. I was just beginning to understand that myself. Our tears washed away our pain. Jake's support and love enabled me to go back to the hospital, where I could safely hide until it was appropriate for me to return home. I had never loved my husband more than I did that day.

Our insurance would pay for two more weeks in the hospital, and I needed to take advantage of this time—time for myself that I knew I would never have again. There were two more mountains for me to

---

[1] In John 8:32, Jesus said, "Then you will know the truth, and the truth will set you free" (NIV).

climb. The first mountain would be the church where Jake and I had 22 years of history I needed to sift through. The second was my relationship with my sister. I loved her and yearned for us both to be free from past hurts. But Barb would not be there to guide me over these steep mountains, where potential failures lurked.

We are now at the final crossroad. Let me speak for a moment to those of you whose lives I call *normal*—those who have not experienced child abuse, especially child sexual abuse. Hopefully, by now, you understand more of what goes on in the mind of a child abuse victim. I do not want to rehash those complexities because by now, I hope you understand that for every abused child who survives, an adult is walking around *trying to do life* with a wounded child living inside them. You can believe me when I say you are standing near at least one person like me at almost any given time. We are everywhere.

Hopefully, you now understand why the AAC acts out in so many different ways, most often contrary to the adult you outwardly perceive that person to be. Wounded adults must find a way to appear to be normal. But as you can now see, they are not normal because they were abused as children, and abuse is *never, ever* normal. As I have previously said, we who are victims of violence are overly complex people.

As you continue my journey with me, please keep in mind all you have learned about the secrets I carried as I tried so hard to walk through life with my head held high—pretending, denying, surviving in the best way I knew. You must grasp that the rest of my story is about the wounded child trying to exist in the skin of an adult and in a world that often just brought more pain, confusion, and victimiza-

Chapter 14

tion. That's important; before we move on, you need to understand what I am saying.

Now I want to speak to those of you for whom I tell my story. You are not crazy. You are not alone in the world of abuse, and you are worthy of love and protection. The precious wounded child that lives within you deserves to be healed and set free. Above all, God loves you and offers you hope.

Let us pause for a few moments of reflection. We have spent a great deal of valuable time preparing the canvas for this portion of my life story. All this preparation was designed to help you understand the inner turmoil I experienced, so you could see how I struggled to keep the threads of my life from fraying into oblivion. It is here that the ugly, twisted effects of childhood abuse stormed into my life, even as the all-consuming love and power of God imparted tender mercy to me, His precious wounded child.

We have washed across the canvas, sketched in the background, filled in the shadows, splashed about colors of despair and hope. But how do we paint the centerpiece of this story: the little girl who has become a woman, the AAC I so desperately want you to know before we put on the finishing touches of the painting? What colors do we choose? Which brush strokes will expose the confusion of a mind that must escape its existence in a black hole so deep and vast that only by the grace of God will the light of hope survive? How does one paint spiritual warfare?

It will take unwavering faith to continue as I reveal God's redemptive work through my spiritual experiences, my final journey before leaving the hospital. Once again, it will not be easy, but it will be victorious. It is the most difficult to tell, in many ways, because this is where all the wounds of the AAC festered.

I can begin again

With the passion of a child

My heart has caught a vision

Of a life that's still worthwhile

I can reach out again

Far beyond what I have done

Part three:

The AAC and the Survivor

Chapter 15

The Imperfect Church, God's Training Ground

Becoming a Christian or a Christ-follower is a choice, not something into which you are born. In the Bible, Matthew tells us that our Father in Heaven is not willing that anyone is lost.[1] His desire is for all humankind to accept His love even though we cannot fully explain what happens when we step out in faith and believe in someone we cannot see. Yet supernaturally, we who have done so know that Jesus Christ is present within us the instant we choose to believe in Him, to believe He is who He says He is. At that moment, we may not be fully aware that our eyes are opened to the knowledge of God the Father, God the Son, and God the Holy Spirit, but in time we steadily gain understanding about the Triune (three-in-one) God. Water does not

---

1 Matthew 18:14 "In the same way your Father in heaven is not willing that any of these little ones should perish" (NIV).

try to be water. Air does not try to be air. God does not try to be holy, and Jesus does not try to be God. It is as it is; air is air. Water is water. God is God, and Jesus is the exact revelation of who God is. If you want to know God, look at Jesus Christ.[2]

I remember my own experience so well. It was the moment when love came in and when seeds of faith were planted within my tender child spirit. I heard God's call, accepted His invitation, and believed in Him—not because I was waiting on Him to accept me, but because He was *waiting on me* to receive Him.

When I was a teenager, I began to walk away from the principles of my faith, but I never let go of my belief in God throughout those tumultuous years and into my early twenties. I know the faith in Jesus planted within my soul as a young girl enabled me to survive.

After my divorce, I found myself surrounded by Christians, and I began to feel God calling me to return to Him. I yearned to find the love and peace I had once known. That is when I walked back into His grace, and that is also when Jake walked into my life.

When we met, my spiritual maturity was far from consummated. I brought into our relationship unreal expectations and the naive notion that all people who go to church are loving, kind, and sinless. I thought that going to church with my family would somehow protect and heal all the ills of my life, but I became stuck in the suspended spaces of those expectations as I put on a large facade that covered my own deceptions.

However, just as sure as the powers of darkness roam this earth seeking those whom they can devour,[3] the Spirit of the Living God

---

2 Ephesians 3:11-12 "according to His eternal purpose that He accomplished in Christ Jesus our Lord. In Him and through faith in Him, we may approach God with freedom and confidence" (NIV).

3 1 Peter 5:8 says, "Be self-controlled and alert. Your enemy, the devil, prowls around like a roaring lion looking for someone to devour (NIV).

roams this earth seeking those who have a heart for Him.[4] The holiness of God pushed through my disobedience, saw my faith, and honored my heart for Him. I could never have imagined just how much I would need Him. I will be eternally thankful that He never let me go and that I never abandoned my faith in Him. I am here to testify that mine would be a vastly different story had I not chosen to accept God's gift of love and forgiveness.

Shortly after Jake and I met, I began going to church with him. His parents went to church faithfully and raised their children to do the same. This was extremely important because I wanted my future children to have spiritual roots that I didn't have until a neighbor took me to church.

Jake's protestant denomination was hugely different from the church of my childhood, where I found the character of holiness. My initial response to his church's service itself left me feeling awestruck— the silence, the kneeling, the liturgy, Holy Communion, the reserved sacrament. It all created an atmosphere of reverence that deeply touched me. However, it took little time to observe that the pious reverence displayed on Sunday mornings did not always reflect the character of holiness in the lives of the people who worshiped and served there.

Although it has taken a lifetime to learn the difference between judging and discerning, I rightly discerned from the very beginning that there were disturbing issues within those walls of worship. I felt something was out of sync, and it grieves me sincerely to say that Jake's church eventually became another dysfunctional family in which I had to learn to survive.

---

4 Hebrews 11:6 says, "And without faith, it is impossible to please God because anyone who comes to Him must believe that He exists and that he rewards those who earnestly seek him" (NIV).

Jake and I became engaged only four months after we met. We promptly made an appointment to discuss wedding plans with his priest, whom I deemed the next best thing to God. Whenever I was around this man, I would practically shake in my shoes for fear of doing something wrong. I had erroneously created a holy illusion about priests because of a new term I had learned: *apostolic succession*, meaning hands were laid on our priest by a bishop following a succession of bishops leading directly back to the 12 apostles and Jesus.

We were unprepared for the ultimatum the priest gave us: I must go before a committee of priests and have my first marriage annulled before we could be married in the church. I must also go through confirmation classes and be confirmed by a bishop before taking communion at our wedding. I wanted to rebel, to protest, but I did not. I agreed to the priest's demands. *The mask of denial was always around to do the AAC's bidding.*

We set a June date for our wedding, so I only had a short time to meet the demands placed upon me and plan the event. I attended weekly confirmation classes at the church, and as required, I accompanied Jake's priest to the annulment hearing. As we traveled down the busy expressway to the cathedral, I could tell my emotions were shutting down. It was another of those times when everything around me went black.

When the interview began, I disappeared somewhere into the background around me. The all-too-familiar panic told me to run out the door. But I could not run away. *Controlled panic attacks were not uncommon for the AAC when she felt unsafe. They left her without boundaries. Depression followed closely behind the panic.*

In my mind's eye, I see about 20 men, dressed in ominous black with their white collars radiating out into my darkness, staring at me and judging me as though I were on trial for some heinous crime. But in reality, I think only about six men were present.

They began to probe into my past and ask me personal questions. I refused to tell a bunch of strange men things I could not even share with my future husband—or, worse, some things I could not even face myself. I held my head high and, with justifiable dignity, avoided telling them what they wanted to hear. In other words: I lied! I was sure God would strike me dead. *The AAC would do anything to avoid the truth. She was unable to face making an honest confession to anyone.*

Confirmation classes should have been another warning. I don't know what I expected, but they had nothing to do with developing my relationship with God. Disturbingly, they were not even about God. The classes were about how to "do church." I was never once asked about my relationship with Christ, or even if I believed in Him.

I began asking the priest and Jake questions that I viewed as essential to my faith. I wanted to know why we were not studying the Bible. Although I loved the beautiful prayers in the prayer book, I wanted to understand how children were supposed to learn to talk to God if all their prayers were read from a book. Since I was a little girl, I had been talking to God and had never once needed to use a book to get His attention. (I have since come to believe that all prayers said from the heart are heard by God.)

I was having trouble understanding the significance of everything tossed at me and expressed my unhappiness to my future husband. With hindsight, I have wondered whether Jake's father, realizing I might walk away, put pressure on the priest to ease off the rules—because finishing confirmation classes suddenly did not seem so important to him. He changed his mind and allowed us to get married before my confirmation, and I was also permitted to take communion at our wedding.

Once married, Jake's family connection to the church made it easy for us to get involved, and we quickly became part of the church's core. Jake was elected to serve on the vestry (like a deacon board in most protestant churches), and I went to work in the church office.

When we attended social parties held by church members, I was shocked to witness leaders and members drinking excessively and exhibiting what I considered inappropriate behavior. Many of those same people would serve Holy Communion and read the scriptures, all piously going through the liturgical rituals on Sunday morning.

Some of the young men on the vestry belonged to a nationally recognized philanthropic organization, which Jake joined. While they and their wives carried out many excellent community services, they also loved to party. Alcohol flowed freely. *When the AAC was around groups of people drinking, anger brewed. But no one would know this because she smiled and wore the mask of deception.*

The effects alcohol had previously had on my life meant I wanted nothing more to do with it. Above all, I feared exposing my future children to drinking as a socially acceptable practice. Unfortunately, Jake could never understand my fears, even when I almost broke off our engagement after realizing his family's apparent acceptance of alcohol. And now I watched as it spilled over into our church and social life. *The AAC put on the mask of disdain. A war began within her between the good and evil she saw in behavior she did not understand. The confused survivor could not find where she belonged. A new wave of anger consumed the wounded child.*

And so it was that early on in our perfect marriage and our perfect life, alcohol's cruel influence began to nibble away at the sweet love we had for each other. Unsuspecting spiritual battles, for which I was ill-equipped, stepped into my path. I appeared to be an attractive, happy young woman, but lies from the enemy of my soul fueled simultaneous conflicting emotions and feelings. I desperately wanted to be good, but freedom from my past still eluded me. I had hoped to find that freedom in Jake, his family, and his church. Tolerance won; I closed my eyes and sometimes even joined in the thing I detested and feared. *The survivor's perpetual shift in and out of God's truth, of right and wrong behavior, was unavoidable. It was impossible for her to control. The abused adult child did not understand that no human could fix her.*

Apart from the presence of alcohol, I found it hard to believe the church could be anything but a loving, safe place for anyone. However, all too often, I did not see the character of Jesus expressed there. There were no Bible studies, no prayer groups, and no Sunday school classes. The priest loved his pipe organ, and the people loved to party. Disunity was evident. Except for a few, I found little spiritual connection with people in the church.

In time, within the church's ambiance, I began to understand that spiritual warfare is real. Satan's work is to seek and destroy the church, the Body of Christ. Within this particular church, I saw those dark forces at work in the lives of well-intentioned but uninformed people. *The AAC became a victim of the dark powers, while the wounded child listened to the lies and acted out in every way she had learned—depression, ambivalence, anger, confusion, and denial. She repeatedly screamed out to be loved but would push people away if they got too close. The wounded child guarded God's Spirit within her. The survivor emerged strong and wore all their faces well.*

However, God loved me too much to allow me to stay trapped in the twisted betrayal of abuse. He used my church experience as a training ground for the spiritual battles I would yet face. Slowly, He pruned the dead branches of my life away from the places where my sins and those of others rotted. In contrast to my wounded child's behavior, He showed me that the strength and character of Jesus coursed through my veins and flowed into many areas of my life. He revealed that I had the goodness of heart for those who suffer, and He gave me opportunities to exercise my faith in Him.

During this training time, God led me to venues outside our church that provided spiritual teaching I did not otherwise have. This was the preparation I desperately needed for the battles to come. I honestly do not know what I would have done without Christian radio and television.

Insight for Living with Chuck Swindoll taught me God's Word, which has spoken to humanity throughout the ages to reveal who God is. Chuck taught me God's precepts—principles that work and do not work for us in this life. I listened intently to James Dobson's *Focus on the Family* radio program. His interview with Ted Bundy gave me insights into a sexual predator's mind and the evil power of pornography, and his programs on child abuse, marriage, and raising children became invaluable to me. Eventually, evenings would find me watching the Christian Broadcasting Network on television, praying with Pat Robertson and the CBN family. These godly men became my teachers, my counselors, my prayer partners, my lifeline to God. They fed my thirsty, immature spirit.

On the battlefield between good and evil, I would learn the value of listening to and obeying God's still, small voice, and I would discover, with great dismay, how easy it is to fall short of doing so. I would realize that my choices, both good and bad, always have consequences. Over time, I would learn my spiritual battles are God's to fight and not mine. I had to learn to surrender my struggles to Him.

I also learned that God never closes His heart, and He patiently waits for me to follow where He wants to lead. The Triune God has been the one sure thing in my life that has sustained me. As we continue, you will experience God's faithfulness to this wounded child.

Chapter 16

Yes, Life Can Get Worse—and It Did

We were delighted when I became pregnant only eight months after we were married. Born two weeks after my due date in November 1969, our daughter weighed eight pounds, four ounces, and was much too large for my petite frame. It was a difficult labor.

We named our baby girl Katherine, which means pure. Katherine is also the middle name that was given to me when I was born. *The abused adult child struggled against bringing an innocent baby into a world filled with so much darkness and pain. The wounded child desired to give her name to her child in the hope of defining a new pure life for herself.*

When Katherine was only a few months old, my brother-in-law appeared on our doorstep with his camera equipment in tow to take pictures of my baby girl. I still cannot believe I let him in the door. The entire time he was in our home, repressed raw rage clawed the inner walls of my skin, begging to be unleashed. As he was leaving, untapped strength surfaced. I looked him in the eyes and declared, "If you ever touch her, you will regret it!"

There was no response; he just left. Shortly afterward, he was diagnosed with cancer. He died a few years later. *The AAC had no power over her abuser, except when it came to her child. She resolved never to let the man near her and felt relief when he passed.*

Delivery amnesia kicked in, and six months later, I was pregnant again. The blessing of having Katherine in our lives far outweighed the struggle of getting her here. We did not realize then that her difficult entry into this world was only the first of many battles for our beautiful, golden-haired baby who would touch many lives.

When I took Katherine in for her nine-month checkup, our pediatrician sent us to a nearby lab for blood tests because he thought she looked a little pale. The results did not show anything significantly abnormal, and we laughed it off; fair skin was a trait that ran on both sides of our family.

It was about this time that I began to have premonitions—consumed by feelings of inexplicable dread concerning my baby. Sudden unexpected moments of panic and fear engulfed me. I would hold her close to me and weep, crying out to God to protect her.

The day finally came when I had to face stone-cold reality. Dread crept over me as I looked purposely at my child. I had noticed she was bruising and had dark, bluish-green circles under her eyes and on her cheeks and arms. Instead of her skin being a pretty baby pink, it had a greenish tint.

I quickly made an appointment to see her pediatrician. Physical pain crushed my chest until I could hardly breathe as we drove into town later that day. A familiar, foreboding presence sat beside me and mocked me. *Denial stuffed every persuasive thought and every dark emotion deep down into the center of the AAC's soul. Her baby needed her, and she could not think about herself. She could not disappear.*

I checked in with the receptionist and settled into a chair in the waiting room. Katherine laid her head on my chest as she caressed the satin binding on her soft blanket—her thumb giving much-needed comfort as she gently nursed it. My chin nestled over the top of her head as I wrapped my arms around her. I was desperate to protect her from the ominous cloud that had followed us for weeks.

A nurse called Katherine's name and directed us into one of the small examination rooms. Dr. Stein, a young doctor who had a reputation as the best pediatrician in the area, greeted us. I would come to believe that divine providence had led us to this wise man.

He examined Katherine and then cautiously suggested we take another look at her blood count. He seemed to be paying close attention to the lack of color under her fingernails and eyelids, and he questioned me about the bruises. I refused to let my thoughts linger as I carried her to the laboratory for another blood test.

I firmly held my baby's hand, trying to console her as the technician stuck her tiny finger with the sharp metal object. Blood rose to the surface of her skin. Tears rolled down Katherine's round, flushed cheeks as she looked at me in dismay. *The familiar darkness that provided refuge for the survivor tried to give her a place to hide, but she could not, would not, go there—not this time.*

I wanted to comment on the blood's color as I watched it going into the small vial, but I was afraid of what the response might be. The last time I had seen my daughter's blood, it was bright red; this time, it looked like pale pink Kool-Aid. Her white cell count was so high that the technician just stopped counting. But I knew, and I ignored the look of concern on the technician's face as she handed me the results and directed me back to the doctor's office.

Noticing my condition as he read the report, our doctor asked me when my baby was due. I appeared to be more than four months pregnant. He told me that Katherine was anemic, and it was vital for us to find out why. He suggested that we go home; he would call when he could arrange for a doctor to see her at the hospital, perhaps on Monday. He was gently preparing me.

The trip home seemed much longer than the journey into town. As I pulled into the garage, I could hear the persistent ringing of the phone. I struggled to pull Katherine over my growing belly and out of the vehicle. The steep steps leading into the house were like giant obstacles trying to hinder me from getting to the phone.

When I answered, the gravity of our doctor's voice betrayed the significance of the call. He told me he had spoken with Dr. Rodgers at Children's Hospital in Dallas, and he was willing to wait for us to get there. Dr. Stein did not wait for me to respond. He told me I should leave immediately for the hospital and instructed me to go to the emergency entrance. It was already close to 5:00 p.m. I called Jake, and he came home to make the trip with us.

Upon arrival, we found our way to the emergency room, where a nurse paged Dr. Rodgers. The head of pediatric oncology wasted no time meeting with us. I instantly felt a peace about this man who had an air of gentleness about him.

When he told us he wanted to admit Katherine into the hospital, I protested.

"She doesn't have any pajamas to wear, and she hasn't had her supper, and it's close to her bedtime!"

The doctor assured me the hospital had plenty of pajamas, food, and beds. *The survivor could not stop the inevitable.*

Jake went to the admitting office while a nurse escorted Katherine and me upstairs. That short walk from the emergency room to the

Chapter 16

third floor made me painfully aware, in no uncertain terms, that only the extremely ill resided in this place.

I tried to ignore the needles that disappeared into tender flesh and the sadness in the eyes of the parents who hovered near their young ones.

Once settled into a room, a nurse took my baby from me. The transition happened so professionally that I hardly had time to think about what they might do to her. Katherine did not protest. She was so trusting. My child's sweet innocence did not know what was in store for her. *The survivor resolved to stand firm. She would not feel. She watched her baby disappear without emotion, numb.*

Deafening silence greeted Jake when he found me alone in our room. We embraced. There was nothing to be said, no words to speak, each grasping for something to hold on to, hoping to comfort and reassure each other as we tried to cope with our fears. We cringed at the news that Katherine would receive a pint of blood plasma; the process had already started.

When she returned to my arms, I carefully wiped the tears from her crimson cheeks. Her golden hair, much longer than most eleven-month-old babies', was drenched with sweat. Long dark eyelashes were matted against closed eyes. She had fallen asleep from exhaustion and sighed every few minutes, her body trembling with each short breath. The nurse put her in the cold, uninviting bed, where I covered her to make sure she would be warm. I was still fretting that she had missed her supper.

I examined the patch on her head where they had shaved off some of her pretty hair, amused by the fact that a Dixie cup, cut in half and taped to her skin, protected the needle that now penetrated her scalp.

I familiarized myself with the machine that monitored the dark red liquid flowing from the clear plastic bag held high above my head by the icy steel pole. I ignored the needle that dug into her tender flesh. Intuitively, I knew that death was knocking at our door. *The abused adult child would be everything her baby needed her to be. She would let no one see the agony that ripped at her soul as she stood and watched her child through the long darkness of night.*

Occasional soft flutters from the new life growing within me reminded me of its presence, momentarily drawing me away from the unforgiving truth I did not want to face. Did my unborn child feel my sorrow? Did it sense what I sensed: the gravity of its sister's condition? Was its little soul grieving with me, or was it trying to offer me comfort and hope for life, not fear of death?

I looked at my daughter and prayed for them both.

Numbness from the past and strength for the present merged that night as the abused adult child emotionally separated from her daughter; the fear of losing her was too much to bear. It would be the only way to survive—the only way she could be strong enough for her baby, her unborn child, and her husband. She was a survivor, and that is what survivors do. Whatever it takes.

My parents came to the hospital early the following morning, Saturday, to be with their ninth grandchild. Tired and weary from lack of sleep, I stood in the hall outside Katherine's room, staring out the window at the tops of October trees. The oranges, reds, and golds blended together while thick clouds hung low in the sky. Sudden, light rain tapped on the protective glass, sending a chill throughout my numb body—drawing my attention back into the hallway.

Without emotion, I returned to the colorless room and looked firmly at my husband. "It can't be leukemia!"

I fell into the familiar warmth of my young husband's arms. His glassy, blue eyes reflected my secret thoughts. *Perhaps now it won't hurt so deeply when we finally hear the truth.* We were given, at that moment, the first of many large doses of grace. *The AAC's tears would flow no more. The survivor could not afford their luxury.*

Noon arrived, and as expected, Dr. Stein and three other doctors walked into our small space and gathered around us. Mom and Dad quietly slipped out of the room. I could not begin to imagine how difficult it was for these men to hand over their verdict.

"Your daughter has acute lymphoblastic leukemia. There is no cure. For now, the blood transfusion will temporarily sustain her life."

Broken only by a soft whimper of distress from our baby, uncertain silence hung in the air. The metal bars of the jail-like bed kept me from quickly comforting her. I struggled to get the barrier free, lashing out in anger at the bed. *The wounded child displaced her anger, just like she had always done in the past, not wanting to look at the source of it but consistently placing it somewhere else.*

With tears in his eyes, Jake asked what kind of expenses we would face. Jake explained he had resigned from his job just two weeks earlier, and the insurance on Katherine had terminated at midnight Friday, the day before. The doctors were sympathetic but told us to expect a minimum of $15,000—nearly Jake's annual salary—for every year she lived.

Hesitantly, his lips trembling and his voice shaking, Jake asked the hardest question of all.

"How long will that be?"

The news was difficult to hear. If Kat could tolerate the medication and stay in remission, she might live for 12 to 18 months. If not, it could be a matter of weeks or even days.

The doctors explained the treatment plan for our baby girl, kindly leaving out the gory details; those, we would experience soon enough. I can find no human words to adequately define the impact of what our ears heard, or what our hearts felt, or what our senses wanted to scream out. I only know that God's grace was sufficient for that terrible moment. *The survivor began preparing herself for unknown territory even as the AAC succumbed to the numbness.*

The doctors left the room, and we struggled to give my parents the dreadful news. Dad and Mom stood silent with their thoughts—most certainly reliving the death of their own baby girl. I was too numb to feel their sorrow. They stayed with Katherine while we left the hospital to tell Jake's parents; it would have seemed inappropriate to deliver such heartbreaking news over the phone.

Before getting into our car, I turned to my husband and looked with determination into his eyes. From some sacred place I didn't even know I possessed came steadfast words: "Jake, God is going to take care of Katherine. I don't know how, but I know He is going to heal her."

Seeds of faith sown in my simple child-heart so many years ago, when a little lost bird flew down from a distant tree limb onto my shoulder, were now beginning to grow like an acorn that had lain dormant in the soil of my soul. Sprouts from within began to search for light as they reached toward Heaven for nourishment. From that moment on, I walked in complete faith and belief that Katherine would not die.

In the days and months that followed, I shared with everyone I knew this unwavering faith I had in Jesus to heal our daughter. But I was not prepared for the lack of faith that surrounded me; everyone thought I was in denial and that Katherine was doomed to die. *The survivor did not understand others' lack of faith. Her faith had overcome denial. The wounded child secretly harbored anger toward those who scorned her faith. But she knew God hears and answers prayers.*

So many times, God imparted mercy to Katherine. An unexpected rise in her blood count prevented the doctors from cutting into her

Chapter 16

ankle in search of a vein robust enough for yet another transfusion, so we were able to take her home without additional treatment. She tolerated the toxic drug, vincristine, forced into her tiny, fragile veins and the weekly oral medication I gave her. I had to accept the warning that any trace of the oral drug, methotrexate, in my body could damage the baby growing inside of me. Everything within me wanted to rebel. I did not want to put my child through this nightmare.

However, Katherine's own God-given ability to endure allowed her to be happy, despite the necessary, seemingly abusive things she had to go through. Her strength and joy carried me through. *The AAC would not allow her feelings to dictate the necessary choices she made. Feelings would no longer be permissible where her child was concerned. And after all, she was an expert at not feeling.*

God met our financial needs in ways we could not have imagined. A thoughtful neighbor wrote an article about Katherine, and several local newspapers published it. Consequently, we were given gifts from people we didn't even know. Envelopes filled with loving thoughts and cash arrived in our mailbox; they never had return addresses. We received a free turkey for Thanksgiving and a free dry-cleaning service. The list went on and on.

Mr. Gaddi, who owned a fireplace business close to our house, kept a picture of Kat beside a fat red piggy bank on his countertop. Patrons tossed their coins—and sometimes their bills into the slot of the smiling pig until it could hold no more. You cannot imagine the surprise and awe-filled thankfulness we felt when, one day, this humble man knocked on our door and presented us with his money-stuffed, pot-bellied gift.

One of the most amazing "Godcidences" came through a young woman whose husband I had once dated before they were married. She worked in the lab, where we had to make weekly and sometimes semiweekly visits. When she realized we had no insurance on Katherine, she went to the lab owner and petitioned him to drop all our charges; we were faced with a minimum bill of $40 a month in lab fees alone, which was substantial. Thankfully, he agreed to this arrangement, and we were never charged for services, no matter how many times we needed them.

Many people touched our lives, whom we will never repay directly or tell how much we appreciate their kindness. But in time, we would return their thoughtfulness in the only way that we could—by helping others in need.

In March 1971, we welcomed the quick and easy birth of our son. The pain of Kat's illness only multiplied the blessing we felt in having our baby boy. Katherine desperately needed a playmate. She adored Jay and could not give her little brother enough attention.

Now, not only did I have a sick child to care for, but I also had the added stress of a new baby. *There was no place for the AAC's self-pity. She could not be self-absorbed. The survivor stayed in control.*

Several months after Jay's birth, we received a call from our pediatrician. He informed us that St. Jude Children's Research Hospital in Tennessee had released its experimental treatment for leukemia to hospitals around the country. He wanted us to consider taking Katherine back to Children's Hospital to discuss entering this program. We did not hesitate; we felt we had no choice but to try anything that might save her life. She was one of the first children in the Dallas area to receive this treatment.

But this mother's heart did not like what she was hearing. A complete bombardment of Katherine's cells was the proposed solution for a possible cure for our daughter. They were striving for a five-year remission with only a 5% chance that she would live beyond that time. If she survived the initial treatment, she would be on maintenance drugs for two and a half years and then taken off all medication because her body would not tolerate the drugs indefinitely.

Katherine went into the program; however, years later, Dr. Rodgers told me they almost did not move forward with our daughter because she showed signs of a relapse. "For some reason, we decided to take a chance with Katherine, and I'm so glad we did."

This treatment protocol typically excluded children showing signs of a relapse from further treatment because they never did well; such treatment would only prolong the suffering, the inevitable. This was yet another extension of God's immeasurable grace toward Katherine.

Three months of intensive treatment began. The protocol included repeating the original intravenous drug, five spinal injections, and a series of high-dosage radiation treatments to Katherine's brain. Maintenance drugs followed for the next two and half years.

During this time, her features changed so drastically that even family members did not recognize her. She was bloated and puffy and bald, but still the happy, sweet little person whose life became more precious to us with each passing day. *God gave Katherine the grace to endure, and He gave the survivor the grace to sit by and watch helplessly. The AAC lived on prayers of faith.*

I must share one endearing story about this amazing child. I had taken her to the hospital for the final injection into her spine. By then, she was a toddler and talking. Although taken from my arms many times, she never once fussed about it. However, she hit her limit on this last trip and was no longer willing to accept any more pain. When the nurse reached out to take her from me, Katherine threw her little arms around my neck, locked her heels around my waist, and would not let go.

I gently told her, "Katherine, you only need to do this one more time, just one more time! After today, no one will ever hurt your back again. Your back will be all well."

She gave me a look I will not forget and, with childlike understanding, loosened her grip on her mother and reached out to the waiting nurse. I felt an aura of love around my child, which said so much about Katherine's own God-given strength and character.

On the way home, I felt a gentle tap on my shoulder. I turned and looked at my young daughter sitting next to me in her car seat. I asked her what she wanted. She leaned forward with big tears in her deep blue eyes and pulled her little white dress with the tiny blue flowers away from her back.

"My back is all well. See, Mommy, my back is all well."

Overcome with emotion, my voice trembling, I whispered back to her, "Yes, Katherine! Your back is all well!"

She was only 23 months old.

We faced some difficult decisions. One of the hardest was to assess the continuing feasibility of living outside the city, in the country.

Even though we loved our first home and the small country community where neighbors truly knew how to be neighborly, we sold the house and moved into town. I allowed myself to cry when Jake took the cats away.

With the dreadful series of leukemia treatments behind us and finally settling into our new home in town, we had another major decision to make. Often kids with cancer die from secondary infections because the chemotherapy compromises their immune systems. In the 1970s, chickenpox was a deadly enemy to avoid because, for some reason, the virus turns inward, and nothing can stop it. With those threats hanging over our daughter's chance for survival, we decided to isolate our children from the rest of the world as long as Kat was on the maintenance chemo. They would not be allowed to go out and play with other children or go to church or preschool. I would not even take them to the grocery store.

Chapter 16

We accepted our new way of life and settled into a routine for the duration of her treatment. Our big adventure out of the house was when baby Jay and I took Katherine in for blood tests every Monday. The next morning, depending upon her blood counts, I would give her oral medications that would hopefully do their job fighting the cancer but would also lower her resistance to zero.

Kat handled everything much better than I did. She continually offered her fingers to be pricked for blood tests, seldom shedding a tear or offering a protest. She was such an amazing little girl, and her sweet countenance carried me through those tough times. *Grace carried the wounded child and the survivor. But the AAC succumbed to the sorrow of what was being forced upon her little daughter. Depression was ever-present.*

And so began a long journey with my young family. It was a journey that would give me the highest expressions of joy and happiness imaginable, and at the same time, plunge me into the depths of despair beyond description.

I severed ties with the outside world and stayed home with my two babies. It was the best of times; it was the worst of times. *It took every resource the wounded child could draw on to keep from buckling under her conflicting emotions and feelings. She was weak; she was strong. She was happy; she was sad. She was hopeful; she was depressed. But the AAC never stopped proclaiming that God would heal her child.*

Our new city neighbors were unfriendly and distant, and I longed for the country neighbors we had left behind. Jake coped with our situation by staying busy with work, church, and the men's organization he had joined. Unfortunately, this left me at home alone in the evenings far too often. His being at home was my only outlet. *The AAC's loneliness began to feed the ever-present sting of depression that she tried so hard to deny.*

I had never been around children before I had children of my own. Each new thing they learned was a celebration and an adventure for me, and I relished everything we did. We read books, sang songs, played games. They were so teachable and fun; my heart burst with love for them. I did things for them and with them that were not done for or with me as a child. I think, in many ways, I was growing up with them. *The survivor inadvertently nurtured the wounded child.*

I had a spiritual connection with only a few people in our church: Esther, Bera Gaye, Kay, Sandra, and Ruth were my lifeline. Their daily prayers, frequent phone calls, and encouragement helped me through. I honestly do not know what I would have done without these strong women of faith. Otherwise, our church was distant and silent.

The day-after-day living without a break finally began to wear me down. Mom and Dad were getting too old to drive in the heavy Dallas traffic to help me, and my mother-in-law, who lived just three miles from us, had little time for us.

My pride said that if I had to ask for help, I didn't want it. I called upon Jake's mother only when we were in a crisis. Those early years, unfortunately, set the tone for our future relationship. *The AAC's preconceived expectations that Jake's family and his church would somehow be there for her began to unravel, with devastating emotional results. She struggled to cope with her life.*

Isolation framed our lives as days slipped into weeks, weeks became months, and months slid into years. Depression skewed my thinking, while unrelenting exhaustion, loneliness, and physical pain forced me to cling to my faith in God. He used this time to teach me to abide in Him.

Several significant things happened during this period of seclusion. One night, crawling into bed, I cried out to God and told Him that if He did not do something to help me, he could just take me out of this life. *The AAC wanted to die, but she could not. She had to live for her children. The survivor would not give in. She fought for survival. Divine appointments awaited her.*

I seldom trusted anyone to stay with my children, and money was tight, so we hardly ever went anywhere. Occasionally, I would scrape up enough cash for a sitter so we could attend a small church-related sharing group. About a week after my desperate cry for God's help, we were at one of those meetings when a doctor in the group overheard me talking about the severe headaches I was having. Dr. John approached me about coming to his office for a medical checkup. I made an appointment.

Life became manageable after spending a year under Dr. John's care. He became a dear friend and wise counselor. I will always be thankful for his obedience to serve others and grateful to God for sending him to me. He did not know he was the answer to a desperate prayer. *The AAC did not fully understand God's faithfulness; the survivor would learn that hope came through faithful obedience and trust.*[1]

Television became an outlet not only for my children but for me. One day a group of Asian children representing an international children's ministry appeared on the screen, singing a medley of Christian songs. For the first time, I heard a small inaudible voice speak to me. I could not resist its urging to support these overseas orphan children. It was only $10 a month, but it might as well have been $100. I responded, not knowing where I would get the money, yet it was always there when I needed to make the payment. *The survivor did not know God was testing her ears, her faith, and her obedience.*

---

1 Jeremiah 29: 11-13 "For I know the thoughts that I think toward you, says the Lord, thoughts of peace and not of evil, to give you a future and a hope. Then you will call upon me and go and pray to me and I will listen to you. And you will seek me and find me when you search for me with all your heart" (NKJV).

In retrospect, I am not surprised God speaks to His children; however, I find it amazing that sometimes I listen. But what I find astonishing is when I listen *and obey*! I am also in awe that God rewards our small steps of faith—and I do not mean just monetarily.

Chapter 17

A Retreat and a Divine Appointment

About a year after Katherine's diagnosis, our small church, forced to unite with another church, inherited the merging congregation's young priest. He was outgoing, handsome, a gifted communicator, and seemed idolized by those who came with him. Along with the merger came a troubling party spirit, which many in our congregation embraced. Jake remained on the vestry, and the new priest asked him to continue serving as the junior warden.

The church grew by leaps and bounds. It was a busy place with lots of energy, but disturbing issues hid behind the activity. Although Jake was often at the church, only a handful of people knew he had a terminally ill daughter at home. Those who served with him on the new vestry made no effort to reach out to us. The new priest never came to our house to check on us or pray for Katherine. I believed God would heal her, and somehow I sensed

He wanted people involved in praying for her. But the corporate church was oblivious to that possibility. It was apparent that our situation was not regarded as being of great importance in the scheme of things.

I tried to be obedient to Jake. In the Old Testament, Sarai obeyed her man, Abram, and followed his mission—and like Sarai, I stayed with my man and his church. I like to think that, in the long run, God honored my obedience to my husband.

Within a year, most of the families I had a spiritual connection with left the blended church. No matter how much I complained about my unhappiness there, my husband defended it. He seemed blind to the unhealthy spiritual condition of the church and had no plans to leave.

The roots of bitterness that had already taken hold grew deeper as suppressed anger raged deep within. Frustration joined the AAC's masks of bitterness and resentment. The wounded child's confusing unmet needs multiplied.

Katherine's second year in remission rolled around. The isolation paid off as both children remained otherwise healthy. Katherine was no longer bloated and swollen. Once again, golden hair framed the simple beauty of our little girl's happy face. She adored her little brother and loved life.

We continued to isolate the children as much as possible, but Katherine often begged to go out and play with neighborhood children. Rarely did I risk letting her be a normal kid, and I seldom left them, not even with Jake. However, in October 1972, when my friend Bera Gaye invited me to attend a ladies' retreat hosted by her church, Jake encouraged me to go. He knew I needed to get away. With mixed emotions, I decided to join my friend and leave my children for the entire weekend.

Chapter 17

As I piled into a car full of enthusiastic women heading north out of Dallas to search for spiritual refreshment and refuge from kids, husbands, and housework, I discovered the diocese's father confessor was leading the retreat. He would, of course, be talking about confession.

Before Jake and I married, I made it clear that I would not ever go to confession.

I told him, "I don't need to tell my sins to a priest!"

Although slightly annoyed by the revelation, I kept my negative thoughts to myself. The 45-minute trip ended with a bit of a surprise as we pulled onto the premises of the retreat center: it was the one I had visited with JoAnn years earlier.

It was heaven on earth to have adult, female conversations over dinner and to throw my bedding on one of the numerous bunk beds and just hang out with them. The sound of women's endless chatter ministered to my lonely spirit. Their laughter warmed me from head to toe, and their love comforted me.

But during the Friday night session in the large meeting room, I sat rigid until Fr. Bandy's words began to break through my pent-up emotions, breaking down my walls of resistance. When the session ended, we entered a period of silence, which forced me to be still and think about the words offered to me that evening. The relentless, all-loving pursuit of God's Holy Spirit began to tug at my consciousness, and in the quiet of the night, He began to lead. I began to follow.

During the first session of the day on Saturday morning, I began to take eager notes—and by noon, I was making an appointment to meet with this gentle, wise man. If I had heard this message in the past, its importance had escaped me. Fr. Bandy reminded me that Jesus taught we must forgive others as He has forgiven us[1] and that we must confess our sins before God.[2] He taught that the consequence of ignoring God's call to forgive would result in roots of bitterness that would continually haunt and hinder my relationship with God and with others; I would not be able to love as Christ loved me.

But this challenge to forgive the people who had hurt me did not seem possible. *The AAC struggled. How could she possibly forgive people she secretly hated, those whose names she could not mention? The wounded child felt the never-ending pain. The survivor was trying to survive.*

I searched my mind for those who had mentored me, guided me, or taught me along the way during those lost years when I walked away from God. I found nobody; there had been no one there for me. I did not understand why God had left me to walk alone or why I was just now hearing about the importance of forgiveness. Might my life have been totally changed otherwise?

I felt I was like a ship without a sail aimlessly tossed around in a vast troubled sea, the weight of abuse's anger and bitterness pulling me under the churning water. Somehow, I knew I no longer wanted to bear the consequences of unforgiveness. But would I be able to confess my secrets openly to this man of God?

The wounded child wanted to run and hide. The AAC felt incapable of facing her guilt and sins or those of her abuser. She did not understand that God was asking her to depend upon Him for strength and courage. The survivor became determined.

My appointment was not until 3:00 p.m., so I walked down to the

---

1 Colossians 3:13 says, "Bear with each other and forgive one another if any of you has a grievance against someone. Forgive as the Lord forgave you" (NIV).

2 1 John 1:9 says, "If we confess our sins, he is faithful and just and will forgive us our sins and purify us from all unrighteousness" (NIV).

Chapter 17

chapel, where JoAnn and I had ridden our horses years before. The crisp country air, warmed by the autumn sun, calmed my anxiety. And just for a moment, I forgot about the burdens of sorrow I carried. I relived happy and carefree moments that seemed a lifetime away.

The chapel was still unfinished; I cringed at the youthful irreverence we had displayed and wondered what strange fate had brought me back to this place, where I had known such joy. It had brought healing to me then; perhaps it would do so again. I found a sunny spot, slid to the unfinished floor, and began to make notes. Not only did I have my sins to bear, but I had the sins of others to carry as well. Time passed much too quickly.

The knot in my stomach grew larger with each step I took as I crept up the stairs to the small room where Fr. Bandy heard confessions. The all-too-familiar darkness hovered around me, inviting me to join the secrets that hid there. The secrets! How weary I was from carrying their never-ending burden! Conflicting emotions haunted me. Part of me wanted to run up the stairs and confess every cruel thing that had happened to me—all the secret hates I harbored. Other parts of me wanted to disappear into the shadowy comfort of the darkness.

When I reached the top of the stairs, the tall, slender man greeted me warmly and invited me to enter the small room. Long slim fingers graciously motioned for me to sit at the round table opposite him.

The first words out of his mouth were, "I lost my son to cancer."

The darkness retreated as this man of God began to share the heart-wrenching story of his son's illness and death at the hands of this unforgiving disease. The fresh grief on this wounded father's face colored the account of the night his child had left him.

It had been snowing for most of the day. His young son lay watching the large, icy white flakes float softly toward earth from his hospital window.

The child spoke calmly. "It takes so long. It takes so long."

His grief undiminished, the father said, "I knew he meant it takes so long to die."

Sorrow hung in the air as salty tears quietly expressed what this man could not put into words.

Then we talked about my daughter.

God had provided one who could understand the survivor's pain. Her mask of denial was replaced by the face of compassion, allowing her mentor to cry and feel his pain.

Fr. Bandy's transparency assured me he was safe; I could trust him. I looked at my notes, and with childlike whispers, I shared what I had not yet dared to speak to others: "My sister's husband, my brother-in-law, abused me as a child. How can I forgive that?" But I quickly moved on; it would not be safe for me to linger.

In simple bits and pieces, I told the priest about my first marriage and divorce. I guardedly talked to him about my issues with the church and the resentments I harbored because my Christian community had not been there for my family and me. I could only give him so much, not ready to unleash it all, but even the morsels he tasted gave him cause to express grave concern for me. He gave me counsel—words I can no longer recall—and then administered the sacrament of absolution, pardon.

"God, the Father of mercies, through the death and resurrection of His Son, has reconciled the world to Himself and sent the Holy Spirit among us for the forgiveness of sins; through the ministry of the church, may God give you pardon and peace, and I absolve you from your sins in the name of the Father, and the Son, and the Holy Spirit. Amen."[3]

---

[3] Only God can forgive our sins. However, I believe He knows our hearts and hears our sincere prayers. I believe my feeble attempt at confessing and forgiving and the prayer said for me from a prayer book, on that day, did not go unnoticed by God.

Chapter 17

Forgiveness to receive. Forgiveness to give. I did not fully understand the importance of my divine appointment with Fr. Bandy, but it would soon become apparent in the following events.

It was a new beginning for the AAC, but it would be an exceedingly long time before understanding would come full circle—before forgiveness would be completed. The survivor and the wounded child felt the impact of the moment.

I had wept bitter tears the night I was given my daughter's death sentence. That was the last time I had allowed myself to cry. Fr. Bandy clasped his large hands around mine and looked sorrowfully into my eyes. I thanked him, then hastily opened the door, ran down the stairs, and crossed the narrow dirt road. I entered the monks' small circular chapel, where candles cast soft flickers of light. I flung myself across the simple wooden altar rail and sobbed deep, cleansing tears. Bera Gaye had followed me. My sister in Christ gave me what I desperately longed for—arms of reassurance, comfort, unconditional love, and friendship. Looking back, I believe that was the day my recovery process first began. It was the beginning of a new spiritual awakening for me, and it set the stage for the months and years that followed.

I can begin again

With the passion of a child

My heart has caught a vision

Of a life that's still worthwhile

I can reach out again

Far beyond what I have done

Part four:

Finding God

Chapter 18

Such Faith Is Sure to Be Tested

In February of 1973, Katherine began to show signs of liver damage from the toxic medications. The alternatives were to leave her on the meds and risk permanent liver damage or take her off the meds and risk a relapse. Neither seemed a good option to me; however, the doctors chose to give her liver a two-week reprieve.

One of the medicines, Cytoxan, was extremely bitter. She received two large tablets every Tuesday if her Monday blood count was not too low. I would grind the pills into a fine powder and then mix them with something I hoped would disguise the taste. It was an impossible task; nothing I tried worked. By the time she managed to get the last of it down, we were both a mess.

Although I was not happy about the reason for stopping the medication, I relished the joy of giving Katherine some much-deserved relief from the stress and being made to feel ill.

During the 1970s, a great revival swept over our country. What was known as the Charismatic movement became widespread. There were many reports of miracles, healings, conversions, and renewal experiences in the Christian community. Fr. Kempsill, who lived in Colorado and was in Dallas for a convention, heard about Katherine. He called and asked if he could come to our house and pray for her. I was ecstatic! I quickly agreed to his request and called Jake, who left work and came home so he could be in on the visit.

We loved Fr. Kempsill from the moment we met him; he exuded the very presence of Christ.

After a short visit, he asked Jake and me to consider having Katherine take Holy Communion regularly as purification of her blood through the blood of Christ. I told him I had reservations about his request because I did not share his faith in communion. Our denomination taught that when consecrated, the bread and wine are transformed into the real presence of Christ, but I believed communion to be an act of remembrance for what Christ did for us.

I explained the unacceptable behavior I had witnessed by some church members who took communion every Sunday. I had seen no evidence that communion made any difference in people who took it. Consequently, I considered it nothing more than a ritual; I was not sure I could believe there was actual power in the sacrament.

I also reported the resentments I'd had toward our church and told him our current concerns about Kat's treatment. "Our daughter is facing relapse because of built-up toxicity in her liver, and our church is not even praying for her. I know God wants to heal Katherine—He wants people to be praying for her—but they're not."

Fr. Kempsill bore witness to my faith. He, too, believed God would heal Katherine, as a testimony to the healing power of Christ, and that lives would be touched, especially within our church. With excitement and conviction, he encouraged us to go to our priest and ask him to get the people in our church involved in our lives.

Before he left, he gathered our daughter in his arms and spoke a simple but powerful prayer.

The following Saturday morning, we met our priest in his office. We told him about the potential threat of Katherine's relapse, my frustration that few people in the church even knew about her diagnosis, and the resentment I felt because our congregation was not praying for her. He expressed surprise when I told him about my grievances, the retreat I had attended, and Fr. Kempsill's visit.

"I assumed you were being taken care of."

As we continued talking, he too caught my faith vision for Katherine, vowing to have a prayer card made up for her and to send it to everyone in the church.

The following day we took our children to the early morning service, where three-year-old Katherine received her first communion; all three services were dedicated to her healing. True to our priest's promise, he mailed prayer cards to the congregation with a letter explaining our circumstances. He urged everyone to place it where it would be a daily reminder to pray for her.

James 5:14-15 appeared at the bottom of the card. "Is anyone among you sick? Let him call for the elders of the church, and let them pray over him, anointing him with oil in the name of the Lord, and the prayer offered in faith will restore the one who is sick." *Unaware of God's plan, set into motion when the power of prayer was unleashed, the survivor was grateful.*

Katherine's lab results were within the normal range at the end of two weeks, and she resumed treatment. Years later, I asked Dr. Rodgers why he thought she had no further problems with her liver.

He shrugged his shoulders and said, "You know, I can't explain it. When these problems start, they get worse, not better."

I knew his answer before I even asked. I just wanted to hear the doctor confirm my belief that God had answered our prayers.

March 1973 came roaring into our lives as my young son, who was only a few days away from turning two, began to run a temperature. I made a late-afternoon appointment with our pediatrician so that Jake could come home and stay with Katherine; I refused to take her into an office with a bunch of sick kids.

Dr. Stein examined Jay, then told me chickenpox was going around. Fear gripped me as I thought about what this could mean for our daughter. The doctor told me what I should look for, but I felt miffed that he didn't just give Jay an antibiotic to take care of whatever he might have. *The wounded child was always miffed about something.*

Later that evening, after putting the children to bed, I suddenly had a nagging feeling about my son. Jake had gone to a meeting, and I was home alone with the children. I went into Jay's bedroom and quietly reached over the rail of his crib. Immediately, I knew he was in trouble; he was blazing hot. I grabbed the thermometer: 105 degrees. His body began to jerk; he was having convulsions.

I went into complete survival mode, and only in retrospect did I realize God gave me wisdom I humanly did not possess. In fact, I had no experience in dealing with the events of the following 24 hours. I hastily undressed my baby and began to bathe him alternately with cold water and alcohol. His fever came down to 102 degrees. Not knowing any better and waiting for signs of chickenpox, I put him back in his crib, praying and trusting in God's protection for my son. I shudder to think what would have happened if I had not looked in on my son when I did—if I had just gone to bed—if I had not responded to the nudge.

Chapter 18

The next morning, when I gave him a sip of 7UP, it came back up. Instinctively, I knew that was not a good sign and retook his temperature; it was still 102 degrees. I called the doctor's office and was given another late-afternoon appointment.

Throughout the day, Jay would whimper and say, "Oh, my back hurts." I continued to offer him sips of 7UP every 15 minutes, which he managed to keep down, but his diaper remained dry the entire day. That deep sense of dread, an uneasy knowing, began to settle over me.

Many times during the day, I shook my head, disbelieving that anything could be seriously wrong with my son. But the feeling was all too familiar. Again, Jake came home early to stay with Katherine while I took Jay back to the doctor. *Fear, denial, hope, and faith struggled within the AAC, who was physically and emotionally drained and just wanted it all to go away. The survivor vowed to be strong. Their son needed them.*

When Dr. Stein came into the examination room, he asked me to lay my hot, feverish child on the cold, paper-covered table. Jay was alarmingly lethargic, his chubby cheeks were bright red, and his clear, blue eyes were glassed over, dazed.

Our pediatrician placed a firm hand behind Jay's head and attempted to push his chin down to touch his chest. I watched in numb disbelief when Jay's head would not bend forward. His neck was stiff.

Dr. Stein looked at me and said gravely, "I think Jay has spinal meningitis."

"What is that?"

The look in Dr. Stein's eyes said it all. I am sure he held thoughts of my seriously ill child at home as he explained that spinal meningitis is a disease of the central nervous system. He took control of the situation.

"Jay has deadly bacteria in his body, and you must get him to Children's Hospital immediately. Your son is critically ill, and you must not stop for anything. Call your husband and tell him to meet you at the hospital."

I quickly gathered my little guy into my arms as he clung to his favorite blanket, his bottom lip neatly tucked over his top lip and tears rolling over his flushed cheeks. I did not fully understand that I was about to drive down the Dallas North Tollway for the second time with a dying child. My mind has lost that space of time. I do not remember the long drive to the hospital.

The now-familiar sights and sounds of the hospital for sick and dying children swam around me as I tried to reason through the moment. I cradled Jay close to my chest—oh so tightly—refusing to give in, refusing to hear, and refusing to believe my son could be taken from me. But I knew. Denial served no purpose. Death was knocking on our door again.

I pleaded, "No, God, please no!"

I handed him over to the forever kind doctors and nurses. I was no longer ignorant of what they would do to him or what he would endure.

Jake arrived after taking Katherine to his mother's house. The seconds dragged. The doctors returned. The news was not good: Dr. Stein's suspicions were confirmed. The deadly bacteria had gotten into Jay's bloodstream, and his spinal column had become utterly clouded with the deadly killer. A powerful intravenous antibiotic was now coursing through his veins, but his condition was critical.

Dr. Stein, who had come to the hospital to check on Jay, was the one who gave us the total picture, gently but honestly. He told us Jay might not live, but would probably be mentally and physically impaired if he did. The bacteria could cause abscesses to form in the brain, resulting in impairment. Hopefully, the antibiotics would stop the bacteria's progression and limit the damage. Dr. Stein went on to explain that if he had given Jay antibiotics the day before, they would have hidden his symptoms, and he would have died before we even knew what had happened.

For a moment, I stopped breathing. I stopped hearing. I could not even pray. I would not, could not, accept our doctor's proclamation. My mind raced with questions. *How? Where? When? He never went anywhere! He hasn't been around anyone! How could this be?*

Again, I received no answers. When they told me my baby girl would not live, I locked up my emotions. I would lock them up again for my little son. *Every skill the AAC had learned for survival came to her aid in that dreadful hour, and she became very still. The survivor held on to her faith in God. The wounded child was numb.*

When Jay was returned to us, exhausted and fast asleep, his blonde hair was drenched with perspiration. His eyes were closed, his long dark eyelashes clumped together. He sighed every few minutes, his body trembling with each short breath. I covered him to ensure he was warm, and I fretted because he had missed his supper. I examined the all-too-familiar patch on his head where they had shaved off a part of his light blonde hair. *Déjà vu* did not even begin to describe it.

No longer amused by the Dixie cup cut in half to protect the needle penetrating his scalp, I refamiliarized myself with the machine monitoring the flow of the powerful antibiotic from the plastic bag on the cold steel pole. Once again, pain from the past and strength for the present merged as one as I faced another long night of uncertainty. I stood over my son and prayed. Faith, born in the heart of a child, held fast. God's grace was sufficient.

The following morning, I discovered that one of our little friends with leukemia was critically ill and hospitalized. I had heard about Fr. Nelson, a priest who held regular Friday night prayer and praise services at his church, where miracles were happening. I called and asked him to come pray for the little boy with leukemia. I also mentioned my daughter's situation and our current crisis with our son. Fr. Nelson did not waste time getting to the hospital but came straight to our son's room.

He said, "Let me pray for your son first."

Our priest had not visited us; no one from the church had visited us.

Jay's healing came gently as he slowly came back to us. His fever gradually declined, his color returned to normal, and he charmed the nurses with his ability to communicate. Each time he went to the treatment room for a change of his IV, another patch of blonde hair was shaved from his head. Each time, he would exclaim, "Oh no! Not more hair!"

On the tenth day of his hospital stay—his second birthday—nurses gathered around his bed to sing "Happy Birthday" and present him with a cake made especially for him.

The AAC walked in a daze, numb, doing what she needed to do. The survivor felt the peace that passes all understanding. Somehow, she knew Jay was going to be okay. She remained steadfast.

Dr. Stein commented on my consistent calmness and told me it was my excellent care of Jay in those hours before taking him to the hospital that had contributed to his recovery. This illness is a fast and unrelenting killer and crippler of mind and body that almost claimed my son's intelligence, his life. But I can take no glory; I know it was God's strength and God's wisdom, not my own, that carried my precious son past death's dark door. Shortly after that, we returned home with a perfectly healthy, rambunctious two-year-old. There were no signs of physical or mental impairment—just a partially shaved head.

Jay's illness had come and gone so suddenly that I hardly had time to think about it. I had to move right back into motherhood and life with Katherine and her condition. We settled back into our routine.

Chapter 18

However, one Tuesday morning, six weeks after I brought Jay home from the hospital, the still small voice within me spoke very clearly as I opened the cabinet door to retrieve Katherine's pills.

"Do not give her that medicine today."

For reasons I cannot explain, I took my hands away from the bottles, closed the cabinet, and walked away. The temptation to skip the hated meds happened weekly, but I had never reneged on my duty—until now. On this day, even though haunted by the message, I did not question it.

The abused adult child took her emotions and disappeared into her place of refuge. The survivor remained strong. She would not allow the AAC's emotions to override her action, even though she did not understand why she put the pills back.

The following day, Katherine began to run a low-grade temperature, and by late evening, she started to make a strange sound when she breathed. I slept with her that night, frequently waking to check on her. The familiar dread, the familiar numbness, the familiar denial began to run through my veins again. As morning dawned, I quickly dressed, fed Jay, and made plans to get Katherine to the doctor.

Instinctively, I grabbed a pillow on the way out the door and placed it between the seat and the car door. Once I had Katherine in the car, I propped her up against it, tilted her head back, and belted her in. I was subconsciously trying to open her air passage to help her breathe. *God's wisdom led the survivor. His mercy kept the AAC from anticipating the unavoidable trial ahead of her. The wounded child worried.*

This time I did not even bother to call the doctor's office. We were on his doorstep when he arrived.

His immediate reaction came in the form of a deserved reprimand. "Why didn't you call me last night?"

I could not reply, because I did not know why. I was devoid of any ability to reason, and I could withstand no more. For the first time, this doctor saw my tears.

Dr. Stein scribbled a picture of the epiglottis: a flap that keeps food from entering the trachea. He explained Katherine's problem: this flap was infected and had become inflamed and swollen to the point of shutting off her air passage. This condition would be profoundly severe for a healthy child—but for Katherine, it was deadly.

"She will probably need a tracheotomy. She is in critical condition, and I want you to leave immediately. Do not stop for anything. I will call Children's Hospital and tell them you're on the way."

Once again, there are no human words to describe that moment in my life.

The AAC did not want to hear those words again. She wanted to scream and take her child and run away to a place where pain did not exist. She did not want any part of this. She was so afraid. The wounded child felt the anger brewing inside of her. The survivor was quiet and subdued. It was far too much to take in.

I called Jake and told him to meet me at the hospital. I was in survivor mode. *The survivor had no choice but to shut down the emotions of the AAC. She must take complete control, or there would be no control at all. Kat needed her now more than ever before.*

For the third time, I methodically drove down the Dallas North Tollway with a child who would die without immediate medical intervention. Every inch of my body wrenched in pain; otherwise, I was numb. I would not allow myself to listen to the lies that besieged me. I would not let go of my faith. I began to sing. *Jesus loves me, this I know.* I was desperately trying to keep Katherine with me. I could not lose her! Not now!

Chapter 18

I prayed, "God, I don't know why this is happening. I don't know why my children keep suffering, but you have said to praise you, not for all things but in all things, so I praise you now, and I ask you to use this for our good and to your glory."

As I continued to sing to Katherine, peace began to fill the space around us, keeping the ever-present darkness at bay. In peace, I carried her into the emergency room. In peace, I handed her over to the doctors and nurses. My young daughter—tearful, pleading—gazed after me, taken from her mother's protective arms once again. Her bewildered eyes—forever imprinted in my mind; I could not bear to return her gaze. I turned away; she let go of me, and I had to let go of her. God's grace was sufficient.

The doctors confirmed Dr. Stein's diagnosis, but they were reluctant to perform surgery immediately because of her weak immune system and the cancer. She was given a powerful intravenous antibiotic and put under an oxygen tent. We prayed the antibiotic would cause the swelling to go down.

I confessed to Dr. Rodgers that I had not given Katherine her medications on Tuesday. He acknowledged that I made a wise decision: the meds would have wiped out her immune system, putting her in greater danger. I don't even want to think about the consequences had I not listened to God's voice. I was in awe that He had spoken to me in such a direct and powerful way. The fact that I obeyed still astounds me. *The AAC wondered how many other times God had spoken to her. The survivor wondered how many times she had failed to listen.*

The long vigil began as the nurses settled Katherine in a big-girl bed. Our daughter was no longer a baby—she was a three-year-old little girl. It had been a long morning, and it was not yet noon.

The part of me that was strong remained stoic. Faith stayed intact, but that fragile, fragmented part of me plunged into unspeakable depths of despair as I watched over this little one. She looked so helpless and vulnerable in the large plastic oxygen tent that encased her small body. I could not get close to her. I could not whisper in her ear to reassure her of my presence, but she slept, and I was thankful, despite my anger at this barrier that separated me from my child. *Typically, the wounded child displaced her anger. She stuffed it where no one could see it, but it was there.*

I was surprised to see our young priest enter our room around noontime; he had never visited us before. Yet, he showed more than genuine concern. When he prayed for Katherine, he appeared overcome with emotion and quickly left the room. He had a little girl the same age as my daughter, and for the first time, I realized that perhaps he was putting himself in our shoes and imagining the possibility of losing one of his children.

So I dismissed his rapid exit as a purely emotional response. Still, I was later surprised to learn he had called his secretary and told her to get on the phone and get as many people as possible to the church to pray for Katherine.

He later told me, "I have seen the Angel of Death before, and I knew Katherine was dying."

About 50 people gathered in our church's sanctuary to pray, and donations were collected to help with our financial needs. About the same time, five o'clock in the afternoon, Kat's doctors decided she was not getting better. They feared having to do an emergency tracheotomy in the middle of the night. Surgery was scheduled for seven o'clock that evening.

It would seem impossible for me to cope with yet another crisis. The human spirit can endure only so much before it finally snaps, and I had walked up to that precipice one time too many. But thankfully, God has given to all of us built-in mechanisms for coping with those

Chapter 18

outrageous, psychotic moments that life imposes upon us. For me, I had learned to hide in the unseen domain of depression, even sometimes tottering on the brink of suicide just to escape my circumstances. But always, miraculously, I was pulled along by an unseen, loving force that persistently beckoned me to hang on—to hang on with all my might—and not let go.

For the past three years, I had not allowed my circumstances to be about me, and this moment could not be about me either. Mercy placed a barrier between my child and me—my child, who had fought so bravely and with so much dignity and will to survive. In this, my most insane moment of all, my faith was tested beyond my limits. I could only see my cherished treasure in the hands of my God, the arms of Jesus. Otherwise, I would have gone stark raving mad.

The AAC had survived a horrific childhood, and now she was watching as her child struggled to survive her own nightmare. And though their circumstances were different—the illnesses, the treatments, and the abandonment her young child must have felt each time she was taken from her mother—all of it was perceived in the survivor's mind as abusive. All of it was intrusive, and all of it was trespassing on her child's soul. The survivor grieved. The wounded child wept.

I recall very little about the hours that followed, except that my friend Esther called the hospital to tell me she had contacted *The 700 Club* on CBN. This was the first time I had heard of this program, so she explained that it was a new Christian television broadcast that had recently started to air in the Dallas area.

"The broadcast is live, so when people call in with their needs, they are prayed for immediately. Many people are experiencing miracles."

She told them about our situation and asked them to pray for Katherine when the program began at seven o'clock that evening. I did not realize the real significance of my friend's phone call.

Shortly before seven o'clock, nurses arrived in our room to take my precious gift away. Too ill to speak, bewildered—tears spilled down Katherine's cheeks. She seldom cried and rarely complained, but the fear in my daughter's eyes stared back at me, pleading to not let them take her away from me again.

I was powerless to keep her with me and powerless to stop them from taking her away. This was her normal; powerlessness was mine. I assured her she would be okay, and then I turned away—again—so that I could not see her go. I clung to my husband in grief as we wrapped our arms around each other. When trials come, true love walks in.

Life was calling on my ailing child to be like her mother: a survivor. *The AAC, the wounded child, and the survivor quietly waited. Their facade removed, their masks exposed, they had nothing to hide. They lay prostrate before their God.*

Shortly after *The 700 Club* began its nightly television program, the Lenten ritual of the Stations of the Cross began at our church, offering prayers for our daughter. Others prayed and waited anxiously in Katherine's room with us.

The many blended prayers of faith opened Heaven's door as people of different denominations and diverse backgrounds came together as one in our desperate hour of need. About an hour later, two doctors appeared in our doorway, looking somewhat perplexed. My heart skipped a beat as I demanded to know what was wrong.

One of them spoke, pausing between his words. "Well . . . we've been watching Katherine . . . she started to get better . . . we decided not to do the surgery . . . she's downstairs talking and playing with the nurses. We'll continue to watch her, and when it's safe, we will bring her back to her room. We suggest that you hire a private duty nurse to spend the night in her room, just in case."

Chapter 18

Dr. Stein later told me he had been with Katherine in the operating room as they witnessed a steady improvement of her condition.

I did not fully grasp what had just happened. At that point, I was too numb to feel or think beyond the simple fact that the surgery was canceled, and my child was better. Katherine returned to us, exhausted. She slept. An emergency tracheotomy kit sat on the table beside her bed.

A young doctor appeared in our room and introduced himself. He checked on Katherine every 30 minutes throughout the night. As early morning dawned, I told him she was better and that we all needed some rest.

He looked at me and said, "Well, you are the mother; you should know."

He said good night, and I did not see him again. When Kat awoke later, her happy countenance had returned. Her fever was gone, and the oxygen tent was removed. Her crisis was over. Still cautious, the doctors kept her in the hospital for a few more days.

Throughout our five-day stay, a woman—whom I assumed to be a doctor because of her white jacket and the stethoscope hanging from her neck—would periodically appear in our room, look at my little girl, and walk out.

One day, she proclaimed, "You do not know how sick your daughter was."

I was so taken aback by her accusation that I just retorted, "Well, I guess that I do!"

She stared at me, turned around, and walked out of the room.

I thought I had missed a perfect opportunity to share my faith. But then I realized I did not need to. She witnessed something supernatural that she didn't understand.

Inwardly, I was crashing, but throughout that day when Katherine's life had been hanging precariously on the edge of eternity, I had not been walking in depression or denial. I was not trying to hide from the truth. Instead, I was carried by Jesus as God wrapped His compassion and mercy around His precious wounded child. That day I walked in peace that surpasses all understanding.

Lives were touched even before we left the hospital. God had answered my simple prayer as I drove my daughter to the hospital five days earlier. It was a prayer of thanksgiving, petitioning God to use this deadly illness for our good and to His greater glory. His perfect plan was set in motion. *Life could never be, would never be, the same for the survivor, for her family.*

Chapter 19

It Is Not That You Have Been Waiting on Me—It Is that I Have Been Waiting on You

In the days that followed, I began to seek God passionately. He had my attention, and I could not get enough of Him. Every spare moment found me reading my Bible as I sought to know my God and His Son, Jesus. I could hardly stay off my knees. I was so thankful for all He had done.

One evening, shortly after our last crisis was over, I watched *The 700 Club* for the first time. I was dressing the children for bed in front of the television and was only somewhat engaged in the program until Pat Robertson began to pray. I stopped to listen. Just then, Jake walked into the house. God's perfect timing allowed both of us to hear Pat's words.

"There is a child who has had leukemia."

He paused, then repeated, "There is a child who has had leukemia.

Know that your child has been healed—know that your child has been healed—the Lord has a message for you I don't understand, but perhaps you will. He wants you to know that it is not that you have been waiting on me; it is that I have been waiting on you."

I knew God was speaking to me—but this time, not just to me, but to Jake as well.

I began to realize that the intricacies of the Holy Trinity are profound and full of mystery, but in time, I saw how the various roles of the three-in-one God worked in my life. Jesus was the one who carried me when I could not walk, the one I talked to and depended on, the one who interceded to the Father on my behalf.[1] The Holy Spirit gave me comfort, wisdom, and peace when life was overwhelming, but it was Father God who healed my children and my brokenness. His compassion and love never failed me as He continually waited on me to trust Him with praise and thanksgiving in all situations.

God works in many ways to accomplish his purposes; therefore, I must pause and give credit to the medical professionals at Children's Hospital in Dallas, and Dr. Stein and Dr. Rodgers, for their dedication, knowledge, and commitment. Without them, my children would not have had a chance to survive.

As a young girl, I discovered I could talk to God, and I spoke about having a personal relationship with God through Jesus. Still, I don't think I fully understood what that truly meant until this critical time in my life. God had revealed Himself to me in different, subtle ways. Yet His clear communication to me on that day through Pat challenges my ability to communicate something I cannot even begin to com-

---

[1] Hebrews 7:25 "Therefore He [Jesus] is able to save completely those who come to God through Him, because He always lives to intercede for them" (NIV); Romans 8:34 "... Jesus is the one who died—more than that, who was raised—who is at the right hand of God, who indeed is interceding for us" (English Standard Version).

prehend. Please bear with me as I share my thoughts.

This Holy One, the Creator of all things, cares *personally* about His children. When we invite Him into our lives and seek His precepts, He honors our faith in Him. When we begin to listen to His voice and obey His instructions, He will work in ways that we cannot even imagine. And in those moments when we cannot pray, He listens to our hearts. His patience amazes me; if He can be patient with me, He will be patient with anyone.[2]

As a child, I had given God permission to work in my life when I believed in Jesus. He had been *waiting on me* for all those years to listen and to obey. Honestly, I had been doing a lousy job on both accounts, and I often fall short even now. But when I attended the forgiveness retreat, just months before the crisis with my children, I truly heard the empowering message of forgiveness for the first time. I was given the opportunity to listen to God's voice speaking to me through the scriptures as He asked me to step out in faith and begin to walk in the power of forgiveness.

That October day, I was only capable of taking a small step in that direction. As it turned out, that small step was indeed just the beginning of understanding for me. But at that time, for my children, I believe it opened a pathway to God that set into motion the events that followed, the miracles you have just read. Had I turned away with a

---

[2] Ephesians 3: 16-21 "I pray that out of His glorious riches [to know God], He may strengthen you with power through His Spirit in your inner being, so that Christ may dwell in your hearts through faith. And I pray that you, being rooted and established in love, may have power, together with all the Lord's holy people, to grasp how wide and long and high and deep is the love of Christ, and to know this love that surpasses knowledge, that you may be filled to the measure of all the fullness of God. Now to Him who is able to do immeasurably more than all we ask or imagine, according to His power that is at work within us, to Him be glory in the church and in Christ Jesus throughout all generations, forever and ever. Amen" (NIV).

hardened heart and refused to offer God a spirit of forgiveness, I am not sure the outcome would have been the same. I believe that a hardened heart toward God separates us from Him. He does not move away from us; we move away from Him.

Having said all the above, I need to clarify that I do not believe we can put God in a box and expect to find a formula to fill our wish list. Each of us is made uniquely different, and our lives are uniquely different. There are unique purposes and plans for each of us. God had been *waiting on me* to follow His desired path. Your path will be different, but equally rewarding, when you fully understand that His love for you is personal. He desires to lead you into a deeper relationship with Him.

I also want to clarify that I honor and respect all of God's Church's sacraments and practices, which I believe should not be limited by humans' interpretation of them. I believe that God honors faith wherever faith in Christ is found, no matter how differently we may choose to celebrate that faith. Please understand that I do not wish in any way to dishonor the many diverse observances of God's Church.

I received Pat Robertson's message as words of knowledge from God.

After hearing Pat's message, Jake silently left the room. I finished dressing my children, read them a story, tucked them into their beds, and prayed with them. I watched in thankful awe as they faded into a peaceful sleep. No words can describe what I truly experienced that evening. Pulling myself away, I walked to my bedroom and closed the door. I slipped to my knees and worshiped my Heavenly Father, thanking Jesus for what He had done for my children, for me. My soul burst with thanksgiving and praise; I could not contain the joy, the gratitude, the humility I felt. *The survivor understood that God knew she could bear no more pain. He knew her secrets.*

Chapter 19

A few days later, I was on my knees praying when a vision of Katherine lying in her hospital bed suddenly appeared in my mind. I saw a circle of light around her bed, and I saw black images trying to break through the light. At first, I was startled, but then I began to realize that my eyes were being opened to the spiritual battle fought over Katherine's life.

Through that experience came the knowledge that the dark, oppressive presence that had often threatened me was very real. I had no previous understanding of Satan and his demons, but I was beginning to see they were not imaginary make-believe beings.

My insatiable hunger to learn continued.

I was given the book *Nine O'Clock in the Morning,* by Dennis Bennett, which defined words I had heard but did not understand, such as a *second touch by the Holy Spirit*, *gifts of the Spirit*, and the *fruits of the Spirit*. Its sequel, *The Holy Spirit and You*, taught me about the precious work of God's Holy Spirit and the responsibility that comes with being committed to a relationship with God.

Bennett explained the consequences of continuing to walk in sin and how Satan, the enemy of our soul, can use our sins against us. His books pointed out many things the scriptures taught that I had never heard before. God had my attention.

In the meantime, my friend Martha arranged for different ladies in the church to sit with my children one morning a week. Kat still had seven more months of treatment ahead of her, so even though I had to fight old resentments, I accepted the offer and was thankful for my weekly trips to buy groceries when the sun was shining.

One day, one of the ladies called and offered to keep Katherine and Jay for an entire day. Reluctant to leave them for so long, I thanked her for the offer and said I would let her know. I did not have a clue what I would do by myself for a whole day. But a few days later, Bera Gaye called, asking me to go with her and some friends to a prayer meeting; it just so happened that the meeting was scheduled for the following Tuesday. Godcidently, arrangements for someone to keep my children were already in place. *The survivor did not know another divine appointment had been planned for her.*

Tuesday morning, I joined Bera Gaye and her friends for the short trip south of Dallas. Anxious yet eager, none of us knew what to expect, but we sensed we were on a mission. An hour later, we walked into a large brick home, where I met a group of women who possessed more joy in their little fingers than I had experienced in a lifetime. Songs of praise greeted us as we entered the family room; my heart leaped with a yearning to experience such joy. *The AAC could not experience unadulterated joy; it was impossible. Her secrets held her captive. The survivor watched carefully.*

The woman in charge of the meeting spoke with confidence, teaching from the scriptures. I clung to every word. When she finished, she turned to me and explained that she had heard about my daughter's illness.

She asked, "Have you experienced the second touch of the Holy Spirit?"

I had heard about this special touch and was curious about the experience; I felt compelled to seek it.

"No, I have not, but I want to."

"Oh, honey, your baby needs for you to have this blessing from the Holy Spirit; you need His special anointing. Will you let us pray for you?"

A young woman stepped up to me and said, "You came here today seeking, and God does not want you to go away empty-handed. Will you let me be God's vessel? Will you let me pray for you?"

I nodded slowly. Without any hype or exaggerated emotion, this young lady lightly touched me and quietly began to pray. And gently, ever so gently, I began to feel a release within me, a letting go of my will, seeking the God I longed to know. Simultaneously, I lost all thought of myself as a sweet flow of energy swept through me. I felt removed from the boundaries of this earth and submerged in a peace I had never before experienced.

Suddenly, looking through different eyes, tears that never came easy begged for release, and for only an instant, I was able to give God a tiny crack into the window of my will. That was all the Holy Spirit needed—my willingness to surrender as He anointed me with holy oil, filling me with its warmth, empowering me, calling me into a deeper commitment. I began to worship my Heavenly Father as never before. Just as this experience would prove invaluable to me, this moment would forever change the direction of my spiritual journey. *The wounded child's road to recovery from the wounds of her soul had taken another step forward. She did not know the road ahead would sometimes be very difficult.*

A few weeks later, the brother-in-law who abused me died from colon cancer. His illness had been long and filled with suffering. He reached out to me for spiritual guidance before his death, but I could not find words to help him. If only he had asked me to forgive him.

I struggled with simultaneous conflicting emotions. I had forgiven my abuser. However, I was unaware of the painful emotions that I continued to carry: his shame, his guilt, and the ever-present raging, suppressed anger that secretly taunted me. I was relieved that I would no longer need to worry about him being around me or my children.

Chapter 20

God Sees a Bigger Picture I Cannot See

In the years that followed, we said goodbye to young friends who had endured the cancer treatments with us. Many of their parents had the same firm faith in God as I—but oh, the sting of death, how cruel it is. I often struggled with the impact of their deaths when my children lived.

One such friend was Cheryl. We went to the same lab on Mondays for blood work. Cheryl's mother and I shared our ups and downs, which was a blessing for us both. When Cheryl died, Florence called and encouraged me to visit her at the funeral home because she looked so peaceful, and I understood the suffering that preceded her death.

Because we lived in the same community, we would occasionally run into each other. Florence never failed to ask me how Katherine was doing, always genuinely interested in her health. It took greater faith in God for this young mother to let go of her child than for me to believe mine would live.

John, a teenager who also had leukemia, became my daughter's mouthpiece. One day, he listened to me tell his mother how frustrated I was that I could not get my toddler to eat. He quickly told me that just opening the refrigerator door and looking at food would sometimes make him throw up. With that realization, I stopped trying to force her to eat because she wasn't able to tell me how she felt. Her main staples were Cheerios, milk, SpaghettiOs, scrambled eggs, and apple juice. I never gave her candy!

John's mother called me the day he died. I was grief-stricken for her; it was heartbreaking to say goodbye to John. He was such a special kid. His parents, who were also Christians, believed up to the end that he would beat this child-killer. Although my head knows God sees a bigger picture that I cannot see, my heart does not understand. John did not finish high school before he went home to be with Jesus.

The little boy who was in the hospital when Jay had meningitis died that same year. Erin was terribly ill throughout his treatment for leukemia, and his suffering seemed worse than any of the other children. His parents, understandably bitter, struggled when he passed. My last phone call from his mother was heartbreaking. My sorrow ran deep.

The faces from those inexplicable years will always linger in my memory. At times, the reality of so much suffering and the many young lives lost overshadowed the images of my faith. The sadness I felt for the parents would never leave me.

However, the long drama of childhood cancer had played out for us. The curtain was finally closing, and the time had come for my family and me to move on. *Knowing her daughter would live when so many others had not was difficult for the abused adult child. She would never feel worthy; survivor's guilt lingered.*

Christmas of 1973 was a turning point for our family. Katherine had been on chemo for three years. Her little body could not tolerate the potent drugs in the long term because they killed good cells along with the bad ones. In early December, the weekly oral chemo stopped. I was at peace as we took her remaining pills and tossed them in the trash. It was a day of celebration. Having our children alive and with us was the only gift I needed. It was indeed a glorious, merry Christmas.

I felt so profoundly blessed. Now we could be like everyone else, normal.

But the AAC did not realize that she was not normal, and life would never be normal for her or her family. There were too many things in her life that set her apart and made her different. The wounded child did not know she was beginning another journey.

The desire of my heart was to be used by God and share His story in me. I felt called to pray for the sick, and opportunities to minister to others through prayer came often. Because of my children's miracles, some people mistakenly thought I had the gift of healing or some special connection to God. Even I believed it was true for a while, but eventually, I had to learn that God loved me too much to leave me in a place of pride. I would be humbled to grasp that nothing about me is more special than anyone else.

In time, I discovered my most notable spiritual gifts are my empathy for those who are hurting and my faith/trust in God to hear my prayers. However, in those early years, I reveled when called on to pray for those in need of a miracle. Late one evening, I received such a phone call from a desperate wife asking me to pray for her husband, Sandy, who had terminal cancer. I didn't know Sandy well, but I recalled an incident that God later used to bring forgiveness to three men who had been angry and hurting for many years.

Sandy was super intelligent, knowledgeable of the scriptures, and responsible for conducting a class after church on Sunday. One Sunday morning, he and two other men had an altercation concerning a dispute over some Biblical text. The three men stood outside the classroom, yelling at each other. It was an awful sight and one that increased my spirit's unease about the church still further. The two men who opposed Sandy left our church that day and never returned.

Years later, when I visited Sandy in the hospital after his cancer diagnosis, he began to relate to me the pain he'd carried all those years over that ridiculous incident. I asked him why he was telling me this and told him it would be better if he told those two men how he was feeling.

The next day he called them, and they both came to the hospital. Forgiveness was given; forgiveness was received; relationships were healed. Sandy received his healing in Heaven the night his wife called in desperation for me to pray for him. He died in peace. God sees a bigger picture I cannot see.

Several years later, I received a similar phone call from our current priest.

His voice was solemn, "Marcie has been taken to the hospital, and she asked me to call you. She wants to see you. It doesn't look good."

As I drove to the hospital, I felt sad; I did not want to lose my sweet friend.

I told Jesus, "You keep sending me to people who are dying, and I go and pray in faith, and they die anyway. I just don't understand!"

When I entered her hospital room, Marcie was alone and appeared to be sleeping. I did not know what God's will was for her, but the Holy Spirit did.[1] I quietly approached her cold, uninviting hospital

---

1 Romans 8:26-27 "In the same way, the Spirit helps us in our weakness. We do not know what we ought to pray for, but the Spirit himself intercedes for us through groans that words cannot express. And he who searches our hearts knows the mind of the Spirit, because the Spirit intercedes for God's people in accordance with the will of God" (NIV).

bed and gently laid my hand upon her thin, frail arm, asking the Holy Spirit to intercede through me for Marcie. She stirred briefly.

"Marcie, it's Nola Katherine. I have come to pray for you."

She whispered, "Good—that is what I wanted you to do."

In the hush of yet another sterile hospital room, where death tapped on the door of yet another person I cared for, the same still voice that told me not to give Katherine her medicine on that fateful day spoke to me again.

"It's not about miraculous healings. It's about touching, loving, and caring. It's about being there when called."

God sees a bigger picture I cannot see.

I finally understood that it was not up to me to determine how God would respond to my prayers. My duty was to answer the Holy Spirit's call to go, to pray, to show love. Marcie's passing was much quicker and easier than the doctors had anticipated. *The survivor listened and was humbled to understand that the greatest miracle of all is to be in God's eternal presence, His will.*

A friend whose teenaged daughter had cystic fibrosis only trusted a few other women and me to stay with her in her last days. My prayer became one of freedom from suffering for Christine. She was set free, healed for all eternity. *The survivor was beginning to understand that miracles come in many different packages.*

One of my dearest friends' newborn sons, Adam, was diagnosed with cystic fibrosis. Because of my own experience, I could understand Jennifer's grief and sorrow. The best I could do for her was to pray. Over the years, I watched Jennifer prevail with great dignity and grace. She extended an ever-present smile and a positive report to all who encountered her. She continued to be a tower of strength during her family's struggles, griefs, and sorrows.

For 32 years, Adam found reasons to smile and to embrace life to the fullest. He made those around him laugh, reached out in love to many people, and left this world a better place because he had been here. Despite her loss, Jennifer and her family never lost their faith in Jesus. God sees a bigger picture I cannot see.

Why some receive physical healing but not all is a mystery to me. This dilemma has stretched my faith, and I think it probably tests everyone's faith sooner or later. Eventually, I have had to face my own health issues, often pleading with God to heal me. But more often than not, His answer has been no. *The survivor was learning to be humble and empathic and trust God in everything—perhaps to keep her balanced.*

One exception happened in 1976 when occasionally I was awakened during the night with a sharp pain at the top of my head. I would shoot straight up out of bed and grab my head, my heart pounding wildly in my chest. These episodes, which continued for several months, were terrifying. I was sure I had a brain tumor.

Jake was without a job, and we had no insurance, so I went to a charity hospital in Dallas for tests. Every person on the planet should experience a charity hospital at least once; it is a humbling experience that will teach you to be thankful for your problems and that patience can be a virtue.

During those long hours of waiting to see a doctor, I met a sweet old gentleman named Clayton. I will never forget this man of meager means who was rich in his faith and love for his Heavenly Father. We shared Jesus stories, and he promised to pray for me.

Several nights after meeting Clayton, I must have had another episode in my head, but this time something happened that I cannot explain. I felt my body ascending rapidly.

Suddenly I heard a voice. "You can't come yet. You must go back."

I felt myself descending . . . and that is when I suddenly woke up.

Chapter 20

There was no pain in my head, and my heart was calm. I didn't know what to think as I told Jake about what happened. I returned to the hospital for the scheduled brain scan and EEG. The results proved that I did have a brain, but that was all. And I never had another of those episodes.

I have often thought about Clayton and have wondered whether my meeting with this prayer warrior was another divine appointment or if he was an angel. Or did my recovery happen because, in me, God had a life to redeem, a story to tell, a book to write? God saw a bigger picture I could not see.

I have just one more story to share. Jake and I received a phone call about a young mother from East Texas who had leukemia and was in a Dallas hospital. Her husband's job prevented him from spending long hours in Dallas with her, and the grandparents were taking care of her young children. They knew no one in the Dallas area; we went to the hospital to meet her.

I realized right away that Pam was a very sweet, private person who had a strong faith in God but was awfully ill and terrified. She needed a friend to walk through this journey with her. Pam opened her tender heart and accepted my offer to help her get through the long months of treatment. I held her, I cried with her, and I prayed with her.

One day, doctors came in to extract bone marrow from her hip. They asked me to leave the room, but I insisted on staying with her; she had been tearfully dreading the painful extraction, and I could not bear to see her go through the procedure alone. The doctors relented.

I laid my head down on the bed beside Pam's head and gave her my hands to squeeze. I have never witnessed anyone endure so much pain. It was a harsh reality for me to realize that my little daughter had suffered this same anguish—without her mother's hands to hold.

Eventually, Pam received a bone marrow transplant and has remained in remission. We celebrated this victory together at her journey's end. In retrospect, I believe God gave Pam to me, more so than He gave me to Pam. I was able to see firsthand the procedures that I had not witnessed with Katherine.

By walking with Pam through her pain, the survivor finally allowed herself to grieve and weep over the pain-filled journey of her young daughter, who had been much too young to articulate while her mother had been much too numb to feel.

As I rapidly approach 80 years of age, I find many names to recall and stories to tell. I am blessed to have had the privilege of carrying so many on the wings of prayer, with the understanding that God's mercy extends to everyone in different ways. Even though others' circumstances may differ from my own, when I am willing to let Him, He will use my sorrow, pain, empathy, understanding, and love to reach out to them. The lessons I learned from those who shared their lives with me forever changed me. *The survivor walked a different path after she understood that God sees a bigger picture she cannot see.*

I can begin again

With the passion of a child

My heart has caught a vision

Of a life that's still worthwhile

I can reach out again

Far beyond what I have done

Part five:

The AAC'S Journey

Chapter 21

Connecting All the Dots—the Church, the Abuse, the Enemy of My Soul, and Jesus

The AAC's journey to find her freedom began here.

The stories I shared in chapter 20 occurred during the years I am about to take you through. I felt it important for you to get to know the tender, caring side of the AAC before further introducing you to the dynamics of the adult and the wounded child in relationship to the survivor who was *trying to do life* during those years.

Until December 1973, my life had been anything but typical, as you will have realized from reading my story so far. Undeniably, I looked through different eyes and changed in many positive ways. However, two sides exist to every coin.

Once again, please understand that I genuinely struggle to share the following 17 years of my life, from 1973 until I entered the hospital in 1990, with you. However, I cannot leave these pictures off my life's canvas; if I did, it would be incomplete, and you would miss a valuable part of the AAC's journey that ultimately led her to freedom.

In retrospect, I realize how vulnerable I was to the powers of darkness that joined the forces of abuse to surround and control me. My husband had no understanding of his responsibility to be the spiritual head of our family, and our church did not teach him otherwise. We were clueless and powerless when it came to combating the world's evil.

The abused, wounded child living inside me was far from being healed from the scars of abuse. Trying to raise children when I did not have a clue how to rear children, trying to be a wife when I had no role model to follow, trying to have healthy relationships with people who walked in and out of my life, and even trying to be the Christian I professed to be, were all monumental tasks for me.

However, this was my life, and all that I knew to do was to continue as before. I would wear my many masks over my facade, hold my head high, and trust in my God. I was a survivor; I was a wounded child; I was an adult; I was a victim. In many ways, my struggles to survive and be restored were just beginning when God gave us the miracles of our children in the early 1970s. Yes, my journey was far from over.

I cannot paint this part of my canvas quickly, so I hope you will hang in here with me as we complete the longest session of all. Remember, as we work, the life situations I depict here can manifest in an AAC in the home, the workplace, school/college, or any organization—anywhere that an adult within whom lives an abused child must deal with people. Mine just happened to be within my church family.

It is important for you to understand that writing about the church Jake and I attended for so many years felt like a betrayal to my God, until one day, I realized I am not writing about the church as a whole. I am writing about Satan, whose sole purpose is to destroy that which God has established, the corporate believers in Jesus Christ—

those most vulnerable to his evil snares. My prayer is that God will take what Satan intended for evil and use it for good.

Let us pick up our brushes once again.

By the end of 1973, I was on such a spiritual high I could not see the forest for the trees. I sincerely thought life would be perfect for my family and me. We would have no more problems, and I would have the spiritual life I desired.

Because I experienced God working to change me, I expected Him to do the same in Jake, our families, and the people in our church. All I wanted was to experience the goodness of God and His love. I never wanted anything in my life again that would burst the joyful bubble in which I lived.

But bubbles burst, and you can't put your faith in a bubble. *Unrealistic expectations, foreboding, dark forces, and secrets from the past slowly began to chip away at the survivor's newfound joy and peace. The AAC was, once again, rendered powerless. She wore the mask of the victim.*

Ironically, just as I had unrealistic expectations of our church family, some people had unrealistic expectations of me. I found myself placed on a strange pedestal. Occasionally, someone in our church would come up to me and say something that surprised me.

"You have such great faith in God."

"You are such a special person."

"God must love you a lot."

A young priest who temporarily helped with our growing church approached me after one Sunday morning service. "I've been watching you, and I see something special about you."

And for a while, I even believed I was special and chosen by God to do great things for Him. I longed to be that spiritual person, but secretly I knew I did not belong on anyone's pedestal. *The AAC feared being on a pedestal because she knew that sooner or later, she would disappoint those who had placed her there. The survivor would learn that pride does not fall gracefully. The wounded child was fragile and wore her feelings on her shoulders.*

People began to come into my life who wanted spiritual bits and pieces that I was incapable of giving to anyone honestly. Yet subconsciously, I felt an obligation and a responsibility to live up to the reputation created around me. Consequently, the facade I wore had to become thicker.

Some in our church did not know what to do with my spirituality, and I sometimes felt consuming rejection. I did not fit their mold.

Our priest told me that I needed to sit on my enthusiasm because "It turns people off."

I began to feel like a deflated balloon, my spirit crushed by others' judgment of me. After what He had done for my children, that anyone could even think I should be less than enthusiastic about God was unimaginable and painful.

One time, I received a phone call accusing the small prayer group I attended of being merely an opportunity for gossip. I was shocked and hurt.

Jake and I played bridge with some other couples in our church. I considered these people to be friends, but once I tried to explain to one of the ladies in the group that I suffered from depression.

She quipped, "Well, we all think you are strange!"

I mentally played those words back every time I was with that group of people, and I never felt safe around them. *The AAC was vulnerable and incapable of handling unkindness. The slightest infraction sent her spiraling out of control. The survivor could not trust.*

Chapter 21

My lack of boundaries kept me going back for more unkindness. *The survivor rode the roller coaster of ambivalence: rejection and acceptance, love and indifference, joy and sorrow, fear and faith, good and evil.*

If someone hurt me, I would inwardly build barriers to keep them out of my space. *The victim loathed being judged; criticism felt like poison in her veins.*

Occasionally, in roundabout ways, I tried to explain that I had childhood issues that had impacted me. But my needs were always quickly dismissed, and I would often end up listening, sometimes for hours, to others' problems.

One person even retorted, "You don't have any problems! Let me tell you what I've been through!"

The AAC was always looking for someone to understand her. The survivor was an attentive listener—but sometimes a resentful one. The wounded child wore the mask of anger while the victim twisted everything into self-pity.

Although God enabled me to serve Him in many ways as I slowly grew in my relationship with Him, our church's unhealthy atmosphere fed the depression that continued to suck the life out of me. Those unseen midnight forces that wanted to hinder my testimony slowly began to steal my joy.

Even though, at times, I would prove to be poorly equipped to handle the spiritual battles and adversities that whirled around me, my faith in God did not waver. He had proven Himself to me over and over, and I did not doubt Him. *The wounded child would falter as she collected additional wounds and held on to them. The AAC would rely upon her many masks to see her through. The survivor trusted her faithful God.*

Our children's miracles impacted many, and it seemed spiritual growth began to happen within our church. Some in our congregation became interested in an international renewal movement that made its mark in the Dallas area in 1975. Jake and I were scheduled to attend the third renewal three-day weekend event where laypeople, with guidance from a priest, became the facilitators. However, a ruptured artery in my nose and two trips to the emergency room prevented me from attending. Although I was disappointed, it turned out to be good for Jake to go without me; he needed his own space to grow. At the end of those three days, a changed man returned to me.

He confessed, "I always knew about Jesus, but I didn't know I could have a personal relationship with him."

The scriptures tell us that understanding is the beginning of wisdom. Godly wisdom comes to us when we accept, by faith, the truths God gives to us in His Word, the Bible. The renewal experience opened Jake's eyes to these truths, which he had not known, even though he had been going to church regularly all his life.

For the first time in our married life, I began to understand why my husband and others looked at me as though I was from another planet when I started talking about having a personal relationship with Jesus. Every decision concerning Jake's spiritual life was made for him, and he did what was expected of him. He had no concept of his need to commit his life to Jesus, to be spiritually *born again*. And he had little knowledge of the scriptures.

Two months later, I made the trek to the now-familiar retreat center. The Friday night session began in the chapel, its walls finally erected. The finished altar, now surrounded by glass, looked out at the clear, star-filled night. I wondered again at what strange fate kept drawing me back to this sacred place where I had once found so much joy.

The chapel was eerily silent as 40 or so people gathered for the service. I mainly sat among strangers as the 30-minute meditation began to fill the serene space around us.

Chapter 21

The meditation walked us through the life of the Messiah. He had been unjustly accused, sentenced, and finally handed over to be crucified. He had gone through the suffering of the cross, and the agony of conquering death, a death that we cannot comprehend.

Some of his friends came to the tomb to prepare his body for burial. They wrapped him in a white shroud, laid him in the tomb, and removed the wedge that held the heavy stone. The stone rolled forward and sealed the tomb. The meditation reflected these thoughts, and its closing words brought everyone in the chapel to the foot of the cross, to the crucified Jesus.

> As cold and empty and silent as the tomb has been my heart—it has been locked up in my sin, and I have refused to open my heart to the quiet knocking of the love of Christ. I have chosen to be dead to His love and dead to life. Oh Christ, strike down the door of my unwillingness to know you. Dissolve my stubbornness. Call me forth from the tomb of my sin and bring me to new life in you.
>
> While on earth, you never mentioned your agony, your death, and your burial—without mentioning your resurrection into the glorious presence of your Father God. And you have promised that for me too if only I would believe in you—if only I would take up the cross and follow you.
>
> This is your mystery, Lord Jesus—the mystery that you are now holding out to me. The mystery you want to share with me if I will follow in faith, hope, and love. I accept by faith, Lord, that you are the way, the truth, and the life. I trust by faith in your love for me because you proved it on the cross, and I trust that you are God-made flesh who offers me redemption from the sting of sin and death.

> I desire to begin to walk on this road of love to you, Lord, and I want to give you the only thing that is truly mine to give you, and that is the total gift of myself—my will—given in love, received from you.
>
> I understand that this road I choose may not be easy, and I am not brave. I ask you humbly to be with me on this road to you. I ask you to please carry me to my final destination—to the dawn of resurrection.[1]

I could hardly breathe as the impact of its message reached out to a roomful of spiritually hungry souls, including my own. It was the most spiritually convicting thing I had heard in my adult life. Many around me found they could not control their tears as the meditation ended, and quiet sobs echoed around the spirit-filled chapel. No one spoke; the silence was welcomed. We were asked not to talk to each other until we gathered for breakfast the following morning. For many, it was a long night of wrestling with God.

The common room with the massive rock fireplace became the heart of the retreat. We gathered early Saturday morning, seated at large round tables scattered around the spacious room, to hear laypeople give structured talks that allowed space for them to interject their personal experiences.

By the end of that day, we had entered a mystical realm that is difficult to describe. A spirit of commonality and community blanketed the room and tugged at our heartstrings. Unconditional love filled us with a peace that could only be a human semblance of what Heaven must be. We were unaware of the hundreds of people praying for us long before and now throughout our weekend. By the end of Sunday, no one wanted to leave.

---

1 Taken from *This is the Way it Was* booklet by Virginia F. Randall, Ph.D.

Chapter 21

The AAC feared going back into a world whose challenges could steal away the love that Jesus had once again poured into her wounded spirit. The survivor did not want to leave this place of peace and safety. The wounded child begged to be noticed. The victim was quiet.

Jake attended the final closing communion service on Sunday afternoon. When we arrived back in the city, we went directly to a "welcome back" party hosted by those who had previously attended one of the renewal weekends.

A laughing woman greeted me at the door with a bottle of wine, who promptly pulled me aside to tell me all about her marital problems.

Startled at this, I realized this gathering would not be like the weekend renewal, but just another party where doors were held open for the powers of darkness to steal the joy of the Lord. I had come here expecting to be embraced by the same love I had felt over the weekend, with everyone eager to talk about and praise God. *The AAC stuffed her disappointment. The survivor felt resentment. The wounded child tasted their anger. The victim did not understand.*

Jake and I became more and more involved in the renewal movement, which required a lot of our time. I learned to play the guitar and participated in the monthly Sunday morning folk masses and other renewal-related gatherings. We both became licensed lay readers and chalice bearers, which meant that one or both of us would be serving at the altar on Sunday morning. Jake regularly presided at the altar at the monthly renewal closing service.

We went through training and served on staff as leaders during the renewal weekends. Jake thrived in the leadership role he assumed, and I did what I most wanted to do: I gave talks that allowed me to share my faith and tell of the miraculous things God had done for my children. We attended as often as possible. *The AAC was unknowingly seeking self-worth and approval. The survivor walked in spiritual pride. The wounded child tried to be happy but failed miserably.*

But all was not well. Initially, people could bring their own bottles of liquor to the renewal weekends. I had begrudgingly resigned myself to the seemingly acceptable practice of drinking during church activities. However, the first time we served on staff for the weekend, the designated lay leader walked around with a glass of scotch in his hand for the entire three days. He would have ruined the weekend completely except for divine intervention.

I went to the priest in charge and expressed my objections. God used my voice to promote change. After that, only wine was allowed on the premises, and it was served only at the Saturday night celebrations. *The AAC had learned at an early age that she had no voice. But the survivor sometimes wore the mask of courage and was learning to speak out. The wounded child waved a huge red flag and wore the mask of unhappiness. The victim didn't understand.*

My enchantment with priests waned over time. On one occasion, when Jake and I were serving as part of the staff during a renewal weekend, the priest assigned to the table I was facilitating seemed determined to bring disorder into the whole experience.

From the word go, his off-color language was disruptive, and his actions were inappropriate. I was disgusted by this man's demeanor, but by God's grace, I managed to interact with him in such a way that by the end of the weekend, he sought me out.

He said, "I think you're one of the few people I know whose baptism actually took!"

I was so shocked that I could not even take the remark as a compliment. Instead, I shook my head in sadness; his declaration painted a picture of the church's heart condition and that of the people in it.

Chapter 21

Intertwined with the good that resulted from our church's renewal experience were rumblings of discontentment, divisiveness, and eventually immorality. Worst of all, our children began to take second place in our lives. Any parent who was actively involved in the movement had neglected children at home. It seemed we were always going somewhere, doing something—but instead of finding satisfaction, I found frustration. And although spiritual growth was happening in our church due to the renewal experience, the after-meetings and weekly gatherings continued to become excuses to have a party. Wine flowed freely, hugs became too friendly, and affairs happened.

To make matters worse, the people in our church who did not participate in the renewal movement began to resent those involved. The meetings' secretiveness and close relationships became sources of contention and division, and people often approached me with complaints. What I saw happening within our church was beyond irreverent.

Unknown to those around me, the depression that consumed me pushed me deeper and deeper into its black pit. I did not fit in. I did not want to be there. I would often go home from the meetings crying angry tears. I did not like what our involvement was doing to my family and me. Eventually, I chose to back away. No one, least of all my husband, understood my unhappiness.

Something created to bring glory to God became a tool of the dark forces in this world because humans allowed the darkness to enter their personal spaces. In time, those powers of darkness won, and the renewal movement in our church died.

The survivor grieved. She was confused and struggled as she juggled the many masks behind her facade. The AAC's constant conflict with ambivalence was maddening. She hated what she witnessed within the church—she loved the church. The wounded child connected the actions of a few to the whole, condemning them all.

I Can Begin Again

Recognizing the trouble in the church and its impact on me

During our involvement with the renewal movement, Jake felt led to become a priest. I supported his decision, and our priest was delighted that another from his congregation would be going to seminary. We were both invited to join other candidates for the priesthood for a weekend retreat where a group of priests would interview us and evaluate Jake's calling. Those priests would then send their evaluation to the bishop, who would decide the authenticity of Jake's call.

I had reservations about this process; I did not feel any human had the right to judge a person's call to ministry. *The AAC unrealistically perceived that they could make things better together if her husband were a priest.*

February in Texas is often the coldest month of the winter. Brisk winds whistled their chilling songs around us as our car pulled into the retreat center's parking lot. Once again, I pondered the strange forces that kept calling me back to this beautiful, peaceful place.

I had not been feeling well when we arrived on Friday evening; once inside the building, I was delighted to see the huge rock fireplace in the common room offering the comfort of firewood warmth. My husband, being warmer by nature, found a place at the opposite end of the room. I quickly claimed the chair closest to the roaring fire and nestled in for the first session, and I retained the same spot for subsequent sessions.

On Saturday morning, husbands and wives were separated into small groups for the weekend. Almost immediately, I began to get bad vibes from the priests who were interviewing my small group. When we broke for lunch, I mentioned my thoughts to Jake. By nature, he is not as intuitive as I am, but he admitted to having the same uncomfortable feelings.

Chapter 21

One priest had caught my attention when we first arrived. His macho demeanor caused apprehension about being in a meeting with him. When it came time for him to interview my group, he had everyone sit on the floor in a circle. He began asking questions, expecting each of us to give him an answer. One of those questions was, "What do you expect out of a priest?"

When it came my time to respond, I said, "I expect the priest to be guided by the Holy Spirit."

This man, whose position should have defined him as godly, banged his fist on the floor, swore at me, and made a derogatory remark about the Holy Spirit. The men and women sitting on the floor around me cringed, as I did, at his reaction.

I am sure my mouth dropped open as the space around me turned black. *The AAC could not stay where she felt unsafe. Her hiding place waited for her. This time, the survivor went with her, right along with the angry wounded child and the victim.*

During each break, Jake and I would compare notes and express our bewilderment to each other. We kept saying, "What is going on here?"

Our last interviews on Sunday evening were one-on-one. The priest scheduled to interview me appeared friendly and spoke to me kindly. "I see you grew up in the Pentecostal church."

The victim in me rose to the occasion. He showed me the form our priest had filled out. It suddenly became apparent why this group of men had been rude to Jake and me—miracles were often associated with the sometimes controversial Pentecostal/Charismatic movement. They probably thought I was a babbling, ecstatic, holy roller who handled snakes (which, by the way, is a total misrepresentation of the Pentecostal or Charismatic churches). Voice raised, I defiantly explained that I did not *grow up* in any church.

Not only was this misinformation a factor, but the priest also pointed out that Jake and I did not sit together during the session, which caused the men to question our relationship. I set him straight on that issue too. Unbelievably, they also had issues concerning our children's healings and my open enthusiasm for God.

We were eager to get away from this peaceful place that sadly felt uncharacteristically unsafe. It was a disappointing experience; however, because Jake had a relationship with our bishop, we quickly secured an appointment to discuss the weekend event.

During a meeting with our bishop, we learned the priests who interviewed candidates were not necessarily people who were qualified to make lifelong decisions for others. We were most grateful when the bishop recommended that we attend another evaluation weekend in a different diocese. We later learned that our voices helped to make needed positive changes in the interviewing process.

Within a few months, we were enduring another weekend of questions, but the atmosphere was entirely different from our first encounter. We respected those who interviewed us, and we accepted their recommendation.

The interviewers were concerned that Jake felt a need to repay God for healing his children. Additionally, they either wisely understood or foolishly assumed that engineers are not always personable. Engineers are, however, great administrators and organizers. They kindly suggested Jake needed a little more time before making a final decision.

But they also questioned my enthusiasm. I just didn't get it; I could not understand why everyone who called themselves a Christian was not enthusiastic about Jesus, about God.

When Jake told our priest he had once again been denied entrance into seminary, he received a reprimand. (Until that point, the priest had sent someone to seminary from his congregation every year during his tenure as our priest.) "Well, you've just ruined my record!"

He offered no consoling, no love, no sympathy, no concern expressed for what Jake was feeling.

Neither of us understood the call Jake sincerely felt. Perhaps God was testing Jake's obedience to follow His voice. Or maybe God was calling Jake into a deeper relationship with Him or teaching him to trust. Nevertheless, Jake did not pursue the priesthood again. In hindsight, it appears to have been the best decision in the long run.

God saw a bigger picture we could not see.

The AAC secretly knew neither she nor her marriage could have survived the priesthood. The survivor had to pretend that all was well but was fearful of having her secrets exposed. The victim did not feel worthy of being the wife of a minister.

I became deeply troubled as I witnessed the quenching of God's Holy Spirit around me. Like the renewal movement, I became a topic of controversy. I was labeled as too fundamental, too far-reaching in my beliefs, and too extreme about God. I never ceased to be shocked by the unkindness of the people with whom I worshiped. Unkind remarks occasionally traveled back to my ears. I often felt a general hostility toward me, and I felt so misunderstood. Dark, unseen forces continued to steal my joy.

I thought the people around me could have come to terms with my children's deaths easier than their miracles. One person callously asked how I could justify my children's healing while others died. Another asked what I did to bring all of *this* upon my children.

A local newspaper magazine published a story about the healing of our children. The article mentioned *The 700 Club* and our church. At that, the church secretary sarcastically said the article made our church sound like a bunch of holy-rollers, which was far from the truth. The magazine simply told of our journey and the power of faith and prayer.

The AAC's hurts continued to multiply and burrowed deeper, her facade challenging her to keep them secret. The wounded child could not accept others' opinions. She rebelled in inappropriate ways, magnified criticism, and often expressed her frustration in anger to those around her. The survivor did not know which mask to wear. The victim felt defeated.

People talked and gossiped; people judged. People still do.

Eventually, I became aware of a small group of people within our church who desired a deeper walk with God. Jake and I were asked to host a weekly prayer meeting.

Getting the demon out

Several significant things happened to me during this period. One day, I had gone to the church to work on a project with several other ladies. As we were standing at a long table, suddenly I felt someone pat me on my bottom. When I turned around, I saw a priest passing behind me. The horror of that moment is indescribable.

When our eyes met, he just laughed and said, "I couldn't resist."

He disappeared around the corner as I stammered for something to say, to hide my humiliation.

I was enraged and confused; I did not understand why men felt they had a right to own me, to use me for their amusement. I was not a raving beauty—I was attractive in my own way, but I did not exude sexuality; I ran from it. So why did these kinds of things keep happening to me? This was not a new reality.

The AAC had learned to deny her disgust for men's unwanted attention and could not face reality. Denial never let go of its grip on her.

Chapter 21

She continually heaped new insults upon the old, causing the scars of her wounded child to fester. They were raw to the touch. Being the constant victim of others was making the survivor physically ill.

When Jake got home that evening, I told him what happened, sobbing on his chest. "Why do men keep coming on to me, Jake?" I pleaded. "I did nothing. What is wrong with me?"

Despite my walk with God, I had often felt some controlling force, a veiled darkness that hovered around me. An inner conviction told me that something out of my control had drawn this man, whom I believed to be sincere about his faith and not a bad person, to carry out this shameful act toward me.

Drew, who led our little prayer meeting, taught us about Jesus's ministry concerning the demonic influences that roam the earth. He knew a man named Steven, who had a deliverance ministry. After much discussion, Jake and I agreed that perhaps we should seek Steven's counsel. We arranged a meeting with him at our house.

I had no idea what to expect from my visit with Steven and his wife. I felt embarrassed and humiliated as we discussed what this priest had done; undeserved guilt overshadowed me. I admitted I had often felt a dark presence around me. They asked permission to pray for me.

Jake, Drew, Steven, and his wife laid their hands on my shoulders and began to pray. Right away, I started to sense the familiar darkness. The more intense the prayer grew, the stronger the darkness. I became fearful, and I told everyone what was happening. They each acknowledged feeling the same disturbing presence.

Intense prayer continued until Steven discerned what was happening. He explained that a demonic spirit, which he called a whoring spirit, was tormenting me, but it was not defining me as such. He believed the spirit had attached itself to me through some means and caused men to be inappropriately attracted to me.

The sexual predators and the perverse pornography to which I was exposed as a child flooded my mind. I could feel their vile evil, and I knew Steven was correct, even though I didn't understand it. Neither Steven nor Drew knew anything about my secret past.

Not wanting to give up, Steven and his wife continued to pray, but for some reason, Drew stepped back and said, "It's getting late, and nothing is happening. I think we should stop."

The unwelcome presence, given a reprieve, seemed to disappear—but I knew it was not gone. Fear did not come close to defining what I was going through.

Drew and the others left our house, and as the front door closed behind them, my worried husband took me in his arms and tried to comfort me.

"Jake, what am I going to do? You felt it too. This thing is real. In some way, it's hanging on to me or around me."

Jake had no answers for me, but as always, I had his unconditional love.

Panic gripped the AAC. Terror consumed the survivor as the wounded child disappeared, and the victim felt hope because someone else acknowledged the unseen.

After a long, sleepless night, I put on my facade and went on with life—breakfast, lunches prepared, kids to school, Jake out the door, my youngest Kim and I off to work.

I was the director of our church's Mothers' Day Out and preschool program, and I had to be there. *The survivor was very responsible and capable of rising to meet almost any demand placed upon her, no matter the cost. But the AAC felt no peace. The victim began to have understanding.*

I put on my friendly demeanor and proceeded to gather my teachers for prayer, greeted parents and kids, conducted the chapel service, collected tuition, and smiled as though I did not have a care in the world. This was the story of my life—the mask of deception I wore. I could never let anyone know I was dying inside while trying to live life on the outside. At the end of the school day, I couldn't wait to pick up Kim from the nursery and get home. When we arrived, I put her straight down for a nap. I had serious business to confront.

I went into our living room, fell on my knees, and prayed as never before. I learned from Drew that Jesus took authority over demons, and before His death, He gave this same power and authority to His disciples who cast out demons in His name.[2] I reasoned that because I had invited Jesus into my life, the Holy Spirit of God lived within me, so I must undoubtedly possess this same power to overcome the tormenting spirit. I stepped out in faith and commanded the whoring spirit to leave me in the name of Jesus. Immediately, I felt the power of God rising within me as I commanded the evil spirit to be bound and never to return to me again. Instantly, I physically felt the ominous presence flee from me. I can explain it no better than that.

Exhausted, I fell asleep, and when I awoke, I knew without a doubt that I was set free.

Time confirmed that men were no longer improperly attracted to me.

This part of my story is shocking—even to me—and will no doubt bring about lively discussions; it certainly did within my own family when my now-grown children read my manuscript. I sometimes think that if we could see into the spirit world around us, we would all be

---

[2] Luke 9:1 "When Jesus had called the 12 disciples together, He gave them power and authority to drive out all demons . . ." (NIV); Acts 5:12 [After Jesus's resurrection and after they received the Holy Spirit] "The apostles performed many miraculous signs and wonders . . ." (NIV); Acts 5:16 "Crowds gathered also from the towns around Jerusalem, bringing their sick and those tormented by evil spirits, and all of them were healed" (NIV).

terrified. Even though I do not understand why it is so, the scriptures teach that Satan and his demons have permission to roam over this earth. They can torment, tempt, and oppress believers in Christ. However, they cannot possess the soul of a true Christ-follower. Powerful tools were given to us to stand against the fiery darts of the enemy.[3]

Think about it: how many times in this book have I written that I felt a dark presence around me? Since I was a young child, I had been held against my will and innocently drawn into others' evil.

Recognizing the avenues that allowed darkness in

But how was it that evil surrounded me when my abusers were not around? I sincerely believe that pornography was the conduit by which this spirit entered my life, where the effects of sexual abuse controlled me. As an adult, I unknowingly invited evil to have a foothold in my life, where its purpose was to tempt me, draw me into, and keep me in bondage to pornography.

As a young Christian, I was not taught; therefore, I did not understand the seriousness of my choices. Be aware that not only will pornography invite dark forces into your life, but many other decisions allow evil spirits to get a foothold. It can happen when you surrender control to alcohol, drugs, or perverted sexual practices, or when you become involved with occult practices such as reading horoscopes, fortune-telling, Ouija boards, tarot cards, or witchcraft. It was not until I finally understood these truths and renounced the few I had dabbled in that I found freedom from many of my struggles and a deeper, more meaningful relationship with God.

---

3   Ephesians 6:11-12 "Put on the full armor of God, so that you can take your stand against the devil's schemes. For our struggle is not against flesh and blood, but against the rulers, against the authorities, against the powers of this dark world and against the spiritual forces of evil in the heavenly realm" (NIV).

Please, hear me when I say I am not one to look for a demon under every rock or behind every bush, but it is essential to be aware of the schemes of the enemy of your soul. Above all else, know that the name of Jesus has all power over this enemy, and conviction by the Holy Spirit moves us to repentance. When we choose to yield to God, we will turn away from the sins of the flesh, leaving a place where God can fill us with His light.

Finding peace in my group

Our prayer group continued to meet for several years, and we were strengthened in faith. The needs within this small body of believers were many, and we needed and invited the Holy Spirit's gentle, loving presence to minister to us and through us. One person in our group was a man named Jonathan, who had been shot during a robbery. Even though he remained wheelchair-bound, his joy and love for Jesus were reflected in his forever contagious smile. He died during my six-week stay in the hospital. He was truly a great prayer warrior, a man of faith, and my true friend. I still miss him.

One of the women in our group had terminal cancer, while another grieved over a troubled son who eventually took his own life. One in our group would die unexpectedly in his early 40s with a brain aneurysm. It was not common knowledge that three adults abused as children were in our group, searching for inner healing. We were all strengthened in our faith. I have often wondered how anyone could have found fault with our meeting together, but some did.

Eventually, I accepted the reality that Christians are not exempt from sin, sickness, or painful trials. Life is not perfect, nor are Christians. My own story bears witness to this truth, just as it bears witness to the redemption Jesus offers us and the strength He gives us to walk through the uncertainties of life. Answered prayers come in many different packages.

The survivor was beginning to learn the difference between judging, discerning, and unconditional love. The AAC had a long way to go before she would finally put it all together.

Sinking into depression

As sure as summer follows spring and fall follows summer, the darkness of winter will follow them all. Our young priest had enjoyed great seasons of success—until his winter season fell hard when he was caught having an affair with a woman in our church. His youth, inexperience, and vulnerability to the unseen dark forces around him ultimately became his downfall.

Strong winds of despair and disbelief carried the dead leaves of this man's actions to many who had put him up on a high pedestal; for others like me, who had discerned the darkness within our walls of worship, enough was enough. The unhealthy atmosphere led yet another group of my brothers and sisters in Christ to leave. Once again, I felt alone. I pleaded for my husband to do likewise, but he would not leave. Jake's roots were too deep.

Instability roamed the premises of our church as the vestry searched for a new priest. In the meantime, I continued to build the Mothers' Day Out program. When I first became the director, it was mostly a childcare program, and it struggled financially. My organizational and bookkeeping skills, prayer, and desire to serve God turned the program into much more.

I met all the city and state requirements to open a preschool, raised money for furnishings, hired degreed teachers, and established a music program. Before class each morning, I met with my teachers for prayer and led a weekly chapel service for the older children. I attended workshops with the teachers, and I published a monthly newsletter.

The Mothers' Day Out/preschool program ministered to children in our congregation and the community. New families joined our church due to the program. It also ministered to me. It was a wonderful healing experience, and I loved every aspect of it.

The survivor found great joy in sharing her faith, especially with children. She was a good teacher/communicator and very capable of being a leader. The AAC and the wounded child tried to behave themselves. The victim let her guard down; she should not have.

A retired bishop was temporarily in charge while the church searched for a new priest, but instability prevailed. My world began to change when I hired a man recommended by a church member to install a chain-link fence around the playground. He messed up the project, and when I refused to pay him, he threatened to sue the church. I gave him the money to avoid a lawsuit, and he attempted to mend his mistakes. The fence was functional—just not very pretty.

Everything I did moving forward was challenged, and the joy of the position began to ebb away. *The AAC could not get away from the victim role in which she often found herself.*

Even now, I struggle to understand the events that follow.

At the end of the school year, a school board member approached me about getting an early childhood development degree. The church would pay my tuition. I was excited and grateful for the offer, but I was concerned about taking on additional responsibility and said that I wanted to wait until my youngest started school.

Just before the fall session began, I received a call summoning me to the church. The school board had held a meeting without my knowledge. Consequently, I received a pat on the back and a raise in salary. However, I also received an ultimatum: either acquire a certain number of hours toward continuing education by the end of May, or I might not have a job.

I am not sure why, but not being invited to the meeting and having my request ignored sent me over the edge. Perhaps it was just the straw that broke the camel's back. Suddenly, the suicidal depression I had fought since my childhood began to overpower me. *The AAC did not know that depression was a prominent symptom of many underlying problems. It was so easy just to give in to its power, and she did.*

Several weeks after the fall session began, a trainee priest stopped me in the hallway. He told me I was doing a great job and encouraged me not to let people in the church get me down. We talked for a while, and I thanked him for his encouragement and support. But it was already too late. An emotional downward spiral had begun.

The people in the church *did* get me down. *Encouragement! Defeat! Confusion! The AAC was drowning. The wounded child wanted to give up. The survivor was silent. The victim was tired of being a victim.*

The school year continued, and my facade remained intact. I struggled, but no one suspected. I chose not to enroll in the continuing education classes. Being a good mother was the most important thing in the world to me, and putting my family through the stress of me working and going to school was not an option, even if not doing it meant losing my job.

By midterm, the demon of suicide had methodically built a haunted house in my mind. The monsters that lived there sought to destroy this child of God, telling me I did not want to live. I had fallen into an indescribable abyss and could not see a way out. I told Jake to put his guns where I could not get to them. He often traveled away from home, and I feared what I might do in a moment of no-return despair. Suicidal depression could not be trusted under any circumstances.

Chapter 21

The AAC could not control her thoughts. She could see only the negatives in her life; they canceled the positives. The wounded child was slowly slipping away. The victim was indefensible and subject to attack. The survivor tried to hold on for all of them.

Fortunately, I had my husband's attention. One morning, in desperation, Jake pulled me to the side of our bed, and for the first time in our marriage, he knelt with me and called out to God for help. He mentioned my state of mind to his mother, who told me about an article she had read which highlighted a book by Dr. Orian Truss called *The Missing Diagnosis*.

Dr. Truss, a doctor in Alabama, had written an article entitled "Tissue injury induced by Candida albicans: Mental and neurologic manifestations"[4] (which eventually led to a book called *The Yeast Connection*, written by Dr. Crook), which discussed the possible harmful effects of antibiotics;[5] one of the side effects is depression. When I called the phone number mentioned in the article, I was told to contact Dr. Manaberg, whose office was "Godcidently" only three blocks from home. I called immediately and took the next available appointment.

A new diet to help with the physical side of depression

I eagerly clung to every word Dr. Manaberg spoke as he shared parts of his professional journey. Like Dr. Truss, he had become frustrated with the medical profession's use of medicine and its inability to help people get well. Dr. Manaberg explained the vicious cycle that can re-

---

[4] Orian Truss, "Tissue injury induced by Candida albicans: Mental and neurologic manifestations," *Journal of Orthomolecular Psychiatry* 7, no. 1 (1978).

[5] For additional information, go to www.knowthecause.com and listen to Doug Kaufman. He has done research on fungus/yeast and the human body and has valuable resources and a daily program that you can view online.

sult when antibiotics promote an overgrowth of yeast in the intestinal tract by destroying the good bacteria we need to keep us healthy.

Unaware of the deadly condition developing within us, we add sugar and other simple carbohydrates that cause the yeast to grow, crowding out the good bacteria that fight harmful bacteria that invade our bodies.

Dr. Truss believed the overgrowth of yeast gives off toxins that cycle throughout the body, causing a breakdown in the immune system. Fatigue, moodiness, depression, confusion, poor concentration, poor digestion, bloating, gas, poor nutritional absorption, sinus infections, and overall poor health can result. He described many of the physical symptoms I had struggled with most of my adult life.

Since no specific test could tell if the condition existed, the doctor would treat me based on my history. I reported that I was 12 when my tonsils and my appendix were removed, and I was hospitalized with the flu that same year. Back then, it was the norm to give penicillin shots every three to four hours around the clock. Later, I took birth control pills, which worsened my problem because they caused infection with the yeast Candida. Yeast needs warm, moist places to grow, so it made perfect sense to me that it could become out of control in the intestines.

Diet was another factor to consider. I watched a deep furrow form between Dr. Manaberg's eyes as I confessed to having been raised on fried chicken, fried steak, fried potatoes, fried okra, biscuits, gravy, pecan pie, peach cobbler, and vegetables doused with bacon grease and cooked until limp. As an adult, I added a daily sugar-filled Dr. Pepper. Of course, I fed my growing family accordingly. The doctor politely but sternly suggested I needed to change the way I cooked. I don't think he was raised in Texas.

The doctor instructed me to eliminate all processed white foods and eat a high-protein diet with fresh green vegetables and nut meats.

That meant no sugar, white flour, potatoes, fruit, juice, or dairy products—and definitely no fried foods!

I was given a prescription for an antifungal drug and instructed to take a few tablets each day, gradually increasing the dosage to avoid a die-off reaction. The doctor sent me to a lab for blood work to determine the nutrient levels in my body and then put me on dietary supplements and probiotics to restore the good bacteria.

I told Jake about the change in diet when I got home.

He laughed. "Why live if you can't eat all those things?"

I had turned my northern-raised husband, who had never eaten anything fried—especially fried steak or fried okra before we were married—into a genuine Southerner.

Two weeks after I began the new regimen, the deep suicidal urges miraculously disappeared. I felt like a different person, and for the first time in my life, I did not feel I had cobwebs in my brain. Getting the overgrowth of yeast in my body under control and changing my diet saved my life.

I am not a doctor, and this is only my observation and opinion. We have long been a society that lives on antibiotics and cortisone. Antibiotics are handed out like candy, and no one can deny that depression and poor health are epidemics in this country. Many doctors are beginning to take precautions and advise their patients to take probiotics when prescribed antibiotics, but many do not believe in this diagnosis. The internet has a lot of information about the effects of yeast growing in the body.

When the depths of suicidal depression lifted, new life emerged for the survivor. It was another step toward recovery for the AAC.

Once again, God showed mercy to me, His wounded child. The deep suicidal tendencies have never returned since I was treated for this overgrowth of yeast. I will admit that I don't adhere to this strict diet consistently but have discovered that sugar is not my friend. It causes mood swings.

However, this was not the end of the depression—the kind that came from my wounded soul. It was a Band-Aid that temporarily covered up the oppressive emotional and mental pain that seemed like it would never, ever go away. Depression was the place where I hid.

Standing against the evil in the church

In the meantime, our church hired a new priest, the school progressed, and the deer-hunting season began. Jake frequently hunted with a group of men from our church, and occasionally, he would take one of our kids with him. After one of his hunting trips, I sensed something was wrong. In all the years Jake and I had been married, he was never intimately aggressive toward me. His understanding and patience were his gifts of love to me. But when he returned home, he was intimately different with me. *The wounded child took refuge in her denial that something was different.*

Several weekends later, we were at a social gathering when one of the hunters' wives asked if I knew our vestry's senior warden had driven his motor home to the hunting camp and had shown X-rated movies on his VCR. Unaware of the bomb she was setting off inside me, she jokingly began to describe the orgies our husbands had watched.

Jake was in earshot of the conversation. He turned and looked at me.

When our eyes met, I saw red. I shouted, "Where was my son?"

My husband came to my side and assured me that Jay had been in bed, asleep.

"And where was Joe?"

He told me that Jay's friend was also sleeping.

Chapter 21

I shook my head, fearing the answer to my next question. "And where was Phil?" He was the son of one of the men who had watched the videos.

By now, the blood had drained from Jake's face. He said nothing.

"Don't tell me you allowed a 16-year-old to . . ." I disappeared into my dark hiding place.

I was beyond angry, and I honestly do not know what I did or said after that moment. These were men chosen by the congregation to be leaders. Some of them regularly read the scriptures and served communion on Sunday mornings.

Although I had been aware that some men in the church watched pornography with their wives, I had no right to judge them because of my previous history and lack of understanding. However, this was where I drew the line. Exposing a child to porn was inexcusable and intolerable. I could not be silent. *The survivor raged. The abused child grieved for innocent children who depended on adults to protect them. The wounded child lost all control. The victim could not be found.*

The following Monday morning, I received a phone call from the church secretary, a trusted friend. She told me the newly hired priest was saying I was emotionally and mentally disturbed. I could only imagine what the senior warden had told him about me. But if being mentally disturbed meant speaking out against leaders in the church who were exposing children to pornography, then so be it.

I already had a reputation to live up to: I was the complainer, the one who could not keep silent when I saw the ever-present darkness working in the church, wounding God's children—the Body of Christ. I did not understand the raging war inside me, and unfortunately, those around me did not understand it either. Sadly, there was always a price to pay for my inconsistent personality—rejection, and I was powerless to control its cost. *The AAC wanted to fight, and she did.*

The survivor did whatever she had to do to survive. The wounded child, as usual, acted out her hurts.

I could not stay silent when a visiting priest spoke to the congregation about stewardship and spewed swear words all over the attendees during his presentation. I voiced my objection to this man's inappropriate language to our priest and the bishop's office, and I wrote a letter to the guilty priest. No one bothered to respond.

When a young woman who worked at the church came to my house and fell into my arms sobbing because the senior warden, in the presence of our priest, had verbally chopped her into tiny pieces over a minor incident—I was not silent. She felt targeted because she was Charismatic.

When the men's group gathered monthly to drink beer and play poker at the church, I frequently protested. At almost every church-related event, alcohol flowed freely. I could not control my anger and made no excuses for it.

When a girl in the youth group told me one of the boys molested her, I confronted his parents. I was ignored. When my children came home from Sunday school telling me they were told it didn't matter who they believed in, Jesus or Buddha—I raged.

When a shaman was invited to speak to the congregation about healing, and he said that it did not matter what *medium* they believed in—I really lost it.

Worst of all, when I heard people in the church talk about my children's miracles, God—and certainly Jesus—did not get the glory. Instead, I heard, "Look how great *we* are! Look at what happens when *we* pray!" It was a place that glorified itself instead of God.

Chapter 21

When some of my church friends became involved in a questionable religious movement, I attended a weekend event to understand its purpose. I was shocked at the mind control, manipulation, and spiritual deception I witnessed. After returning home, I felt compelled to express my concerns to my friends and our priest. My words fell on deaf ears.

I discovered that many involved in this movement, which began in 1971 and ended in 1984, were Christians. If leaders fail to teach about the snares of the enemy of the soul, if they do not warn people to be watchful and pray for discernment, if they do not demonstrate how to be grounded in God's Word, those under their leadership will be easily swayed and deceived.[6] There will always be consequences for willful disobedience.

Before long, just like his predecessor, the new priest who deemed me mentally ill had an affair with a woman in the church and was fired. The wife of the senior warden who exposed the teenager to porn at the deer camp divorced him. He left the church.

---

[6] Jesus warns us in Matthew 7:15, "Watch out for false prophets. They come to you in sheep's clothing, but inwardly they are ferocious wolves." And 1 John 4:1–3 says, "... Do not believe every spirit, but test the spirits to see whether they are from God, because many false prophets have gone out into the world. This is how you can recognize the Spirit of God: Every spirit that acknowledges that Jesus Christ has come in the flesh is from God, but every spirit that does not acknowledge Jesus is not from God ..." Finally, 2 Peter 2:1–3 reminds us, "But there were also false prophets among the people, just as there will be false teachers among you. They will secretly introduce destructive heresies, even denying the sovereign Lord ... Many will follow their depraved conduct and will bring the way of truth into disrepute. In their greed these teachers will exploit you with fabricated stories. Their condemnation has long been hanging over them, and their destruction has not been sleeping" (NIV).

I suppose some would judge me as crazy, considering the childhood issues that controlled my sometimes inappropriate responses to different circumstances. I desperately needed something in my world to be surefooted, to help me and keep me safe. When the church failed me, and when I could not fix its failure, I crashed.

However, I could never accept the carnal behavior exhibited within my church family. What I witnessed over the years was sacrilegious, irreverent to that which is sacred. The propensity toward alcoholism ran through my children's veins, flowing from both sides of their family, and I feared they would slip into its grip. They would soon be teenagers, and their constant exposure to casual drinking troubled me. And now, a child exposed to pornography by church leaders was the last straw.

I had seen what pornography does to children at the hands of a pedophile who used porn to entice me to accept his advances as normal. I knew firsthand just how vulnerable a child's mind is and that those first sexual triggers will be the very thing they keep going back to for sexual pleasure. I knew that young souls soon become trapped in the grip of the images they see, and innocence cannot discern or process the right or wrong of it. I knew that pornography is addictive, like drugs and alcohol. You cannot unsee what you have seen; once it gets into your mind, you cannot get it out, and it takes more and more to satisfy the need for it. I knew the evil that lies therein, the demonic power that dances with pornography. The natural beauty of sex is vulnerable, courted and swayed and twirled around and around to the music of pornography's deception; music that entices rapists, murderers, and abusers into the dance of death—death of mind, body, and soul. Pornography invites unsuspecting, innocent men, women, and children to be its partners. Worst of all, it distorts the human perception of God and hides His face from view.

Chapter 21

No matter how crazy I may have appeared in the past, this time, my reaction was utterly sane and justified—but what was I supposed to do now?

I wanted my children to have what I did not have as a child: a solid spiritual foundation on which they could stand firm throughout their lives. I always felt unprepared to guide my children spiritually—and Jake, who spent his entire life going to church, was even more ill-equipped. It seemed the only time Jake and I ever fought was over things that happened in our church.

I found myself at crossroads. Emotionally and spiritually, I was in a good place. I saw things more clearly, and I did not care what anyone thought about me. I told one of the school board members I was resigning from the Mothers' Day Out/preschool program. Her response was an ugly expletive. I turned and walked away without a word. Eventually, this successful program dissolved because those who had personal agendas controlled it without seeking guidance from God.

To counteract the negative influences, I decided to put our children in a Christian school. As far as I was concerned, I was through fighting, through being judged, and through being defeated. I told my husband the children and I were leaving his church; I would no longer keep them somewhere Jesus did not reign as Lord and Savior. The children and I started going to the church associated with their school. No one reached out to stop me. We left; Jake stayed. I was not surprised when those who called me a friend criticized my decision.

I was not emotionally healthy

You may be wondering what took me so long. That is a good question and one that I eventually had to answer for myself. An emotionally healthy person would never stay in such a toxic environment, nor feel the *need* to fix everything around them. But child abuse creates emotionally unhealthy adults who inappropriately act out, make inept decisions, and create more inward suffering for themselves and sometimes for those around them. They will continue to do so until they take back their power, find their precious child, love their wounded child, and change their behavior. Because I was not emotionally healthy, I stayed in a place that was not safe for me. Consequently, I lost the precious gift of joy that I had found in knowing Christ.

The AAC stayed in familiar situations because, in her twisted thinking, she thought she had no choice. In her mind, the familiar was safe because she wore the mask of denial. She had no understanding of her need to try and fix whatever she perceived as broken—when she could not even see the brokenness of her wounded child.

In retrospect, I believe God was teaching me to walk in spiritual balance. Eventually, when I became serious about studying the Bible, I realized that controversy existed in the early church. Even then, Christians were encouraged to seek balance and unity. Some denominations today focus on salvation, some on liturgy and communion, some on the gifts of the Holy Spirit, some on theology/religious studies, some on works. Ultimately, the Body of Christ, the church should embrace all the teachings of Jesus. Often, it does not; therefore, we have division and unrest. We are out of balance.

It would be many more years before my husband and I became unified spiritually, but I will save that story for another day because I am about to take you back to Unit 3E.

Reflecting after my time in Unit 3E to find my precious child

I welcomed the punctual knock. Sharon's inviting smile peeked through the gap in the door as she pointed to her watch, reminding me it was almost time for our small group session. I gave her a thumbs-up and paused to reflect.

I had just climbed over the top of what seemed an impossible mountain, the weight of child abuse tied to my ankles, life's circumstances standing on my shoulders. The struggle had been enormous, and I was so very tired of digging through the twisted threads of my life. I wanted to be done with it all, but I knew I was not finished.

I had allowed myself to get in touch with memories, feelings, and emotions that touched the very core of everything that culminated in this pivotal moment. I came to terms with many obstacles and sorted out the unbearable pain I bore. But in the face of the craziness, I also found victories and blessings on my faith journey.

I am humbled to realize the Creator of the Universe has gone to a great length to reveal Himself to me—this Holy Being, who is not the Universe, as some proclaim, but the One who created it. It is difficult to comprehend God's great love for humankind. It is like the wind; it moves all around us. We can feel it, but we cannot see it. Its strength is so powerful it can turn the worst of human nature into the sweet submission of compassion and forgiveness. We all know it is there, and even though we may try to ignore it, it will not go away—it cannot. Love is the very nature and character of God—to create, not destroy.

Which of us can even begin to perceive this Holy God who designed this one of a kind, singularly made planet among unknown numbers where He breathed His breath of life and love into existence in the form of the nature we enjoy?

Who can grasp, except by faith, this Creator of all things who birthed His own Spirit into humanity, becoming the man—Jesus, the sacrificed lamb, the object of our faith? How can we comprehend His birth, His death, and His resurrection? He was *born* to give us new life, right standing, and a personal relationship with our Creator/Heavenly Father. He *died* to provide us freedom from the darkness of this world and grant us forgiveness of our sins, which keep us separated from God, and gave us the grace to forgive those who hurt us. When *resurrected*, He gave us the promise of eternal life. Honestly, I cannot wrap my mind around these things, but I know the power of my story lies within these holy mysteries.

On the other hand, how can we begin to understand the opposing forces of evil? We also cannot deny these forces or their power as they whirl all around us, unseen but deadly to the human spirit, taking their wickedness and turning it into cancerous malevolence. I cannot deny the presence of both good and evil in this world. The evil I have seen and experienced in my life is real. Evil is not an illusion. Evil things happened to me. The ungodly acts I witnessed within the Christian community expose the power of these evil forces. They seek to thwart God's plan of salvation and His great love for humanity. Man created religion, and man sadly pollutes it.

I cannot explain how, but I know He knows me. I feel so unworthy, but I know that His great redemptive love covers my unworthiness. He has given me free will, the choice to make wise and unwise decisions. I made plenty of foolish choices, but when I strayed from His divine course, He patiently waited on me to respond to the unconditional love He cannot withhold from me.

Had I put my faith in the religion of Christianity, I would have walked out a long time ago. I repeat: had I put my faith in the *religion* of Christianity, I would have walked out a long time ago. But my faith is not in this religion. It is in its object: Jesus Christ. Carried to this moment by God through faith in Christ, my faith in Him was stronger than ever.

The scriptures teach that I am to remove the log from my eye before taking the speck from the eyes of others—a truth I needed to heed.

But in my brokenness, I had not understood how this truth related to my walk with my God or others. Our churches and the world as a whole are full of hurting and needy people. It follows that my wounded child was often in conflict with other wounded people around me. Hurting people hurt people.

I had been looking for self-worth, trying to make my imperfect world perfect. I desperately wanted *people* to love me and heal my hurts, rather than looking only to God to fill and heal the voids in my soul. I expected Jake, his family, and members of the church to make me happy. But no human can make another happy; happiness grows within from a relationship with God. I had been searching for significance and acceptance. Now, I had to face that I had been doing so in all the wrong ways. But that is what adult abused children do and will continue to do until their wounded child is healed—until they find their precious child. To be honest, I had to admit to my shortcomings: the church, the Body of Christ in which I sought to serve God, may not have been there for me, but at times, I was not there for the church.

In no way do I condone the inexcusable behavior of those who hurt me. I am not their judge; I am only responsible for my actions.

Christians are called to be a conduit of love. But when we fail in this, we hurt each other, and we hurt the cause of Christ. In no way does this mean that we turn our heads and ignore the sins of others because to ignore sin is to ignore God's call to love one another honestly. I believe the scriptures teach us to find balance—and the time had come for me to begin walking within that balance.

Sitting on the bed, I looked down at the sheet of paper I clutched. I had been making a list of all the people who had hurt me, those toward whom I held resentments, bitterness, and anger. The list had become unbearably long, and now I realized I paid a great price for withholding forgiveness. If unconditional love walks in forgiveness, then the principles of my faith hung between the two and were at stake if I failed to forgive. I had to make a choice.

The AAC knew the answer all along but had failed to connect all the dots until now. She had been so tangled in the wounded child's twisted threads that it was impossible to move into a place of peace and live within the boundaries of unconditional forgiveness. She was set free spiritually but not emotionally. Her threads were no longer twisted; she could now move on.

I gathered my furry friends into my arms and held them close. I slipped off the bed that had become my holy space and fell to my knees. My hospital room was suddenly serene, with only faint sounds filtering down the hallway and through the door. Soft shadows danced in the sunlight that shone through my single window. The chill from the air-conditioning unexpectedly felt warm. Tears welled up as I buried my face into my hands. Agonizing groans came from deep within my spirit as I laid my life at the foot of the Cross once again.

It had been almost 20 years since Pat Robertson had spoken a word of knowledge to me after Katherine's and Jay's healings. He told me he had a message from the Lord that he did not understand, but perhaps I would. I can still hear his words to me.

"It is not that you have been waiting on Me; it is that I have been waiting on you."

When Jesus was dying on the Cross of Calvary, He prayed to his Heavenly Father to forgive those who rejected him, beat him, and crucified him: "Forgive them, for they know not what they are doing."

At that moment, while I was on my knees, I believe that Jesus was asking my Heavenly Father, "Please forgive her because she did not know what she was doing."

Throughout my journey, God had continually waited on me to hear His voice, to follow His call, to learn His precepts as taught in the

Bible. Ultimately, He had been waiting on me to recognize that Jesus is the one who holds the key—forgiveness—that unlocks the door to unconditional love. The great mystery is that He died for the forgiveness of my sins. Although I had understood the eternal value of forgiveness, I had missed its earthly importance. Without unconditional forgiveness, I could not love others unconditionally.

For so long I had failed to grasp just how sin separates us from God and each other on this earth. God gave us a history book, the Bible, which reveals to humankind what works and does not work in life, in relationships.

What works is kindness, compassion, honesty, gentleness, temperance, self-control, purity, respect, generosity, and forgiveness. These attributes walk toward love.

What does not work in relationships is hate, rudeness, self-centeredness, immorality, drunkenness, bitterness, lying, cheating, anger, gossip, and deceit. These traits walk toward depression, suicide, guilt, self-loathing, unhappiness, hate, broken relationships, divorce, murder, addictions, abuse, and poor health. God calls these actions/choices sin, and sin separates us from each other and God.

The root of my sin was bitterness. My sin became inappropriate anger, and its tentacles reached deep into every area of my life. I had come to this place to find answers because I wanted to live—not just survive. It was time to step into that place of healing and to move forward.

"Oh Lord, my God, please . . . forgive me for the bitterness and the anger I have held on to for so long against so many—those who have felt anything but love from me; they did not understand me. And for those who have hurt me so deeply . . . give me the grace to forgive them; I did not understand them. In Jesus's name, forgive me." And He did.

I can begin again

With the passion of a child

My heart has caught a vision

Of a life that's still worthwhile

I can reach out again

Far beyond what I have done

Part six:

Reconnecting With My Precious Child

Chapter 22

The Canvas of My Life Completed—Well, Not Just Yet

I was almost always the last one to arrive at my small group meetings, and this day was no exception. I slid onto the nearest waiting chair, attempting to smile back at the questioning eyes that gazed at me. Many faces had come and gone within our small group during the past month and a half. Some of them had changed; they reflected a hint of peace. Some had stayed the same; their depression manifested sorrow. New faces mirrored fear and anxiety. I understood them all.

I liked Michael, the unit coordinator and the facilitator of my small group. He had been a solid rock, a good listener, stern yet fair in his responses to everyone. He knew that my stay on 3E was coming to an end.

"Nola Katherine, tell us what is going on with you today."

Most of them had heard bits and pieces of my story during the past few weeks, but none of them, except for Sharon, were fully aware of the work I had done. Like me, they were trying to find their way. I struggled to find my voice; my emotions were all over the place. I chose my words carefully, telling them much of what I had learned.

> I have been at war with myself, but I have finally found balance in my life—letting my strengths overcome my weaknesses and my weaknesses become my strengths.
>
> Today, I accepted responsibility for my poor behavior. Although the anger and bitterness I concealed against others were justified, I could no longer afford the luxury of nurturing them.
>
> Forgiveness set me free.
>
> I took off my many masks—all of them—so that I could truly be who I am.
>
> I am more than a survivor.
>
> About six months before entering the hospital, I attended a workshop for survivors of abuse, and around the same time, I had a disturbing dream. The dream and the workshop were instrumental in leading me to seek help.
>
> I dreamed I was standing on the shores of a large lake, watching a little brown dog drown. I kept going out into the water and rescuing the little dog, but it just kept going back into the lake. Finally, I just let it go and let it drown. I became the little dog in my dream, and I felt the sweet release of leaving my pain-filled life—letting it go. When I awoke, I recognized that I was both the one drowning and the one rescuing. I knew that if I did not get help soon, I would drown, and the survivor in me was unwilling to let that happen.

Chapter 22

> Today, I realized that small brown dog was my precious child—the little one I have been trying so hard to find. She has been with me all the time. We have been clinging to each other and rescuing each other all my life. She is the core of who I am—my soul, my spirit. She is a unique part of who I am, and she is truly precious.

Michael picked up on my words and explained that he rarely used the words *intestinal fortitude,* but when he was writing about me, that is the term he used. He observed that I was unique because I lost my core, the essence of who I was as a child, and somehow I got my core back and then worked on the child abuse issues.

I will never forget his next words to me.

"Nola Katherine, I am genuinely concerned about you. I have seen you go to such depths of despair that I was not sure you would be able to come back. It is like an archeologist who can dig and dig through centuries of treasures, but then after a while, he must stop searching because the treasures he finds begin to crumble. I think it is time for you to stop digging."

I knew Michael was right. It was time to stop searching, and it was time for me to move on with my life. I told my small group I would be leaving soon. I was showered with hugs and well wishes as the session ended. Michael put his arms around me. I had seen tears in his eyes more than once when he talked to me.

"You have made a tremendous impact on my life."

We both knew I had one more obstacle to face.

Since I had entered the hospital, no one on my side of the family had contacted me. I am not sure why; possibly it was because Mother did not tell anyone where I was. Perhaps fear and denial kept them away. However, I could not delay the inevitable. Before I left the security of the hospital and my therapist, I knew I needed to confront my sister.

The knot in my stomach tightened as I picked up the phone to call her. She willingly agreed to come to the hospital, but she was unprepared for what was coming. I did not want to hurt her; she had come from the same family as I, so her life could not have been easy either. Her second husband had just passed—I needed to tread carefully.

Perhaps subconsciously, I hoped that through me she would see that she, too, needed healing. I earnestly wanted us to have a healthy relationship. But I knew that would never happen if I did not talk to her about what her first husband had done to me and her part in protecting him but not protecting me.

Small rooms designated for therapy sessions lined the hallway just outside the locked doors leading into Unit 3E. Long narrow windows on the doors allowed visual entrance into the rooms. The elevator on the opposite wall guarded these small rooms, each of which allowed just enough space for four chairs and a table. I waited for my sister in agonizing silence with my therapist.

During the workshop I attended earlier, Mia told me I had no boundaries. Anyone could get into my space, and I would not object. But now, I felt strangely uncomfortable with the proximity between Ron and myself. I was not afraid of him; I respected him, but I was suddenly aware that I didn't want him so close to me, even though he was sitting opposite me. *The survivor understood and felt a sense of relief; she was experiencing healthy boundaries.*

Chapter 22

A gentle tap on the door broke our silence. Sis stood peering through the window, and Ron motioned for her to come inside. She smiled like she always smiled—like I always smiled—as I introduced her to my therapist. For the first time in my life, I looked at my sister through different eyes. She seemed old, drawn, and tired; her shoulders slumped slightly forward.

Nothing about our appearances would connect us as sisters. She was five inches taller and carried a larger bone structure. I was short and petite. She had just turned 60, and I had celebrated my 47th birthday while in the hospital. Even though her auburn hair had turned white, her complexion remained flawless. She inherited the enviable darker skin of our native American roots and tanned beautifully. In contrast, I inherited dark hair, fair Irish skin that burned, blistered, and peeled when overexposed to the sun, and skin cancers. However, I got great high cheekbones!

Ron explained to my sister that I had been working through child abuse issues, and I had some things I needed to talk about with her.

With her smile still in place, Sis replied, "Okay."

I did not know for sure what my sister knew about my abuse issues. However, I strongly suspected that she knew—how could she not? Still, when I asked her if she knew that her first husband had abused me, she denied any knowledge of the abuse—just as I expected she would. As I disclosed snippets of information, her smile turned harsh, and she even tried to blame me.

"You always wanted to go with him! You were always sitting in his lap! You always have had an overly active imagination! It was just photography when he was taking pictures of you!"

Her accusations caused me to catch my breath. When I gave my therapist a sharp, panicked look, he quickly intervened.

"Unhealthy attention will be perceived as acceptable if a child is not getting the healthy attention one needs. Young children will almost always turn to their abuser for attention."

The air in the room turned thick and heavy with anger and denial.

I asked her, "Did anyone ever sexually abuse you when you were a child?"

I saw a flicker in her eyes that said *Yes*. Her answer was emphatic. "No!"

It was not a pleasant encounter; we resolved nothing. We hugged, and Sis left the confining room, angry and hurt. I do not know what I felt as I returned to my chair and sat silently.

Ron wanted to know what was with the hug.

He did not understand that I loved my family, despite everything. *The adult abused child understood that she could not hate the ones she understood. The wounded child, the survivor, the victim—they all understood her sister.*

I did not know my sister was deathly ill with cancer, and I would not get another chance to tell her I forgave her or another opportunity to ask her to forgive me—because I knew my bad behavior toward her my entire life had hurt her too. *The survivor would live with that grief for a long time. It's hard to forgive yourself.*

Dr. Kamen took me off all medications. We both felt I no longer needed them and could make it on my own. He made the necessary arrangements for my discharge. Caution was extended, and a warning was given. The world I left behind had not changed because I had changed; people would have me in a box and would not want to let me out. I could not help but wonder what the days and weeks and years beyond would bring.

Healthy, ambivalent feelings raced through me as I began to pile my belongings onto the metal cart that would transport them to my car. One of the nurses on staff appeared in my doorway to escort Jake and me off the unit. She remarked that I sure did have lots of cards and flowers for someone who did not feel very loved when they came into this place and that I'd had more visitors than anyone she had witnessed on this unit.

The wounded child had only focused on those who rejected and hurt her. The AAC could not see that others loved her. The survivor now looked through different eyes. The victim saw hope for new beginnings.

The sound of the large metal doors clanging behind me as I left Unit 3E for the last time was music to my ears. The familiar rattle of keys remained on the inside as the door closed behind me. I lost my precious child, but now I had found her. She had been a prisoner, but now she was set free.

My husband, my soulmate, the love of my life, took my hand as we disappeared into the elevator. He could not see the little girl holding my other hand. He could not hear us singing . . .

The passion of my precious child had caught my vision for a life that is still worthwhile. We joined our hands and reached out far beyond what we had done. Like dreamers, we had awakened to the new life that was yet to come. For new beginnings are not just for the young.

And so together . . . we began life again.

Well, our journey together has come to an end. Thank you for taking the time to bring added life to my painting. As I stand back and examine this remarkable work of art, I thank God for the privilege of being the artist's brush and giving me friends along the way to help me. And although I would never have chosen this canvas for myself, I would not trade it for any other on this planet—because the picture stories on it made me who I am today.

I know the canvas of my life is far from being complete. Wisdom, not fully revealed, is waiting for more truths to unfold. Much more living will come my way; more sketches to draw and more canvas to paint. The good news is that whenever I make a mistake, I know I can begin again, and someday, when this life is over and the canvas completed, the Master Artist will say, "Come home, my good and faithful servant. Come home."

I can begin again

With the passion of a child

My heart has caught a vision

Of a life that's still worthwhile

I can reach out again

Far beyond what I have done

Part seven:

Guidelines to Help You Begin Again

A poor past is a poor excuse for poor behavior.

If you are an AAC—an adult abused as a child—I hope you will pick up your own brushes, prepare your own canvas, and seek others you can trust to help paint your unique personal picture. You are precious, and I cannot emphasize enough how heavy my heart is for you. I understand you, and I know your pain and confusion. I pray, ever so fervently, that you will find freedom from the devastating grip of your abuser(s).

I will always be an AAC; you will always be an AAC. That will never change. But your knowledge and perception of the abuse, and your power over it, can and must change. You do not need to live in defeat. You do not need to remain stuck in your pain.

Medications are often needed to help with the recovery process. If you suffer from depression, I encourage you to seek professional help to determine whether you need to be on an antidepressant. Sometimes we just need some help to get where we need to be.

The following guidelines are suggestions to help you take those first steps toward freedom. Each of us travels down a different path at a different pace. Be patient and take one step at a time.

Not everyone has insurance or the financial ability to check into a treatment center or see a therapist. But it costs nothing to take a step of faith and trust God to provide what you need. I believe He will meet you exactly where you are and help you let go of your past to become all He created you to be.

I am not a licensed professional; therefore, please understand I give you these guidelines out of my own experiences and from my heart's desire to use those experiences for good. I want to help you do more than just survive. I want you to live life fully. If recovery is to come, you must be in a place wholly committed to doing the work; you must choose to let go of your pain and decide to be set free. I pray that the following suggestions will be of some help to you and those who love you.

Prayer

When I first began to take seriously the reality that every horrible thing that happened to me as a child affected and controlled every area of my life as an adult, it was overwhelming. I did not know where or how I would get help, but I knew I could not go down that road without God. I memorized the following prayer, and I said it over and over every day. I honestly do not recall how long, but I know that God did answer this prayer in time. I urge you to memorize it also.

> *Come Holy Spirit and heal my understanding.*
> *Heal the deep, innermost realms of self.*
> *Heal that which only you can heal.*
> *Heal the dark unconscious cellars of my mind.*

Heal my hurtful memories.
Heal my hidden griefs and sorrows.
Heal my wrong desires and ambitions.
Heal my disappointments and vain strivings for those things that I should not have.
Heal the pangs of frustration.
Gently release the chains that bind me.
Lead me into the light and freedom of your sufficiency so that I shall be filled with joy all the days of my life.
Amen

—Author unknown

Prayer is the key to Heaven, but faith unlocks the door. Put your faith and trust in God, and He will lead you. God loves you in a way that no one on this earth can love you. Believe in Him to answer your prayers. His mercy has no boundaries, no limits.

Explore your history of origin

If you have abuse issues in your family, find out as much as possible about your parents, grandparents, and siblings. How were they raised? What happened to them as children? This information will bring an understanding of the way you, in turn, were reared. I didn't get this chance. I let time pass, and then they were gone; it was too late, and I live with regrets that I didn't press them for more information. Out of my family of seven, I am the only one still living. My father passed before I went into the hospital, and I didn't realize that, eventually, I would want more information from my mother and siblings. Please, if possible, don't put off getting the answers that will help you understand who you are. Ultimately, it will bring needed awareness to your wounded, abused child. However, there is a warning: tread lightly. You may be opening a can of worms and met with rejection and anger.

Write

Write about your abuse. Spare no details. Express how you felt at the time of the abuse and how you feel about it now. Express your feelings toward the abuser. Do not try to imagine something that is not there. Be honest. However, physical memories are significant; do not discount them. You may not recall who hurt you or the details of what they did, but you may remember physical or emotional symptoms that are very real. Ask the Holy Spirit of God to reveal the truth to you. If they are genuine memories, you will eventually have peace about them, one way or the other. Writing is safe and can bring valuable healing to the AAC.

I must caution you to only share your personal information with those you can completely trust. People are too quick to judge, and you don't need further rejection. You will only feel safe to share your story more openly after you turn that corner and start walking in freedom.

Talk

Find a safe and trustworthy person who will listen without judging you. Such a person will encourage you to keep talking and not give up. Remember that you are as sick as your secrets, but they are no longer secret once you speak of them, and they no longer have power over you.

If your safe person is a friend or family member and not a professional, be careful not to wear them out. Adult abused children have a habit of doing this to those who are willing to listen. Once everything is said, you do not need to keep rehashing the abuse. This is for your benefit too: it is not healthy to repeat the story over and over, again and again. Be done with it. You will know when it is time to stop. In time, when the abuse no longer has power over you, you will be able to share your story with the intent of helping others.

Seek out a therapist who has a plan designed to move you into a place of healing. Do not be afraid to ask for a treatment plan. Find out what methods they use to help people recover. I have known women who have been stuck in therapy for years and have never moved on. If you regularly see a therapist who does not encourage you beyond talking, especially if you have just been talking for several years, find another therapist.

Realize that everyone is different, and everyone moves at a different pace, so please do not look for a set formula or place a time limit on your progress. Just ask for some guidelines so you will know a plan exists. You might even share the guidelines presented here.

In terms of talking in general, guard what you say casually to people you don't really know or even people you think you do know. We are secretly desperate for people in our lives to understand what we have endured. Adult abused children have strange ways of communicating at times. Do not put yourself in situations that will cause you to be judged, rejected, or distressed.

Use discernment because the effect abuse has on children is complicated. Keep in mind that you want *normal* people to understand you, but they do not process life the same way that you do—others cannot fully understand what the effects of abuse entail. They never will. In her book, *Normal is Just a Setting on Your Dryer*, Patsy Clairmont states that "Normal has nothing to do with people. Try as we might, we remain peculiar people with distinct differences." Perhaps a good thing for all of us to keep in mind when judging who is normal or not normal.

Role-play

Role-playing can be invaluable to you as a victim of child abuse. I do not believe it is wise or safe to face an abuser directly. Through role-playing, you have a safe place to verbalize what you need to say to the one(s) who have wounded you; to say what you are feeling. If the abuser is deceased, role-play can be just as effective.

Not only does this exercise allow you to confront your abuser(s) safely, but it will also help you to openly get in touch with the guilt, shame, and anger locked up inside. Role-playing can enable you to identify the emotional repercussions of abuse that have fueled your poor behavior, depression, self-loathing, resentments, bitterness, unhealthy decisions, sexual dysfunction, etc.

Remember that as a child, you were vulnerable and innocent. Adults have enormous control over children, and children lose control when abused. Anyone can get into the space of an adult abused child at any time because the AAC is powerless to say no. You do not have healthy boundaries, and that must stop! A safe person permits you to have good and healthy boundaries and helps you stop playing the victim role. It is your life, and you deserve to be in control of it, to take back your power.

Role-play is not easy. It took me a long time just to open my mouth and speak, and I only touched the surface of my issues at the time. It may take several sessions to work through your problems, but I beg you not to do what I did. I wasted years living in denial and emotional and physical pain before getting the help I needed.

I sincerely hope you will choose to participate in role-playing. If you do, be prepared to work hard and not waste any more of your life carrying another's evil on your shoulders. Be passionate about the process. Put fire in your words when you verbalize why you are angry at the abuser. Speak to the one who has stolen the very essence of who you are, your life—your innocence, your joy, your ability to be intimately healthy. Be specific! Place all your shameful, guilty feelings back on the abuser.

Say, "I give your anger back to you! It is not mine!"
Leave it there and walk away.

Give the shame back to your abuser. It is not your shame that you have been carrying for all those years. You do not own it, so give it back to the person to whom it belongs. You have nothing to be ashamed of, and God covers any shameful thing you have done because of the abuse with His love, grace, and mercy. Please understand this and let it go.

Verbalize it: "I give your shame back to you! It is not mine!"
Leave it and walk away.
Likewise, let go of the guilt and take back the power your abuser stole from you.

Suggestions for the Safe Person
Role-playing can lead to a decisive turning point for your friend, loved one, or patient. Before beginning, remember to always ask for permission to take on the role of the abuser.

If you are not a professional and someone has asked you to step into this role, pray ardently before proceeding. Be prepared to stick with your friend or loved one until the end. Be patient, and please do not judge. Please, give unconditional love. Listen, and don't be too quick to give advice. Let them get their pain out. It takes time and patience.

When you work with an individual, I suggest putting a pillow in their lap. At some point, anger will and should surface, so they may need an outlet to release their anger on, something to punch. The pillow, not the person, will get the well-deserved punches.

Give affirmations:

- I am sorry you were hurt.
- You are safe here with me.
- No one else will ever hear what you say.
- No one will judge you.
- No one will disbelieve you.
- What happened to you was not your fault.
- You did nothing wrong.

Help them to verbalize what they need to say. Ask leading questions:

- Who hurt you?
- What did they do to you?
- How old were you?
- Can you tell me more?
- How did you feel when it happened?
- How do you feel now?
- What do you need to say to the one who hurt you?

Help the wounded adult child get in touch with their feelings—shame and guilt and anger. Help them release that guilt, shame, and anger back to the abuser.

Encourage them to say:

- "I give your shame back to you, I give your guilt back to you, and I give your anger back to you."
- "I take back control over my life, and I take back the power you took from me."
- "I am free from you, and you will never hurt me again."

And finally, help them to choose to turn a corner and move on with their lives.

Please keep in mind that this process takes time and patience. It will probably take many sessions to get through it all. It took me almost six weeks in a hospital to get to this point.

You are a valuable gift to the survivor.

Forgive

Forgiveness is always a choice. If you choose not to forgive those who have hurt you, then you will stay stuck in your pain, and you will not move forward. If you are a Christian, then you understand the unconditional forgiveness that Jesus personally bought for you at a great price. It is part of the great mystery of our faith. We have done nothing to deserve it; we have not earned it; it is a gift. Understanding that, how can you possibly withhold forgiveness toward another human being, regardless of who they are or what they have done? You must choose to forgive. I promise that healing leads to peace in the act of forgiveness. Forgiveness is another step closer to complete freedom from those who have wounded you.

If you have not yet come to understand this great mystery, I ask you to step out in faith and choose to forgive your abuser(s).

Ask God to give you the courage, the power, and the grace to do so.

It is of utmost importance to understand that forgiving is not saying that what was done is okay. Abuse of any kind is never okay.

I love my parents, my siblings, and my aunt. I do not believe they—especially my mother—meant to bring harm to me any more than I intended to bring hurt to my children. While it does not compare, I know that sometimes I did wound my children. But as you have read, my family of origin suffered from its own childhood wounds, and those wounds transferred over onto me. It does not excuse their behavior, but forgiving my family members sets me free to love them. Understanding my family was a huge revelation for me. It is hard to hate those you understand, and you will never be free until you are set free spiritually and emotionally; that is what forgiveness does for you.

And finally, do not forget to forgive yourself. No doubt, you have done many things in your life that you wish you had not done. Let those pain-filled memories go and forgive your wounded child; she did not know what she was doing. Memories never leave us, but we must not let them have power over us. They do not need to plunge us into a dark pit every time we think about them.

Turning the corner

A little bit of caution here. It is challenging to break the pattern of being everyone else's beating post/victim. I have learned I must have healthy boundaries. First, I do not have to be with people in whose presence I do not feel safe—those who do not honor me, respect me, or affirm my worthiness as a human being. Secondly, it is okay to communicate whatever I need to say to take care of myself. Speaking up does not naturally come easy for me, but I fully understand my right to be heard and feel safe doing so.

Finally, approach the wall that has held you captive, turn the corner, and walk to the other side. Take responsibility for yourself and your happiness. And above all, trust God to walk with you. Give yourself time to heal; it takes time. But please, do not stay stuck in your pain. Choose to move on with your life. And do not forget that life on this planet is never going to be perfect, but now you have the power to face life's hardships healthily.

Confrontation

Once you have turned the corner, you may then consider confronting your abuser. However, you may no longer feel that confrontation is necessary. If you do feel you must face the abuser, never go alone; take someone with you. Go empowered and leave empowered.

Be aware that the confrontation may have negative repercussions for you. Your abuser most likely will deny your charges, get angry at you, and possibly further abuse you emotionally.

If you feel a face-to-face meeting is not the solution for you, perhaps you could consider writing a letter to your abuser. Don't mail it right away; you may eventually feel it is not necessary. Just writing it can bring a certain amount of freedom and peace.

If you feel that you have hurt others because of your confusing behavior, be discerning, wise, and cautious about going to them. Some will respond favorably, but some will not have a clue about what you are telling them. Do what is best for you. Again, letters are an excellent way to communicate, but always remember that apologizing is about what *you* have done, not what the others have done. I have found the following statement to be effective: "Please forgive me if you have ever felt anything but love from me." Or be specific if you are aware of a particular offense.

Leave it at that. You do not need to explain yourself. If the person responds, you will know they care and want to have a healthy relationship with you. If they choose not to respond, that is their problem. You will have done what you needed to do for yourself. Move on; you do not need them in your life.

Thoughts for a spouse, friends, and family members

If you live with an AAC, I applaud you for hanging in there; it is not always easy. Just remember, you have someone in your presence whom God highly cherishes. Your loved one holds many admirable qualities, and I hope you acknowledge them. However, those qualities are often unseen because they were tragically stolen and hidden by the effects of the abuse. In other words, a precious child is living inside your loved one, and that precious child is worth finding. It takes unconditional love, and that is what your loved one needs from you more than anything else.

I hope my story has given you a new understanding of past experiences you may have had with the AAC you live with or know. We are, not by choice, complex individuals, but the abused child will always live in us, and we will always look through different eyes. Remember that healing takes time. It is a process. Behaviors do not change overnight.

If you are a parent, a teacher, or a friend who suspects child abuse, please do not be in denial. Get help immediately. It is your place to protect powerless children. Children depend on adults. Act now! Pray hard for guidance and discernment. You can make a difference, and you may be the only hope they have.

Sexual confusion

I want to be very clear that when I talk about sexual confusion, I am not talking about being a homosexual or transgender person. I am talking about how sexual abuse affects children exposed at a vulnerable age—when feelings and emotions are aroused at too young of an age.

We AACs do not respond to sex in a normal way. How can we when our brain chemistry is changed by abuse? Messages triggered by inappropriate responses to sex caused shame, anger, and confusion that, as a child, I was incapable of sorting out. These messages followed me into adulthood, and it was challenging to figure out who I was created to be.

My story confirms that sexually abused children have every right and reason to be perplexed about sex. This can lead to sexual confusion. Every woman I have talked to who proclaimed to be gay admitted she was sexually abused. They alway paused to consider my reasoning that follows:

Because perpetrators are often members of the opposite sex, if we become gay, we can avoid ever having sexual encounters with the opposite gender again. This was my friend Sharon's sole reason for being gay.

On the other hand, if someone of the same sex abuses us, a different response occurs, and there is a strong probability that same sex relationships will result.

My response was somewhat different because I shut down sexually. I didn't respond to men; therefore, the question always in my mind was—am I gay? I didn't go down that path, but I chose unhealthy ways to act out my confusion.

Children are not accountable, but as adults, we become responsible for the decisions we make. It is wise to get to the root of sexual confusion if you are not at peace, not happy with your life. Understand, I am not here to judge anyone.

For those without gender issues, please do not be too quick to judge. We must all reach out in love and leave the judging to the only One who truly knows the human heart, the only One who knows our true stories. God's children deserve our mercy, just as He is merciful to all His children.

Pornography

I wrote the following information ten years ago and have decided not to update it. However, I encourage you to go to Enough.org and read about what is happening to our children. You will be shocked. In 2020 alone, 21.7 million suspected child sexual exploitation reports were made to the Cyber Tip Line of the National Center for Missing and Exploited Children.

I emphasize the importance of this subject because I am passionate about your understanding of the dangers of pornography. Once again, let me be clear: I do not believe in looking for a demon behind every bush. I do not go around screaming and casting out or rebuking demons every time something strange happens. I do, however, understand from experience the battles we mortals face. You must be wiser than the enemy when it comes to overcoming this or any evil addiction.

I know this addiction would come back to me in a flash if I invited it in, and I fear I would never be able to get free again. You cannot play with it, ever! That is how powerful pornography is. Its grip on the human mind is extraordinarily strong, and just like abuse, it will affect every area of your life. And I believe the addiction has the potential to be passed on to your children if it is left unchecked. Please, hear me when I say that your involvement in pornography will adversely affect your family as you invite these powers of darkness into your life, into your home.

I would like you to consider that a story like mine may be behind each pornographic picture or video you view. Do you understand that if you were to look behind the camera, you would find an abuser and a manipulator? You cannot see why or how those women, men, or children are exploited. When you engage with pornography, I believe you are participating in the abuse of the one who is giving you such lustful, self-seeking pleasure. I must ask you—is your momentary pleasure worth the consequences you will bear for choosing to participate in the wounding of those whose bodies you lust?

One Christian college survey revealed that a shocking percentage of men and women viewed pornography at least once a week. These are young adults who were most likely raised in good homes and have Christian backgrounds. You may think that your children, especially your daughters, would never go down that road—but do not be too sure. In November 2009, a popular talk show host reported that one in three women viewed pornography (or erotica, as it is now sometimes deceitfully styled). Ten years ago, Familysafe.com reported the following statistics gathered through several resources listed on their website:

- 53% of men who attended a Promise Keepers weekend, a Christian event held for men, had used pornography the previous week.
- 47% of Christians interviewed admitted to having a problem with pornography at home.
- 72% of men and 28% of women visit pornographic websites.
- The average age of children exposed to internet pornography is 11.

- There are 4.2 million pornographic websites.
- There are 68 million daily search engine requests for pornography.
- There are 1.5 billion porn-related downloads every month.
- There are 116,000 child porn requests every day.

Enough.org reported that child pornography is the fastest growing business online, and the content is becoming worse. In its 2008 annual report, Internet Watch Foundation found 1,536 individual child abuse domains; I am sure that figure is much higher now.

You may say of yourself that you would never have an affair, have same-sex relations, or engage in unthinkable acts such as child abuse or rape, but don't be so sure if you are addicted to pornography. I know that sounds extreme, but porn is extreme. It will rob you of your self-respect, and it will anesthetize your sense of right and wrong. The desire for it, once planted, is insatiable and has the potential of pulling anyone into a self-centered, destructive, bottomless pit. If you are into porn, you have opened a door that I beg you to close immediately. You are inviting the powers of darkness—Satan and his demons—to enter your world, your home, your mind, and your soul. It will touch the people you love the most: your spouse and your children. Our prisons are full of people there because of pornography, and I am sure none of them ever intended it to lead them there.

Even devout Christians are highly vulnerable to the lure of sexual immorality. I want to share the following story to prove my point.

When I was the bookkeeper for my church, a young woman came into my office and closed the door. She began to sob uncontrollably. Her expressions of guilt and shame were almost unbearable to watch. She was a committed Christian and a single mom with high morals. Yet, she was pulled into a relationship that involved alcohol and telephone sex. She was devastated by her choices and did not know how to get out of evil's gripping power. Her need and desire for human physical intimacy had become skewed; it overcame her passion for spiritual intimacy with God. She knew she had broken her relationship with Him, and the agony of that lost relationship left her empty and defeated. The devastation she felt far outweighed the momentary pleasure she found in insatiable, unfulfilling sexual activity. Thankfully, she did get free from her addiction, and today she is a beautiful, joyful, and fulfilled woman.

God desires intimacy with His children. When our spiritual connection with our Creator has broken, intimacy will become skewed. We search for alternative ways to fill the deep void that we feel. Every human being craves intimacy, and sex is the most physical, completely intimate act we experience. However, when sex becomes an idol, as it has become in our nation and throughout the world, it ultimately brings loneliness and emotional bankruptcy—not lasting pleasure or happiness or fulfillment. More than ever before, people are searching for real significance in the idol of sex. If those heavily involved in porn were honest, they would tell you that what I am saying is true: they are not happy or fulfilled. Satisfying sex outside of God's plan is an illusion. Innocent children, whose bodies and spirits are violated, are carrying this idol on their shoulders. I repeat: *innocent children* carry the idol of sex on their tiny shoulders.

Trust me. Only a relationship with God will give you the inner peace you desire. I know I have said it many times already, but I do not want you to forget that Satan is a roaring lion seeking whomever he can devour. Know your enemy, but also know you have a God who roams this earth seeking the lost and seeking those who have a heart toward Him. For this, He gave us Jesus and the healing power that is in His name.

Before I move on, I want to tell you about the rubber band trick. It has the potential to help you. Wear a strong rubber band around your wrist. Whenever a thought comes to your mind that entices you to go to your addiction, pop your wrist with the rubber band. Continue until the idea is lost. Sooner or later, your brain will associate the thought with pain and not pleasure—and let's face it, we humans do not like pain. However, you must want it to work, and you must be consistent to get the success you deserve.

Something goes crazy in our brains when arousal of any kind takes place. We can't fight it, and we can't stop it until that urge is somehow satisfied—except, perhaps with a simple rubber band and the grace of God.

Alcoholic beverages

Drinking is mentioned a lot in my story, but I didn't say much about it. I want to put my thoughts on the subject here for you to consider. Jesus told his followers: "Be very careful, then, how you live, not as unwise but as wise, making the most of every opportunity, because the days are evil. Therefore, do not be foolish, but understand what the Lord's will is. Do not be drunk on wine, which leads to debauchery. Instead, be filled with the Spirit." The Bible appears to make allowances for drinking wine, but it clearly warns about drunkenness. The problem is, anytime you find people drinking alcohol, you will find a measure of intoxication. It is a socially accepted drug that alters the state of mind.

I have been in both camps: I have drunk excessively, and I have sat and watched others get drunk. Neither is a place where I am comfortable. I do not want to separate my mind, my body, or my spirit from God. When we are in an altered state of mind, we are at risk of being disconnected from God and others. However, alcohol gives us a false sense of connection. Countless times, I have watched groups of people hardly speaking to each other when they first enter a gathering—sometimes it appears they do not even like each other—but after a couple of drinks, they're all best friends.

The worst human behaviors start with just one drink—and then another and another. Whatever your basic personality trait is, it will manifest under the influence of alcohol. When your conscience guard is low, your true self will emerge in an exaggerated form because no one is minding the store. If your personality is bent toward anger and violence, you will be a mean drunk. If you are kindhearted and loving, you will be overly vulnerable and become powerless.

I have known people who used alcohol to dull their physical and emotional pain, boredom, stress, loneliness, and insecurities. The problem with this is that you never get to the source of your problems because you just keep drowning them in alcohol and never get real, lasting help. The real danger in drinking is the potential for alcoholism, a devastating disease. Lives are wasted and destroyed; families disintegrated, abuses perpetrated. Car accidents, promiscuity, unwanted pregnancies, rapes, suicides, overdoses—the list is endless. The destruction never ends.

My greatest concern is for children who live with parents who must have "happy hour" daily. Monkey see monkey do, they watch their parents drink and grow up with the idea that this is a cool thing to do. However, the potential for these children to end up as alcoholics or drug addicts is off the charts. I beg you to be an example for your children and educate them about the dangers of alcohol. It is a brutal world we live in, and they are so vulnerable.

During my journey, I discovered the closer I get to God, the less I need other things to fill my life. Alcohol and drugs produce a temporary high that will eventually make you crash and burn. Instead, be filled with the Holy Spirit. It is a joyful and powerful high that will fill your emptiness. And the supply is free and limitless. Please be wise; be discerning.

The Christian community

If you were hurt, as I have been, within the Christian community and have walked away, I am deeply sorry. I encourage you to go back to your roots in Christ and renew your walk with Him. He knows you, and He is *waiting on you*. His arms are always open. You can find many healthy churches with genuine, accountable leaders. The Holy Spirit will show you whether you are in a church filled with genuine Christ-followers. Please, always remember that where there are human beings, there will never be perfection. Christians are not perfect, and sometimes we make awful mistakes, but we are offered the grace of forgiveness. It is for us—sinners—that Jesus came to this earth to forgive our transgressions. I know I am perfectly imperfect.

Pastors, priests, ministers—you are called to lead, to be shepherds. But if you are not accountable, and do not strive to live by Christian precepts, then the darkness you invite into your own life will trickle down into your congregation, into your ministry. As never before in our nation's history, we need the church, the Body of Christ, to be healthy and stable. Teach your congregation how to be faithful disciples of Christ, true Christ-followers.

And finally, before moving on, I want to challenge the Christian community to wake up. For too long, churches have been asleep and silent. In many ways, the Body of Christ is responsible for the evil taking over our land. Life has been too good, too easy for us. We have forgotten that church is not about *doing* church; it's about *being* the church. It is about meeting the spiritual needs of the people who walk through the doors. When you go to church on Sunday mornings, I challenge you to look around you. Find the one who is alone, the one who looks sad, or the one who, perhaps, was abused and needs someone to tell them, "It's going to be okay. I care about you." You may be the first face of grace they experience.

If you do not believe in God/Jesus

If you have never come to know your Creator, God, I pray that something in my story will compel you to seek Him. He knows you; He knows everything about you. He is also *waiting on you* to receive His provision of love. Just because you deny His existence does not mean He does not exist, and just because I believe He exists does not mean He does. Truth is truth; it is objective, unchanging, and not something we can make up. As I wrote earlier, water does not *try* to be water. Air does not *try* to be air. God does not try to be holy, and Jesus does not try to be God. It is as it is: air is air, water is water. God is Holy God, and Jesus is the exact revelation of who God is. God is who He has revealed Himself to be, or He is not. It is that simple.

On your journey to find Him, if you encounter something you do not understand, I encourage you to put your questions and doubts on a shelf in your mind and ask God's Holy Spirit to reveal the truth to you. This has worked for me. In time, God's love will override any confusion you might have.

I ask you to consider the following precepts from the Bible.

"God so loved the world that He gave His one and only Son, that whoever believes in Him shall not perish, but have eternal life."

God's love is personal. God loves you!

"All have sinned and fall short of the glory of God."

"The wages of sin is death."

The problem with humanity is rebellion against God's teachings. This rebellion is called sin, and it separates us from Holy God.

"God demonstrates His own love for us in this: while we are still sinners, Christ died for us." Jesus said, "I am the way and the truth and the life. No one comes to the Father except through me."

The good news is that God sent His Son, Jesus Christ, to pay the penalty for our sins. He lived a sinless life, died on a cross, defeated death, rose from the dead, and offers us the gift of eternal life when we accept Him as our Lord and Savior. He sits by the Father in Heaven and intercedes for His children.

"Yet to all who receive Him, to those who believed in His name, He gave the right to become children of God."

Because of Jesus, we have been made righteous—we are in right standing before our Holy God. We can come to Him with our deepest thoughts and concerns without fear.

If you desire to have a relationship with God and receive the gift of eternal life, you can do so by saying this simple prayer:

Jesus, I accept by faith that you are the Son of God. Forgive my sins and come into my life; be my Lord and Savior.

Invite the Holy Spirit to actively work in your life and praise God for what He is doing in your life:

Chapter 22

Father God, I surrender my will to the work of Your Holy Spirit. Anoint me with your power to overcome temptation and wisdom to know your truth. Holy Spirit, teach me God's precepts, protect me from the enemy of my soul, and use my life to glorify the Father.

Begin to read the New Testament. Ask the Holy Spirit to lead you to a church where Jesus is the central focus, where His truths are taught, and be baptized.

I sincerely hope today you decide to become a disciple of Christ, a Christ-follower. Perhaps someday, you will become the first *face of grace* for another AAC to see.

In closing, please know that I am praying for those of you who have just read my book. If the telling of my life experiences in any way helps only one of you to decide to step out in faith and begin to reweave the threads of your life, then I have found meaning to my time on this earth. If my story ultimately leads you into wholeness and freedom from the afflictions of abuse, then my pain and suffering have value. If my vulnerability leads just one of you to find God, my life has been worth it all. No matter where you have been or where you are today, I pray this adult abused child has helped you begin your life again.

Finally, remember that a poor past is a poor excuse for poor behavior, and what needs to be changed is poor behavior. In time I hope that you can help others to begin changing their behavior.

Blessings, Nola Katherine

Postscript

You have just read a revised version of a book that was first published ten years ago. I have learned a lot about writing since that time, and I realized I could do better by making my story less wordy and repetitious. You are probably laughing now because I certainly gave you many words to read, and some repetitions remain—but for a reason.

You probably have some lingering questions about my family, so I will answer a few. When I wrote the first edition of *I Can Begin Again*, I was 67 years old. I am now 78, and a lot of changes have taken place. I will begin with my children.

At Dr. Kamen's request, we engaged in several family sessions before schools started. Those sessions gave my children the platform they needed to hear and to be heard. Even though they were shocked by the extent of their mother's abuse and how it had affected me all my life, they were supportive. They are great, understanding kids, and we are blessed to have them. They were, of course, spared the details.

Our 13-year-old daughter was vulnerable and affected the most by what was happening in her family. In retrospect, she claims the best thing that ever happened to our family was my going into the hospital. She learned it is okay to express herself, to say no, and that it is vital to have boundaries.

My son was less affected because, when he was about the age of ten, I had seen the telltale signs of withdrawal, and I knew that somehow I had to draw my son out of his shell. I pressed him to talk to me, and slowly the dam broke. From that time on, we were pals, and he told me everything . . . well, almost everything! In retrospect, I am amused by the irony of my wisdom, considering all that I was holding in at the time.

My oldest daughter was a different story. She is the one whom my control issues affected the most. I was unintentionally overprotective, overbearing, and over-everything else that a mother can be. I could not allow life to be anything but perfect for her; therefore, she was not allowed to be anything but perfect. Unfortunately, those unrealistic expectations held devastating consequences for my beautiful daughter and me as she grew up. I put a wedge between us that would take years to remove. It is heartbreaking for me to even think about it because, for different reasons, she too is a survivor, like her mother.

I loved my children more than the air I breathed, and I would have done anything to protect them from ever going through what I had experienced. Despite my dysfunction, I gave them the one thing I knew would sustain them in this life: the knowledge of God's immeasurable love for them through Jesus. I know I have been a good mother by God's grace despite my childhood circumstances. They know how much their mother loves them.

Katherine (Kat) is now 51 and single. She graduated from Southwest Texas State University in San Marcos. She works in the insurance industry; doctors are amazed that she can manage such detailed data given the childhood radiation exposure to her brain. She is a survivor, and I admire her so very much. Kat is a sweet, fun-loving, strong woman who loves to find a bargain and has given us lots of grandcats over the years. She has never had a cancer relapse, remains in good health, and remains connected to a childhood cancer survivor's program through Children's Medical Center in Dallas.

Jay, now 50, is a kindhearted, fun-loving man, a talented musician, and deeply loves his family. He has no mental or physical signs of having had meningitis. Jay graduated in the top ten of his high school class, summa cum laude from Texas A&M, and with honors from the Naval Officer Candidate School. He is currently VP and Chief Technical Officer for an international medical software company based in California; he and his family lived there for several years, but he now works remotely from Texas. His wife, Zoe, also an A&M grad, is a sweet, loving, talented woman who loves and cares for her family well and is my friend. Jay and Zoe gave us our first two outstanding grandchildren: Olivia, in her early 20s, is already a successful computer programmer, while Sam, also a talented musician, is in college. Both are kind, loving people. They have my heart and have given this granny great joy.

Kimberly, our "normal" kid, blessed us all with her sweet, outgoing, sometimes challenging personality. She graduated from the University of Tulsa as a biology major and became a deputy sheriff, with plans to become a forensic pathologist. However, Kim's life changed after giving birth to twins when her firstborn was 18 months old. Even though I was blessed to help her, I am still amazed by how she coped with three little ones. Her husband, Anthony, also a UT grad, is kind, intelligent, loves sports, and is devoted to his family. All three children, now teenagers, attend a Christian school where Kim also teaches. They, too, are outstanding kids, kind and loving. Luke and Hunter love football and being active, while Heather is musical, artistic, and theatrical. Sometimes her brothers join her in the theater scene. They have all brought me much joy and captured my heart.

I am very proud of my kids and their families, and I am blessed they lived close by as the grandchildren grew up. They have all professed faith in Jesus. What more could a mom and granny want?

It became evident to Jake, now retired, that he could no longer stay in the church of his family. We started going to a nondenominational Bible church and have not looked back. We have grown spiritually and relationally, both individually and as a couple, and we have enjoyed many trusting and loving relationships with the new people in our lives.

As for me, I turned a corner and moved on. The joy of the Lord returned to me, and I finally learned to laugh. The memories of abuse no longer haunt me; they no longer have power over me, and they only remain for me to look at when needed.

My fickle handwriting remains a mystery to me. When it changes, I consider it an indication that something within me is trying to get my attention. However, I no longer feel controlled by the fragmented compartments of my mind. I rejoice and thank God that I know who I truly am. Life happens, and if I sometimes find myself slipping in some way, I know I have the power to choose the right path.

Depression no longer gives me a dark place to hide, nor is there inappropriate anger to fuel the depression. I can get angry, but I don't let anger turn into bitterness because I understand that God gave me the capacity for anger. I believe a redemptive side exists to this intense emotion and that God's intent is for us to use it for good, not turn it into something terrible. He has shown me how to use anger in constructive ways rather than allowing it to be destructive. If I acknowledge my anger and do something about it, I can be healthy in mind, body, and spirit. I have learned that I must never sleep with anger; I

Postscript

will get into trouble if I do. I must openly talk about the things that bother me because being immediate and genuine prevents the accumulation of anger's poison. Sometimes I forget, and sometimes I fail, but recovery is quick if I pay attention and deal with it healthily.

One of the biggest challenges for an AAC is overcoming the victim role. One of the most critical tools for correcting victimization is developing healthy boundaries. I trained myself to be aware of circumstances that put me in that mindset. It remains a mystery how others' dysfunction sometimes targets me, but I have worked hard to identify and maintain healthy boundaries. Sometimes, I forget those too, but I know I must not stay around people who do not honor and respect who I am.

I am far from perfect—I am human, and life is not perfect—but I have come so far. I can allow myself to have feelings and not shut them down. I no longer see myself as the same wounded child. By the grace of God, I have changed. Most importantly, I am okay with who I am, the good and the not-so-good.

Before my book first went to print ten years ago, I received an e-mail from a man who had known me between the fourth and eighth grades, the time when most of the abuse I remember happened. Because I blocked out so many of my childhood memories, I did not remember much about the relationship I'd had with him in my youth, even though I had sometimes thought about him. As we began to correspond, we found out a lot about each other. He shared many Vietnam war stories, one of which was extremely important for me.

He had been out on patrol for days. One fretful night, he suddenly awoke thinking about me. He got up and wrote a poem.

He told me, "That night, you brought me peace."

Following is a portion of the poem, which brought confirmation that all I have shared in my book is real and not imagined. I am thankful that Bill found me and opened his heart to me before he died. He was an amazing man who served his country well, and I have the utmost respect for him. Bill's poem was written 11 days before I married Jake. I now share it in his memory with thanksgiving for the few months God gave us to share our stories. I learned that he, too, was a survivor of child abuse.

But something about her was missing from the times that we shared.
Emptiness, darkness, a cover I could not pare.
She held a part of her away from me, but I knew it was not because of me.
Something else within her hides, an ebb and flow of deeper tides.
I could not reach—I could not breach.
I sensed within her a frailness, a sadness, that she tried to hide,
and to bring it out of her, I truly tried.
I gave myself all that I had in hopes that she would no longer be sad with me.
Though my eyes may never again behold her, within my heart, I will always hold her.
Even today, after so many years, she still is with me, so far, yet so near.

Bill LaBaume
18 June 1968, Republic of Vietnam

During the past ten years, I have co-authored a book, spoken to and led small groups, spent time mentoring hurting souls, led Bible studies, been a guest on several radio programs, taken my book to a convention, and loved on my grandkids, a lot. It was not until I injured my back at 75 that I realized I was getting old(er), and if I was going to revise my book, I had better hurry up. Time is running out.

Postscript

I have been humbly encouraged by many who have read my book and been impacted by my story. A therapist told me my book had done more to help her patients than any book she had read. A young mother, whose son was abused by his father, heard me speak on the radio and contacted me. I have walked with her during a long battle to protect her family; we have become friends. I am angered and sad to report that the justice system appears to be failing this family; I pray that ultimately things will change in her favor.

Within a few weeks of finishing my revision, I was contacted by a woman who had recently read the original book. Over lunch, she poured her heart out to me, thanking me for sharing my story and telling me how it changed her. Her eagerness to move forward and reach out to others was inspiring. I believe this lady was placed in my path to encourage me to press on. Her wounds centered around adult abuse rather than child abuse, but abuse is abuse—no matter the circumstances—and it affects all similarly.

Despite continued back pain, a recent recurrence of melanoma, and a blood cancer diagnosis, I am determined to promote my book diligently. Ten years ago, I wrote that the America I grew up in is changing. Now, more than ever before, people need hope. I pray my story will bring encouragement and healing—but most of all, I pray it will bring renewed faith in God to many in our hurting world.

My Family, c 1945

About Three Years Old

My Childhood

School Picture, Nine Years Old

Age 14 With My Niece, Mary Jo

Senior Year

Me With Lady Bug

Billye After Moving to California

My Mother & Her Family

Ancestors

My Siblings: Sis, Alice Ann & Jack

My Dad's Mother

My Siblings With Uncle Ben & My Dad's Dad

Billye, Ruby Ellen, Eva, My Dad & His Father

Nola Katherine and Jake June 29, 1968

Marriage & Family

True Love Walks In

Sweethearts

Katherine's First Christmas After Diagnosis

Katherine Loves Her Baby Brother, Jay.

Katherine Loses Her Beautiful Hair

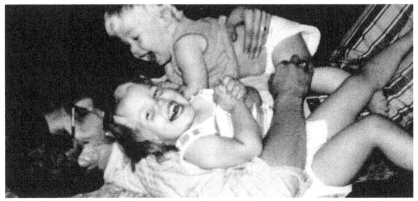
Tickle Time With Dad

God's Grace is Sufficient

A Miracle for Katherine

A prayer of faith will heal the sick, and the Lord will raise him up.
St. James 5:15

Jesus, Son of Mary, You have ordained and constituted the services of Angels and men in a wonderful order: Mercifully grant that as Your Holy Angels always serve You in heaven, so may they guard and defend Your child Katherine on earth. Through Jesus Christ our Lord.

Amen

O Lord, Jesus Christ, who with joy did receive and bless the children brought unto You: Bless Your child Katherine and grant that she may be restored to that perfect health which is Yours alone to give so that she may live to serve and glorify You all her days: Through Jesus Christ our Lord.

Amen

Kat and Jay: Constant Companions with Hair

Cuddle Time With Mom

Just Before Life Gets Really Tough

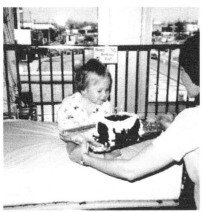
Jay in Hospital on His 2nd Birthday

Our Two Miracles

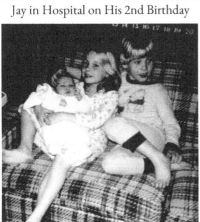
Katherine & Jay Welcome Baby Kim

Kim and a Special Moment With My Parents

My Family – Easter 1990 – Just Before I Went Into the Hospital

Memories

Dickie Bird by NK, c 1955

Chewy and Her 12 Puppies

Jo Ann & I Ride the Old Chisholm Trail

Falling Off the Horse by NK, c 1967

Acknowledgments

Above all, I give praise to God for using my life story to His glory, for my good and the good of others. I will be eternally grateful that He never let go of me. Without Him, there would be no story to tell, no book to write.

For those who helped me in so many ways during the first publishing of *I Can Begin Again*:

I give kudos to my husband, Jake, for his unconditional love, encouragement, and patience with my limited computer skills during the original writing of my book. I have learned a lot since then.

I cherish the time spent with Jake and my grown kids Kat, Jay, Kim, and my daughter-in-love, Zoe, as we waded through my very rough manuscript. We laughed, cried, and shared our souls. I love and appreciate the wonderful people that you are.

I am incredibly thankful to my retired pastor and friend, Dr. Gene Getz, for inviting me to tell my story on his weekly program Renewal Radio. By allowing me to speak openly about childhood abuse, he gave me the courage to move forward and finalize the writing of my story. His advice and encouragement were priceless gifts to me. Thank you, Gene, for being God's inspirational voice to me and so many others.

I am forever thankful for the many close friends who read my story and gave me honest feedback and editing advice. Each confirmed in different ways that I must get my story out there for others to read. They are Lorrie Schnetzer, Jerry Castpell, Trudy Smith, Stefanie Michaels, Dan L.ockhart, Janie Oliver, Madeliene Dickson, Lois Hyatt, Bera Gay Chevers, Pam Evatt, Helen Clark, Clarice Harris, Frances Fassett, Donna Johnson, Jeanne Washburn, Juanita McGinnis, Stephanie Davis, Lois Smith, JoAnn Frances, Linda Ferguson, Carol Lockhart, Beth Crowe, and my nieces Stephanie Davis and Matthea Breuer, and my cousin Cindy Micheals. Iva Morellie and my son, Jay, helped with old photos.

I am grateful for the many prayer warriors who prayed for me, especially the Nelson Life Group. I felt their prayers daily, and I know that I would not be where I am today without them.

Additionally, I acknowledge those involved in the revision of *I Can Begin Again:*

Self Publishing School, Chandler Bolt, https://www.self-publishingschool.com

I can't say enough about Chandler's enthusiasm and sincere desire to help authors get published. I am grateful for the patiences and understanding the SPS family gave this elderly grandmother.

Katie Chambers kmchambers@beaconpointservices.org

Katie is an excellent, talented editor. She has a fantastic ability to organize and search out needed changes. She urged me to pair down my story to make it less wordy and more effective, which is what I knew I needed to do. Katie was also patient and thoughtful; she encouraged me in so many ways. I am so pleased with what she did with my man-

Acknowledgments

uscript, and there are not enough words to express how thankful I am that Katie is my editor.

Stephanie Thompson www.thompsonediting.com

Proofreading is just one of Stephanie's talents. She found errors that needed to be corrected, did some needed fact-checking and encouragement me with her positive comments about my story. Stephanie was very kind and helpful, even after she released my manuscript back to me.

Alejandro Martin www.bloom-designagency.com

I give many kudos to Alejandro who designed the perfect book cover for my story. Because my story entails so much sadness, his artist flare gave my book a much needed hint of hope. He was extremely patient with me during the formatting stage. It was not an easy task because of the unusual way I wrote my story. He graciously took the time to make additional changes and edits. I am very thankful for him.

The Praying Grandmas: Margaret Quinn, Darlene Lynn, Shirley Mobley and Pat Trapp carried me on the wings of prayer during both printings of my book. I love them so much, and I thank God for their unconditional love and support.

I am thankful for the Woodcreek Church Prayer Team, Davis Community Group, and my Book Club whose prayer support during the revision was invaluable to me.

I am grateful to my friend Donna DeCost who took the time to review my manuscript one last time and found what others missed.

Praises for *I Can Begin Again*

"Your book was one of the more socially relevant and inspiring manuscripts that I've read and edited. I felt you; I was close to tears reading and rereading your life story, not to mention your family's story. It's one material from which people can learn, and your readers will surely feel the same when they read it. It was a story of hauling oneself out from the quagmire brought about by the harsh circumstances life has to offer. 'Denial was my game. Confusion was its name.' were two powerful lines that will eventually lead one person to living life again—to the fullest."

—Belle Miles, Copy Editor, 1st addition

I don't even know what to say. Your story is not only parallel with personality traits of my own but also the handwriting thing because I do it all the time too. I could never figure out why my handwriting varies. For once in my whole life, I am sitting here bawling and grieving and comforting my inner child. After years of dysfunction, I have a long way to go. Even my therapist has tried for years to get me to do this; I never really could tap into what she was trying to get me to do. But I'm getting it now. Thank you for allowing me to read your manuscript. A divine appointment has been kept.

—Stefanie M.

"I love your book. It is helping me and drawing me to have more healing. God's love is all over your words, and I am praising Him for your story. The world and the Body of Christ need to hear it. People will get a feel for what goes on in 'our' (survivors of child abuse) heads and hearts."

—Trudy S.

"I just finished reading your book in a two-evening marathon. It was hard to stop at one-thirty in the morning. It was fantastic, very profound, and well written. I particularly liked your painting technique and how you interjected the thoughts and emotions of the adult/abused child and the survivor. It was an excellent rending of your experiences and truth about healing the body, mind, and soul, very honoring to God's work and the love of Jesus. It was very insightful, clearly the hand of the Holy Spirit throughout. It gave me some reinforced insights into the pain and abuse of pornography and awakened some of my own abuse as a child victim myself. I have a lot to process and think about."

—Jerry C.

"Throughout the ages, God had used women to save His people; Deborah, Ruth, Esther, Mary. Each one of them was 'raised for such a time as this.' In each case, God called each woman to step out of her circumstances for the good of many. So it is with you. We know that while abuse is a horrible thing, we also know that God will use your life to His glory. He has a master plan for everything. He knew all along that He had a story of forgiveness and healing, and you had a talent for telling that story. To complete the process, He gave me a knack for editing (1st addition). A divine appointment, indeed! You too 'have been raised for such a time as this.' How beautiful are the feet of those who bring good news, who proclaim peace, who bring good tidings, who proclaim salvation, who say 'Your God reigns!' Isaiah 52:7."

—Linda F.

In the past ten years, I have heard many stories from others abused as children. Sadly, my computer crashed, and I lost many of the responses I received. I am humbled by those responses, knowing that my story has touched so many lives.

One of the lost responses was from a theapist: "Your book as done more to help me than any other book I have read."